Institutional Racism

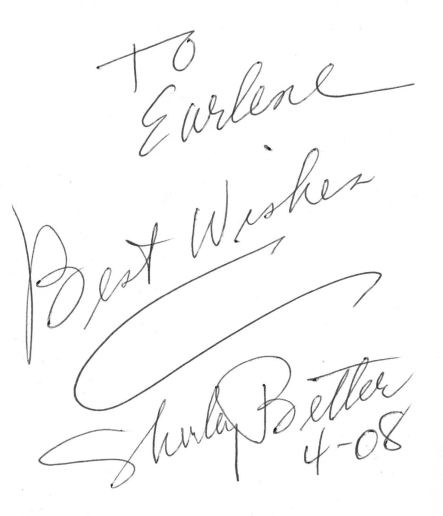

To Earlene

Best Wishes

Shirley Better
4-08

Institutional Racism

A Primer on Theory and Strategies for Social Change

Second Edition

Shirley Better

ROWMAN & LITTLEFIELD PUBLISHERS, INC.
Lanham • Boulder • New York • Toronto • Plymouth, UK

ROWMAN & LITTLEFIELD PUBLISHERS, INC.

Published in the United States of America
by Rowman & Littlefield Publishers, Inc.
A wholly owned subsidiary of The Rowman & Littlefield Publishing Group, Inc.
4501 Forbes Boulevard, Suite 200, Lanham, Maryland 20706
www.rowmanlittlefield.com

Estover Road
Plymouth PL6 7PY
United Kingdom

British Library Cataloguing in Publication Information Available

Library of Congress Cataloging-in-Publication Data:
Better, Shirley Jean.
  Institutional racism : a primer on theory and strategies for social change /
Shirley Better.—2nd ed.
      p. cm.
  Includes index.
  ISBN-13: 978-0-7425-6015-4 (cloth : alk. paper)
  ISBN-10: 0-7425-6015-5 (cloth : alk. paper)
  ISBN-13: 978-0-7425-6016-1 (pbk. : alk. paper)
  ISBN-10: 0-7425-6016-3 (pbk. : alk. paper)
  1. Racism—United States. 2. United States—Race relations. 3. Social change—
United States. I. Title.
  E185.615.B48 2008
  305.800973—dc22   2007027625

Printed in the United States of America

∞™ The paper used in this publication meets the minimum requirements of
American National Standard for Information Sciences—Permanence of Paper for
Printed Library Materials, ANSI/NISO Z39.48-1992.

Contents

Illustrations

FIGURES

TABLE

EXERCISES

Acknowledgments

This book is the culmination of many years of teaching students about racism. Over the years, my students have suffered through my mental gymnastics of thinking through the differences between individual racism and institutional racism. They have had the burden of preparing papers and doing group exercises, which have helped me to understand how best to get the material across in the classroom.

I thank my students over all these years who have given me evaluations of sections of my manuscript that they were required to read. They were always favorable and encouraging.

Special thanks to Christina Ho, Brenda Wang, and Angela C. Santamaria for the research they completed that helped me complete sections of the book.

Thanks also to my friend, Toni Colbert, for having faith in my work and using it as a text in its early rougher form.

Thanks to Essie Seck for helping me to get on the right track early on as I struggled to articulate what I believed.

This revision allows me to make up for the earlier omission of the support and encouragement of participants in my many seminars on this subject at many annual conferences of the National Association of Black Social Workers.

Preface

The second edition of this book continues the focus on understanding institutional racism, an enduring social phenomenon. As we move through the twenty-first century, America is destined to be increasingly diverse—with all the challenges and promises that accompany the cultural change. This edition updates much of the factual data assembled to highlight how institutional racism functions in our social institutions. I have also included a case study, "The Aftermath of Hurricane Katrina: A Case Study in Institutional Racism," that is unfortunately a classic example of how racism can devastate the innocent.

I differ with many scholars in this field who concentrate on the problems that minorities suffer because of racism and direct my attention to the reasons that racism persists in America. This is to encourage us to focus on who gains from maintaining racism, rather than hand-wringing over the victims. Only through this clear-eyed assessment can we produce lasting change. The intent of this book is not to encourage or endorse further separation of the races in America. Nor does the book intend to downplay the importance of other forms of oppression: sexism, classism, ageism, and homophobia. The goals are twofold: to increase the understanding of what institutional racism is and is not and to increase individual and group skills to combat racism at both the individual and the institutional level.

I was inspired to create this treatise from frequent use in the classroom of a now defunct essay entitled, "Institutional Racism in American Society: A Primer," written in 1968 by a group of students at Stanford University and published by the now nonexistent Mid-Peninsula Community House in San Francisco. This student essay provided the seed from which my own interpretation of the issues has grown.

The following is an account of several important changes that have taken place in American society since the 1950s in demographics, social pressures, and the economy. The American metamorphosis has heightened the need to explore the importance of racism as an area of academic study as well as public policy analysis.

KEY ELEMENTS THAT MAKE THE STUDY OF RACISM MANDATORY

The Browning of America

Since the 1980s, the United States has experienced an explosion of legal and illegal immigration of nonwhite groups. Southern California has led the way as the entry point for large numbers of persons from Mexico, Central America, and parts of Asia. Between 1980 and 1990, the white non-Latino majority in Los Angeles County turned into a minority; the county is 43.5 percent Latino, 35.1 percent white, 9.9 percent black, and 11.4 percent Asian. In the United States during this period, the number of Hispanics increased by 53 percent to 22.4 million, roughly 9 percent of the nation's population.[1] Today, nearly one-third of the U.S. population are people of color. Over 11.5 million additional,[2] people of color were recorded between 2000 and 2005—a 12 percent increase. The analysis confirms an increasingly multiracial, multinational, and multilingual nation that will demand new attention from local, state, and federal policymakers.[3]

Government projections predict that Latinos will comprise about 13.5 percent of the population in the year 2010, and 24.5 percent in 2050. "African Americans are projected to increase . . . 14.4 percent by 2050."[4] It is my thought that U.S. projections for 2050 will need to be revised because of the fast growth. The U.S. population topped 300 million on October 12, 2006. Demographer William Frey of the Brookings Institution stated, "I predict it's going to be a Latino boy, born in Los Angeles to a Mexican immigrant mother."[5]

Racism has historically been seen as a black–white affair; however as we become more visibly diverse, the social discourse must encompass a broader society. When groups from different cultural backgrounds begin to inhabit the same space, often there is an increase in tensions. The tensions generally can be attributed to the stress associated with making adjustments to the unknown: unfamiliar lifestyles, language barriers, and unfamiliar religious beliefs. In those communities inhabited by persons with limited technical skills and income, there is the added pressure of competition for scarce resources—goods and services, jobs, housing, and education or vocational training. The unfamiliar and the competition compound the level of tension throughout the community. The 1992 Los Angeles uprising was in part a response to the tension created by the competition for these scarce resources and the internal tension of dissimilar racial and cultural groups occupying the same space. Some Latinos and African Americans resented the fact that Asians were increasingly assuming ownership of small mom-and-pop stores in "their enclaves"; further, there was resentment among some African Americans and Latinos that Asians failed to hire employees from the community. There was growing resentment by African Americans of what they perceived as an invasion by Latinos of former all-black communities. Latinos and African Americans found themselves vying for the same low-pay, menial jobs in urban areas. The looting of Asian-owned stores and the fights between Latinos and African Americans can be viewed as symptoms of this.

The Increased Social Tension in American Society

Because of the changing demographics and changes in the economic structure outlined below, the social pressures have continued to heat up. This is not a new phenomenon for America—no, there have been silent and not-so-silent race wars since the first European settlers began their assault on the Native Americans. The salient difference is that it is no longer isolated to certain geographical areas, or just to whites and blacks or whites and Native Americans. Social pressures have increased the violent interactions across racial, ethnic, and class lines, making the tensions a multicultural/multiracial affair, often spinning out of control.

Los Angeles County is one of the most diverse areas in the country and is a good example of the social tension created by demographic changes. San Gabriel Valley, a large area east of downtown Los Angeles, has had dramatic changes in neighborhoods. Twenty years ago, the city of Monterey Park had a majority population of whites, then the city found itself with a rapidly increasing Latino community. By the mid-1980s, the population was changing again as large numbers of Chinese immigrants and Chinese Americans moved into the area. This has led to pitched battles on the campuses of some high schools—fights between Latino and Asian students as well as fights between white and Latino students.

The Restructuring of the American Economy

It generally has been true that when the American economy is functioning at a relatively high level (production is high, inflation is low, relatively low unemployment, and jobs are being created), there is a relatively high rate of tolerance of racial and ethnic differences. When the reverse is true, tension increases in every sphere of American life. High rates of racial/ethnic conflict occur. It is no accident that the first multiracial "urban unrest"—the 1992 Los Angeles uprising—occurred in the midst of the most severe recession California had experienced since World War II. The 1965 Watts uprising also occurred while there was double-digit unemployment in the area.[6]

Since the 1950s, the structure of the economy has been transforming. Through the 1970s and 1980s, there was a gradual decrease in manufacturing, which threw thousands of low-skilled workers into permanent unemployment or into jobs that paid much less. African American males were disproportionately affected by this economic change for they were heavily represented in low-skilled jobs.[7] A high percentage of black males were employed in car manufacturing, steel production, and other smokestack industries.[8] These were high-paying jobs for persons with limited technical skills. The very industries that provided a strong economic base for the black family were the ones most severely damaged in those decades.[9] The same was true for low-skilled Latino and Native American workers who effectively were segregated into cyclical, seasonal jobs, such as day work and low-skilled factory work, and placed at the mercy of the economy.

Throughout much of the 1990s, California floundered in a lackluster economy; it has since recovered from one of its most severe economic recessions caused by the ending of the Cold War. Cutbacks in military hardware acquisition triggered the recession. California benefited greatly during the Cold War as the war machine generated a sizable portion of its economy. Through 1993, the unemployment rate hovered around 9.7 percent. In minority communities of African Americans, Latinos, and Native Americans, the unemployment rate was twice as high.

Along with the change from war to peace, technological advances and global competition have seriously altered economic activity. During the twelve years of the Reagan and Bush administrations, America ran up an enormous deficit that throttled best efforts at pulling the economy out of the doldrums. In the twenty-first century, we are living with the results of much economic restructuring engineered by large corporations that have followed cheap labor, taking American manufacturing jobs overseas. This has resulted in a complete restructuring of production, distribution, and consumption patterns and thus new social and political structures. The current technological revolution fueled by the microprocessor and aided by jet travel has impacted not only production but also the workplace itself. The vast changes in our society have also spawned an uncertain future. The destruction of the World Trade Center in 2001 and the American invasions of Afghanistan and Iraq have increased uncertainty to its highest level. Will there be long-term growth or deflation? Will there be free markets or regional trading blocs? Will the vast disparity in wealth between the most industrialized countries of the North and those of the Southern Hemisphere be the norm? And finally, what will be the ultimate effect of the threat of terrorism on American society?

A study entitled *The Ethnic Quilt: Population Diversity in Southern California* reveals the depth of the gap between minority and white income.[10] The study states that, compared with whites, minority groups in Southern California earn less today than they did forty years ago. The authors accounted for the widening gap in income by means of such factors as immigration of low-skilled, low-paid laborers, discrimination against minorities, and lower education levels among minorities. Since the Enron debacle of 2002 there has been more scrutiny of CEOs; this examination led to the discovery that some American corporate heads earn 400 percent more in salary than the lowest-paid worker in the company.

This economic upheaval has contributed to an increase in social turbulence that must be factored in by college students preparing for a professional career in American society, as well as all other entry-level workers. Entry-level workers can now expect to encounter a more tense and in some instances hostile work environment. It is now commonly recognized that the future workplace will be comprised of an increasing number of women, American minorities, persons with disabilities, gays and lesbians, and foreigners. This change requires that all workers make unexpected adjustments in communication and work style to accommodate the increasing numbers of women and ethnic minorities. The increased diversity contributes to social tensions in the workplace just as job insecurity and the unpredictable economy do. Because of the change in the overall American economy, and the expansion of a global economy, those with marginal skills now face fierce competition for the scarce jobs that remain. Because of continued corporation mergers and subsequent downsizing, there is growing uneasiness on the part of those employed about if and when they will receive a pink slip. This uncertainty increases the likelihood of racial tension. As we will see later, it is may also lead to an increase in job discrimination, a major component of institutional racism.

The 2000-Pound Elephant

As we explore the ramifications of institutional racism, we will discover that it is analogous to a 2000-pound elephant residing in one's living room. Everyone in the house is disgusted with the elephant taking over the living room. The family is mortified that the elephant is in house, so they pretend the elephant does not exist. All the while the elephant is chewing up the sofa, punching holes into the wall, discharging an awful odor, eating everything in sight, and in every way possible being a general nuisance. Nevertheless, everyone in the household continues to act as if the elephant is not there. Why is this? First, no one wants to admit that they have an elephant living with them that is destroying a portion of their house. Second, no one in the house has the political will to force the elephant to leave. And it never will leave until someone in the house develops the courage to acknowledge the beast's existence and create an action plan to rid the house of it!

CHAPTER SUMMARIES

Chapter 1 defines the central terms that I use to explain racism, both individual and institutional, and provides some everyday examples of how it operates. It explores the difference between action and attitude—a central component in defining racism. A host of theories to explain racial inequality are examined. The importance of whiteness as a basic ingredient in the development of institutional racism is examined.

Chapter 2 explores the reasons why racism persists in the United States even though millions of dollars have been spent in the name of increasing equity and equality of opportunity, and the importance of cultural blindness and deafness. I offer a theoretical model, *The Better Model*, to explain racism and discuss in detail the "positive uses" of racism—economic advantage, social status, and psychic reward.

Chapters 3, 4, and 5 examine the operation of institutional racism within major social institutions—housing, education, employment, law enforcement, and social welfare. Current examples of policies, practices, and procedures within them are detailed to show how they disadvantage members of minority groups, and possible remedies for it.

In chapter 6, I provide another theoretical model, *The Web of Institutional Racism*, which graphically explains how institutional racism weaves through the major social institutions. Through a mythical saga of Franklin and Jose, we learn how racism can trap unsuspecting individuals in a tangle of invisible restrictions that can have a devastating effect on their life chances.

To provide a better understanding of how institutional racism functions in the real world today, following chapter 6, I provide a case study on institutional racism highlighting the tragedy that occurred after Hurricane Katrina. I provide a historical study of the city of New Orleans and examine how policies, practices, and procedures in specific social institutions there contributed to the disastrous aftermath.

Chapter 7 outlines strategies for combating individual racism and institutional racism at the individual and group levels. Cultural competency, the focus of this chapter, is one such strategy. The chapter outlines the skills that need to be developed, the guiding principles, and its limitations. The chapter also includes a personal code of conduct when confronted with racism.

Chapter 8 explores the strategies of negotiation and interracial collaboratives as avenues toward racial pluralism. Diverse racial and ethnic groups value interracial collaboratives for their historical impact on American society and their ability to provide an atmosphere for shared interest and action.

Chapter 9 extends the discussion of strategies for combating racism by examining the arenas where racism is acted out. It explores the home and family, the workplace, the faith community and school, the importance of the vote, and the use of community organization in neighborhoods as methods of social change at the macro level.

Chapter 10 proposes racial pluralism as an antidote for institutional racism—a structural issue that deeply affects all areas of American life. The antitoxin has to be as strong as the social ill. And while it may be impossible to eliminate all vestiges of institutional racism, a heavy dose of cultural pluralism throughout all our major social institutions can reduce the harshest results of institutional racism.

NOTES

1. C. Lewis Kincannon, *Condition of Hispanics in America Today* (Washington, DC: U.S. Government Printing Office, 1983).

2. Applied Research Center, *Tabulations of U.S. Census Population Estimates* (New York, 2006).

3. Applied Research Center, *Tabulations.*

4. U.S. Department of Commerce, *Statistical Abstract of the United States, Table 18* (Washington, DC: U.S. Government Printing Office, 1994).

5. Deborah Zabarenko, "L.A. Welcomes the 300 Millionth American," *LA Health News*, November 2006.

6. *McCone Commission Report*, commissioned by Governor Edmund Brown, Sr., in the wake of the Watts uprising in December 1965.

7. James Blackwell, *The Black Community: Diversity and Diversity* (Bayside, NY: General Hall, 1985).

8. U.S. Census Bureau, *America's Black Population: 1970 to 1982*, Special Publication, PIO/Pop-83-1.

9. James Blackwell and Philip Hart, *Cities, Suburbs, and Blacks* (Bayside, NY: General Hall, 1982).

10. James P. Allen and Eugene Turner, *The Ethnic Quilt: Population Diversity in Southern California* (Los Angeles: University of California, 1997).

I

TOWARD AN UNDERSTANDING OF RACISM

1

Conceptualizing Racism

President Johnson's Commission on Civil Disorders, created as a response to the nationwide violent uprisings from 1965 to 1968, states "This is our basic conclusion: Our nation is moving toward two societies, one black, one white— separate and unequal."[1] This was untrue then and remains untrue and tends to support the historical facade surrounding racism. The operative word "moving" is false. We have *always* been two nations, one white, one of varied hues, one rich, one poor—separate and unequal.

—Shirley Better

UNDERSTANDING RACISM:
KEY CONCEPTS AND CONSTRUCTS

Race: A Societal Invention

While this book focuses on racism, I must hasten to say at the outset that the term *race* is a **social construct**. A social construct is a culturally determined label.[2] That is, the classifying of individuals by external physiological differences is purely a societal product. Race, as used in social discourse in America, is a bogus term. There is no biological validity to the term "race"; the science of biology and microbiology has demonstrated that only slightly beneath the skin there is little difference between the so-called major three races.[3] Current DNA research suggests that all humankind can be traced back to one female. That being said, the reality of our lives is that our opportunity to share in the fullness of life is predicated on this social construct. Thus being born Latino, African American, or Native American in America has immediate and often negative outcomes. American minorities

3

are more likely to be poor, to suffer discrimination, and to earn less income than whites over their lifetime. Consequently, it is of the utmost importance to understand the ramifications of racism and its power in our society.

I view the terms "race" and "ethnicity" as separate and distinct concepts within the discussion of race relations in the United States. Some scholars use the terms interchangeably. I believe that this is done to neutralize the term "race" and thus reduce its importance in American society. While I agree that the term is bogus, the reality is that *race* continues to have an overwhelming influence over all aspects of American life. Therefore the social condition cannot be erased or soften by eliminating the term and substituting ethnicity. **Ethnicity** refers to any social grouping that is defined or set off by religion, language, national origin, and cultural differences, or some combination of these categories.

Race, as a social construct, is an ambiguous and changeable concept, because who is included within each category has changed over time. Hacker points out that Jews, the Irish, and dark-skinned Mediterraneans were not considered white for a generation or more of living in this country.[4] What American history has taught us is that skin coloring is not the dominant characteristic that determines racial classification. The degree of darkness of the skin as a measure of the social status of a person rests entirely on the interpretation of the dominant group at any point in history. Thus, biological variation has no meaning except what we give to it. **Race** refers to differential concentration of gene frequencies responsible for traits that are confined to physical manifestations such as skin color or hair form. It is no more significant to our behavior than the color of our eyes. Having brown eyes or gray eyes contributes nothing to the essence of our being; the same is true regarding the significance of skin coloring to who we are.

The Origins of Racial Classification

It seems crucial that we explore the origins of race. It will surprise many students to learn that race is a relatively current social development. Since race has only been used to categorize human variation in recent times, it is possible to reverse its use in our society. Most historians of science consider that modern categorization of the human species started with Carolus Linneaeus, a Swedish botanist, who in 1735 published *Systemae Naturae*, the first version of a extensive classification plan. Johann F. Blumenbach put forth his systematic racial classification in his 1775 treatise, *On the Natural Varieties of Mankind*. He concluded that there were five human races: Caucasian, Mongolian, Ethiopian, American, and Malay. Blumenbach introduced the term "Caucasian" because he believed the Caucasus region in Russia produced the world's most beautiful women.[5] Other European scientists during this period extended the study of placing humans into groups based upon physical attributes such as skin coloring, hair texture, and body build. Banton and Harwood aver that "Scientific theories of race failed to gain widespread acceptance and importance until 1865, with the emancipation and rise of blacks as a strong political force."[6]

This classification of humans into superior and inferior groupings parallels the age of European conquest of Asia and Africa. It appears that the creation of "races" went hand and glove with the determination of white skin superiority, which supports the claim I make in this book that the use of race is a thinly disguised rationale for economic exploitation. My thesis is that the biological connection of superior and light skin coloring came as a justification to support the permanency of slavery and land acquisition. Smedley suggests that, "By the end of the eighteenth century, the social construct of a hierarchical racial grouping had reached a critical mass. 'Race' became a potentially comprehensive worldview emanating from and compatible with the existing reality of the power relationship [between countries], the goals of European countries as they expanded their control through worldwide conquest."[7] Thus, the racial sorting becomes a convenient political connivance employed by Europeans who were at that time conquering Africa and Asia and subjugating their people. It provided a "scientific" justification for the exploitation of inhabitants of conquered countries by using skin coloring and other physical attributes as a method for supporting white skin domination. Racism is a Western invention coming out of a need to explain the huge gap in the power, wealth, and influence of European countries over the rest of the world.

Race Ideology

Smedley provides an in-depth analysis of race ideology in her book, *Race in North America*, and I will summarize her examination here as a prelude to further discussion of racism.[8] **Race ideology** is defined as the belief in hereditary differences and their immutability. This belief lies at the heart of understanding the persistence of racism in America. Race ideology suggests that physical features such as skin color and hair texture are linked to biology or human nature. Smedley asserts, "We think we see 'race' when we encounter certain physical differences. What we really 'see' is the social meanings that have been imbedded by the ideology of race. Physical features have been institutionalized as markers of lower or higher race status."[9] In short, biology is linked to social stratification. Thus race ideology requires that darker-skinned persons be relegated to the lower rungs on the social ladder. Moreover, through the hierarchy of racial groups, those at the lower end were considered less than human, which allowed for the dual distinction of being somewhat human, but also the property of someone else. Property rights proved to be more powerful than human rights. This is exhibited many times over by the judicial decisions that reinforced the property rights of the English over the human rights of Africans and Native Americans. Over time this belief system has become unassailable as the truth. It is formidable, as we will see throughout this text, because it has been utilized to maintain the wealth and social status of powerful whites. Most scientists will not support the notion that genes and ancestry preordain anyone to automatically have any given traits, intelligence, or lifestyle. Yet most Americans consciously or unconsciously continue to believe that people who are "racially" different are necessarily culturally different.

Two powerful and contradictory forces dominated discussions regarding the hierarchy of races during the early days of American colonization: Judeo-Christian doctrine and "scientific" race ideology (see Figure 1.1). The Judeo-Christian doctrine expounded the sameness of all humans who were created by God. It held that all humans have a soul and certain inalienable rights. However, the plantation owners and others needed to maintain a hierarchical view of humans, for this allowed for the continued exploitation of certain groups, Native Americans and Africans. The dominance of the Christian religion in the colonies compelled the English to justify maintaining slavery.

Representatives of slave owners joined forces with the growing authority of science in the nineteenth century to justify slavery. Scientists substantiated and strengthened the ideology of race, stating that it was a part of a natural ordering system. However, subjugation of the Native Americans and Africans simply reflected the use of superior armed forces, and was not the ramification of a natural classification of human beings.

It is crucial to understand that maintaining permanent enslavement of the Africans was critical to European aims of land acquisition and wealth. Growing tobacco, the main money crop in the South, required a huge labor force. The colonists found it convenient to support the theory that blacks were inferior and not like whites to ensure a supportive social and political environment for slavery. Thus slavery developed a racist characteristic as a means to justify its continuance. Moving the Native Americans off the desirable land was also supported by the dogma of race worthiness. The Europeans lumped to-

Race Ideology	Judeo-Christian Doctrine
"Scientific"	Religious Creed
Physical features linked to worthiness	All humans are created by God with inalienable rights
Property Rights	Human Rights
Social Darwinism	Humanitarianism
Social Construct	

Figure 1.1. Powerful Forces of American Ideology

gether all Indians regardless of cultural and physical differences into one single group of more or less "savage" beings. Race ideology was used repeatedly to support America's policy of broken treaties, stolen lands, enforced apartheid, and impoverishment. It was not until the passage of the Indian Citizenship Act in 1924 that Indians were given American citizenship.

The fierce debate that centered on Christian beliefs and race ideology had the effect of crystallizing the dogma of physical features being linked to worthiness of an individual. On one side were those who support the hierarchy of human groups and met all attempts to establish a culturally pluralistic society with strong resistance, even violence. Examples of American groups who represent this stream of thought include the Ku Klux Klan, the neo-Nazis, and the skinheads. On the other side was the message of equality, freedom, and human rights espoused by the Constitution, the Bill of Rights, the abolitionist movement, and the civil rights movement.

OTHER THEORIES OF RACIAL INEQUALITY

Mario Barrera developed an excellent compilation of theories on the existence of racial inequality in his book, *Race and Class in the Southwest*. A **theory** is the analysis of a group of social phenomena in their relation to one another. Barrera's framework of theories is offered here to expand your awareness of the variety of beliefs that have been developed over the centuries. Many of these theories have fallen out of favor from time to time, only to be recycled and repackaged for use again to justify racism, or to support unfair racial preferences. On the following pages, I have summarized Barrera's more detailed discussion of each theory.[10]

Deficiency Theories

Biological Deficiency Theory

This category suggests that racial inequality can be attributed to genetics and thus hereditary inferiority on the part of certain races. Although these theories are generally held in disrepute, there is a resurgence from time to time, as for example, in the work of educational psychologist Arthur Jensen. In his 1972 book *Genetics and Education*, he dealt with the question of differences between blacks and whites in the measurement of IQ. Jensen speculates that a substantial part of these differences may be due to biological inheritance. His theories are generally not taken seriously. One reason for this is the serious methodological problems such as the heavy reliance on IQ test scores, universally acknowledged now as very imperfect measures of anything that could be considered general intelligence.

Deficiencies in Social Structure

This theory argues that minority racial groups in the United States are held back by problems within the social structure of those groups. Below are two examples.

Daniel Moynihan's 1965 report, *The Negro Family: The Case for National Action*, argues that historical factors have created a weak family structure among African Americans and that this weakness creates emotional and attitudinal problems, such as emotional instability and male role confusion. A vicious circle is set up with economic problems reinforcing their weak family structure. The problem with this theory is that it looks at the glass as half empty. One could look at the African American family and marvel at its strengths. For example, Moynihan stated that black females headed one-fourth of the families, and therefore, the family was pathological. He could have just as easily stated that given the over two hundred years of slavery, the breakup of the family, and the great migration from the farms of the South to the inner cities of the North, three-fourths of all black families remain intact.

D'Antonio and Form's 1965 report, *Influentials in Two Border Cities*, describes the condition of political powerlessness of the Chicano residents of El Paso, Texas. This powerlessness they attributed to such structural deficiencies among Chicanos as a lack of political insight, a "low level of social integration," and factionalism.

The problem with social structure theories is methodological. Social disorganization or political fragmentation might as easily be seen as results rather than as causes of the racial inequality.

Cultural Deficiency

These theories blame inequality on one or more traits of the group in question. They emphasize attitudes and values, rather than social structure, although the two types of factors are often linked together in the models.

Edward Banfield's *The Unheavenly City* argues that inequality is due to a "lower class culture," consisting of such traits as a present rather than future orientation, and poor work habits. Herschel Manuel suggests that Chicanos do poorly because of a language handicap and such values and attitudes as fatalism, present rather than future orientation, dependency, and lack of success orientation that lead directly to problems in school. His theory suggests that Mexican American culture is highly traditional and nonadaptive to the requirements of upward mobility in an industrial society.

Cultural deficiency theories lack methodological rigor. They search the cultural inventory of the group until some presumed traits are discovered that hold the group back from achievement and social mobility. These presumed traits then constitute the explanation. However, the cultural apparatus of any people is so complex that certainly negative as well as positive traits will be found. Additionally, the cultural characteristics they point to can be considered deficiencies only within a given institutional framework. For instance, we know that a Chinese monolingual child will have difficulties in American schools. However, this is a "deficiency" only if the society fails to provide special educational opportunities for the child. If not provided, the deficiency is in the educational system itself.

Bias Theories

These theories consist of attitudes and feelings of the dominant group in the society, and thus tend to put the responsibility on the Anglo majority rather than on the minorities.

Discrimination and Prejudice

A classic work in this area, Gunnar Myrdal's *An American Dilemma* (1944), maintains that racial discrimination itself causes the status of African Americans. He places great emphasis on the concept of the vicious circle, that is, the disadvantaged condition of blacks reinforces the prejudice of whites by confirming their low opinion of blacks.

Discrimination, Prejudice, and Pathology

Kenneth Clark's work focuses on prejudice and discrimination, but he includes a deficiency component consisting of a set of ghetto pathologies that are pictured as mutually reinforcing. While bias theories have their own problems, the general approach is not so much wrong as incomplete. Most—except for Myrdal's—lack a historical perspective.

Structural Discrimination Theories

These theories locate the source of minority disadvantage in the social structure of the society as a whole.

Caste-Class School

In Dollard's 1957 book, *Caste and Class in a Southern Town*, the social structure of the American South is described as a combination of caste and class. Caste was characterized by endogamy (prohibition of marriage outside the caste) and by rigid barriers between the division. Class was seen as nonendogamous and as allowing social mobility. Prejudice was seen as a defensive attitude intended to preserve white prerogatives in the caste situation. The weakness of this theory is the use of the term "caste" which comes from India; there is no exact equivalent in America.

Internal Colonial Theory

Neocolonialism is the economic and political policies by which a more powerful country or entity indirectly maintains or extends influence over other countries, areas, or people.

- Internal Colonialism: Sociologist R. Blauner theorizes that the United States operates an internal colony through its economic and political domination of ethnic enclaves: ghettos, Indian reservations, barrios, and Chinatowns. These enclaves are closely patrolled by local law enforcement organizations. The inhabitants have little voice in the functioning of their communities or the society at large.
- Marxist theories: Supporters of Marxism would accept Blauner's theory regarding ethnic and racial communities, but would add that the colonization is maintained to insure economic domination by the ruling class.

EXPLANATION OF TERMS

Racism is an individual act or an institutional practice that perpetuates inequality, based on racial membership. **Individual racism** relates to individual actions, which may or may not be supported by a personal belief in stereotypes. Figure 1.2 provides a graphic example of the attitudes, practices, and structures for both individual and institutional racism. Many times people who do not consider themselves to be racist behave in ways that disadvantage minorities because their beliefs and behavior have been conditioned over time by racial stereotypes. One example of this would be the comedian Michael Richards, who after a venomous verbal attack in 2006 on African Americans at a nightclub stated the he was not a racist.

Stereotyping is the process of maintaining a standardized image or mental picture of a group or race to which all members of the group or race are said to conform. Individual racist action results in disadvantaging or subjugating the person of the targeted group and/or enhancing the privileges of the person from the dominant group. The store owner who suspects that minority customers are likely to steal and watches them more closely is acting out these beliefs. While the behavior of the store-owner doesn't in a direct way disadvantage the minority person, it certainly produces tension for both individuals. Further, the action of being watched for criminal intent places an undue burden on the person of color, often eliciting feelings of self-consciousness and rage that rob the person of a feeling of well-being. Thus the action by the storeowner in this scenario does disadvantage the minority person, if only to make the person uneasy.

Institutional racism denotes those patterns, procedures, practices, and policies that operate within social institutions so as to consistently penalize, disadvantage, and exploit individuals who are members of nonwhite racial/ethnic groups. (See figure 1.3.) Institutional racism functions to reinforce white skin privilege in all facets of American life.[11] It provides a graphic example of attitudes, practices, and structures for both individual and institutional racism. There are, of course, other definitions for racism, which differ with the above definition. For example, Cyrus proposes that "Eurocentric prejudice and discrimination result in racism."[12] Thus, he gives equal weight to attitudes and actions. Though Hacker supports to a large extent the definition that I offer, he also includes negative feelings and attitudes as the central ingredient of racism.[13] In the seminal book *Institutional Racism in America* by Knowles and Prewitt, the authors devote pages to defining the term through the use of examples within institutions. However, they are generally in agreement with me on the definition of institutional racism.[14]

Wellman eloquently describes white racism as being a strategy to maintain privilege, and this has most successfully been accomplished through social institutions. **Social institutions** are social aggregates of society. Knowles and Prewitt suggest, "They are fairly stable social arrangements and practices through which collective action are taken."[15] Sociologists studying racism in the early part of the twentieth century were not unaware of the structural implications or societal barriers of racism.[16] However, there continues to be an unwillingness to move beyond attitudes and feelings, even as social scientists are more knowledgeable about how social organizations function. This treatise suggests that the central reason for institutional racism is the desire for economic advantage. Negative attitudes and feelings are viewed as a byproduct of the original need to justify the economic exploitation.

Institutional Racism denotes those patterns, procedures, practices, and policies which operate within social institutions so as to consistently penalize, disadvantage, and exploit individuals who are members of non-white groups.

Individual Racism relates to personal actions, which may or may not be supported by a personal belief in stereotypes.

Unfortunately, too many social scientists and policy makers equate prejudice with all racism, and cling to nonstructural (societal) barriers to account for its persistence. Again and again there is the focus on a feature story of a Southern whose racist act startles the country, or use as an example a marginal group like the KKK. Why is this so? Because it is comforting for many Americans to believe that racism is just a matter of ignorance of a particular back-

	Individual	Institutional
Beliefs	Negative stereotypes of "people of color" The presumption of white supremacy Acceptance of social inequality	The presumption of white supremacy Acceptance of social and economic inequality The maintenance of white skin privilege
Attitudes	Hostility Fear Prejudice Intolerance Cultural blindness and deafness to racism	Commitment to maintenance of inequality between the races/ethnic groups Individuals are personally responsible for their own economic outcome
Practices	Negative verbalizations Use of pejorative name-calling Hostile actions	Neglect Discrimination Isolation Segregation Exclusion Exploitation Physical attacks Genocide
Structures	Customs/Traditions that reinforce inequality Informal rules of behavior that reinforce racism Conscious and unconscious behavior patterns Cultural blindness/cultural deafness	Laws (Jim Crow laws) Formal policies, practices, and procedures Informal policies, practices, and procedures

Figure 1.2.   Comparison of Individual and Institutional Racism

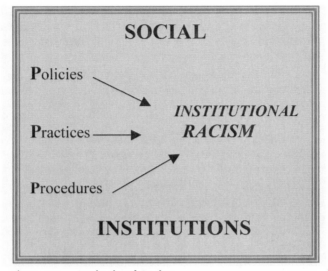

Figure 1.3. Institutional Racism

ward or fringe group of individuals. To accept that racism is purposely in place within American institutions to preserve white privilege would mean to acknowledge that America is not, at its roots, a just and meritorious society. As Americans, we are educated to see our country as a land of opportunity for all who are willing to work hard and abide by the laws of American society. Liberty, freedom, and the pursuit of happiness are such basic values in American society that it is painful to admit that we have not lived up to our credo. It is easier to blame the victims of inequality or lunatic fringe groups than to admit the reality of basic injustice that exists in the United States.

It is exceedingly difficult for us to control our institutions which, being products of their history, cannot but perpetuate practices which advantage the typical white and handicap the typical minority person. Historically, the dominant group in American society, Europeans, has justified its rule and exploitation of minority groups by building into its social institutions ideology as well as practices that supported this domination. Schools, city councils, businesses, county offices, newspapers, congressional committees, and welfare agencies, though often in the hands of enlightened persons, remain dominated by practices that produce racial inequities. This chapter will not examine the historical development of racism, for there are many fine treatises on the subject.[17]

Attitude and Action as a Litmus Test

There continues to be some disagreement over the meaning of racism, which contributes to the continued misuse of other terms often equated with it, as suggested earlier. For example, the terms bigotry, bias, and prejudice are used as if these words are interchangeable with racism. Bigotry, bias, and prejudice relate to acts of belief, judgment, or opinion. Racism denotes actions that have power. It refers to the power to act in ways that exploit another person based on membership in a particular racial or ethnic group. The point to remember is that racism is a negative *action*, which subjugates a race or ethnic group. This permits another race to maintain some form of control over them and thereby secure personal privilege.

Therefore, every person who has negative feelings toward a particular person or group is not necessarily racist. The person may be biased, bigoted, or prejudiced, but that does not give him or her the mantle of racist. To be a racist one must be in a position to *act out* in ways that exploits or disadvantages another person. Further, the negative action must be a con-sequence of the person's membership in a racial/ethnic group. Racism requires the ability to act out negative feelings in such a way as to disadvantage a person or group because of their racial/ethnic membership. Of course, nonaction that results in disadvantaging minorities is also racist. For example, if an employer refuses to hire a person who is Latino/Asian/African American, this would constitute a racist act.

It is not necessary for a person to have negative feelings toward a person of another ethnic group to act out in a racist manner. It is quite possible that a person is entirely knowledgeable about the fact that "race" is a societal term and has little validity biologically. The person may be well aware that there are no differences that matter between "the races." Even so, the person may still use race as a means to exploit another person. For example, suppose we have the owner of a plant who decides to hire only Mexican Americans for his factory because he knows he can pay them lower wages and not provide them with health benefits. Does he have to believe that Mexican Americans are mentally and socially inferior to him to create the disparity in the employment? Of course not. The owner may be fully aware that there is no difference biologically between them. However, he is also aware that he can get away with paying them a lower wage just because they are Mexican American. By maintaining lower wages for the Mexican American workers, the owner is enhancing his own financial status. Thus the owner's racist action does not emanate from negative feelings or stereotyping but from an economic motive. This example points out the importance of the distinguishing between feelings and action in defining racism.

ON THE VALUE OF WHITENESS

Explanation of the Term "Whiteness"

When we focus on race relations in America, we are unaccustomed to discussing whiteness. When we talk about racism, we tend to concentrate on the victims, who are members of minority groups. However, it is crucial to examine whiteness in any discussion of racism. Not doing so would be the same as studying the poor—who are often the casualties of economic policy—and not examining the rich and powerful who develop and control those policies. Euro-Americans must begin to see their role in perpetuating white skin privilege if there is to be a serious dialogue about racism.

Let us first define terms. **Whiteness** denotes a privileged socioeconomic status conferred upon a group often identified by light skin coloring, specifically Caucasians. While this definition is useful in a general way, there are subtle nuances to whiteness. Light skin coloring is not the sole determinant for privileged status. Hacker discusses the historical inclusion of outgroups who currently are perceived as white.[18] The Irish, Jews, Italians, and Eastern Europeans were not considered white when they landed on American soil, even though they were accepted as Caucasian. Only through assimilation over one or more generations were these groups accepted as white. Consider, are Arabs considered white in America at this time? Whiteness is synonymous with racial superiority; it confers on a designated group *unearned privileges*. American society, because of the desire for economic gain, has used skin coloring as a means of creating a privilege status for specified groups.

The Privilege of Whiteness

Euro-Americans rarely refer to themselves as "white." Why is this so? I surmise that this omission is much like the default built into a computer. In the computer, default is the automatic selection by a program in the absence of a choice made by the user. Whiteness is automatically assumed in the absence of a stated classification—the privilege of assumption. Thus, in the media, the term "the white man" is unnecessary, simply saying "the man" implies this. In all other instances the person's race or ethnicity is used to describe him. Possibly another reason that whites stumble over using the term is that consciously or subconsciously there is the realization of the true connotation of the term in American society—that being white means being special. Whiteness is not only supported by Euro-Americans; people of color and European immigrants do as well. European immigrants come to this country and are often marginalized. How do you get on the right side, the white side? You behave like the white side. One way of doing this is to be against those groups that whites are against by adopting racist actions. Thus, American minority groups often find themselves discriminated against by immigrant groups who are not accepted by mainstream society either. Ironically, there are also individuals within American minorities who support whiteness. This is done as a way of gaining favor with those in power. We find high-ranking African Americans and Latinos supporting laws that exploit people of color. In exchange for their support they are accepted and compensated by the power elite.

Another way of looking at the privilege of whiteness is to put it into a historical perspective. All of our social institutions—schools, the criminal justice system, banks, the workplace—have been created and recreated by white men. Thus, there is a natural fit between maleness and whiteness in all American institutions; white males easily succeed in a system invented for them and by them. Recent challenges by women and people of color in the form of affirmative action edicts have pointed up the ultimate control by white males. Whites have special entitlements; however, only those with heightened sensitivity perceive themselves as privileged. Most Euro-Americans think of whiteness as the norm. This unearned privilege equates with the advantages of being right handed. Pick up a pair of scissors, grab a door handle, or sit at a lunch counter. They are designed for "righties." But what right-handed person ever thought of himself as privileged? This unearned special status that permeates our society supports institutional racism. Consequently, white skin privilege cannot be viewed as a quirk of American society.

In her book, *White Man Falling*, Ferber suggests that one way of examining whiteness is to explore the group that most exemplifies the extreme of white privilege—white supremacists. She suggests that they offer a clear doctrine that fiercely defends white skin privilege. Ferber states, "In studying white supremacists groups there has been a tendency to focus on leaders in a particular movement and to explore the character traits that lead an individual to join this movement. However this contributes to the belief that racism is somehow rooted in one's personality rather than institutionalized in our society and culture at every level."[19]

Viewing white supremacy as extremism often results in absolving the mainstream population of its racism. It implies that white supremacists are the racist fringe in contrast to some nonracist majority. One should view white racism as a continuum or a scale with groups such as the neo-Nazis at the extreme of the scale, but all Euro-Americans having some degree of involvement and/or benefit in white skin privilege.[20]

The Capital in Whiteness

Institutional racism and the value of whiteness merge as one, for whiteness is used to maintain unearned privilege through the structure of institutional racism. Institutional racism and whiteness complement each other for the capital of whiteness is generated from the benefits derived from institutional racism. Institutional racism is the mechanism used to ensure unearned entitlements. Lipsitz offers another viewpoint on the maintenance of whiteness in his book, *The Possessive Investment in Whiteness*. He looks at American racial inequality from the vantage point of white skin privilege. Lipitz believes that social, cultural, and micro-economic forces encourage white people to expend time and energy on the creation and re-creation of whiteness.[21] He explains that "whiteness has a cash value; it accounts for the advantages that come to individuals through profits made from housing secured in discriminatory markets. [Advantages] were gained through intergenerational transfers of inherited wealth passed on due to the spoils of discrimination to succeeding generations."[22] Like institutional racism, investment in whiteness is everywhere in American culture, yet is often difficult to see. Lipsitz argues that Euro-Americans are encouraged to invest in whiteness because it provides them with resources, power, and opportunity. Because Americans are ignorant of their history, they are blinded to the systematic progression of the investment in whiteness or institutional racism generated by slavery, segregation, conquest, and colonialism. Both have been elevated, as we will learn, by liberal and conservative social policies. However, because of a contrived history, Americans are unable or unwilling to follow the interwoven system of racism. Instead, we produce largely cultural explanations for institutional racism.

In the past, the power of whiteness depended on not only white hegemony over people of color but also on manipulating disenfranchised groups to fight against each other to curry favor with whites. There is the episode of African Americans, former slaves, riding with the American cavalry throughout the West to conquer the Indian tribes. Native Americans returned runaway slaves because whites offered a bounty for them; some Native Americans also held Africans in slavery. One of the first chartered African American units in the army went to war against the Comanches in Texas. The defeat of the Comanches in 1870 ignited a mass migration by Spanish-speaking residents of New Mexico into the areas of West Texas, formerly occupied by the vanquished Native American tribes.[23] There have been, of course, many examples throughout American history of the American minorities forming coalitions to fight **oppression** and discrimination. The Seminoles in Florida frequently recruited African slaves to fight against abusive settlers. Native American tribes often harbored runaway slaves, an arrangement that benefited both groups.

Eliminating Whiteness

There are an increasing number of workshops and books that focus on this topic. The discussion of whiteness in American society, a relatively new area of study, offers a new way of thinking about inequality. The term "white race" is as much a social construct as the term race itself. The term "whiteness" denotes an unearned status in a society that strives to be a meritocracy, and as noted previously, the perpetuation of this special status has reinforced widespread misery throughout the country. Therefore, if we are to become a true meritocracy, whiteness has to be abolished. To rid our country of racism, we must rid ourselves of the power of the term, the concept, and the reality of whiteness. Opposing whiteness should not be construed to mean opposing white people, but rather opposing the unearned status and rewards conferred on whites. Just as African Americans have abandoned the term "black" to identify themselves, so should Euro-Americans give up the term "white." Both terms contain negative connotations. Several scholars suggest that whites will need to critically examine how whiteness has become synonymous with oppression while creating a space for a white [Euro-American] identity.[24]

As the final admonition in his book, Lipsitz comments on this needed new direction:

> In the years ahead we still have ample opportunities to see what white people are made of, to see whether we can transcend out attachments to the mechanisms that give whiteness its force and power. We need to learn why our history has been built so consistently on racial exclusion and why we continue to generate new mechanisms to increase the value of past and present discrimination. How can we account for the ways in which white people refuse to acknowledge their possessive investment in whiteness even as they work to increase its value every day? We can't blame the color of our skin. It must be the content of our character.[25]

Given the benefits that whites receive in society, one must ask this question regarding the future: why would they give it up?

SUMMARY

This chapter began with a discussion of the bogus term "race" and how it is a social construct. Next we examined the social events fhat brought rise to the creation of racial categorizations. Two major ideologies were explored—the race ideology and Judeo-Christian doctrine—for their contribution to the ongoing debate about racism in America. Offered were a range of theories to explain the presence of racial inequality. This was followed by an analysis of terms the author views as crucial to the discussion and understanding of her two theories designed to explain the persistence of institutional racism in America. Finally, the focus turns to the meaning and value of whiteness and its role in the persistence of racial inequality.

KEY TERMS

ethnicity. Any social grouping defined or set off by religion, language, national origin, and cultural differences, or some combination of these categories.

individual racism. Individual disadvantaging actions that may or may not be supported by a personal belief in stereotypes.

inequality. The pattern of unbalanced distribution of economic, political, and social goods and services within a society.

institutional racism. Those patterns, procedures, practices, and policies that operate within social institutions so as to consistently penalize, disadvantage, and exploit individuals who are members of nonwhite racial/ethnic groups.

oppression. A sense or condition of being forced to assume; a particular stance with respect to oneself, the world, and the demands of change. It is a pattern of hopelessness and helplessness, in which one sees oneself as static, limited, and expendable.

prejudice. An irrational attitude of hostility directed against an individual, a group, a race, or their supposed characteristics; the act of prejudgment.

race. Differential concentrations of gene frequencies responsible for traits which, so far as we know, are confined to physical manifestations such as skin color or hair form, facial and bodily characteristics. It has no intrinsic connection with cultural patterns and institutions.

race ideology. The belief in hereditary (biological) differences between social groups and that these differences are constant and unchangeable.

racism. An individual or institutional practice that perpetuates inequality, based on racial or ethnic membership.

social construct. A culturally determined label.

social institution. Social aggregates that serve to maintain the society. They are fairly stable social arrangements and practices through which collective action are taken. They serve to maintain the society. Major American institutions are education, business and labor, politics, law enforcement, housing, health, and public welfare.

stereotypes. Labels, identities, or "pictures in the mind" that are attributed to different social groups so that the entire group is pigeonholed as falling within a given category. Stereotyping is considered to be pervasive in that almost all groups are subject to generalized classification. Stereotyping can be both positive and negative.

theory. The analysis of a group of social phenomena in their relationship to one another.

whiteness. A privileged socioeconomic status conferred upon a group, and often identified by light skin coloring, specifically refers to Caucasians.

GROUP ACTIVITIES

1. Describe an occasion when you felt you were being treated differently from others because of your racial/ethnic group membership.

2. Find a current newspaper article that exemplifies institutional racism. Discuss within your study group how the article reveals institutional racism.
3. Discuss the differences between biological deficiencies and social structure deficiencies.

STUDY QUESTIONS

1. What is the most important ingredient necessary to act racist?
2. What social and economic factors lead to slavery becoming a racist system?
3. How is bigotry and racism different?
4. Explain the term "whiteness."
5. Why is it that Euro-Americans do not recognize their ethnicity?
6. What is meant when the author says "whiteness" is the default?
7. Define the term "race ideology." What is its relationship to racism?
8. How does whiteness gain capital?
9. Define and give an example of a structural discrimination theory.

NOTES

1. Report of the National Advisory Commission on Civil Disorders (New Times Co., 1968).
2. Philip Popple and Leslie Leighninger, *Social Work, Social Welfare, and American Society*, 2nd ed. (Boston: Allyn and Bacon, 1993), 357.
3. Ronald Takaki, *A Different Mirror* (New York: Little, Brown, 1993), 24–50; John Kromkowski, *Race and Ethnic Relations 95/96* (Guilford, CT: Dushkin Publishing, 1996), 10–16.
4. Andrew Hacker, *Two Nations: Black and White, Separate, Hostile, Unequal* (New York: Ballantine Books, 1995).
5. See chapter 7, "The Rise of Science: Sixteen- to Eighteenth-Century Classifications of Human Diversity," in Audrey Smedley, *Race in North America* (Boulder, CO: Westview Press, 1999).
6. Michael Banton and Jonathan Harwood, *The Race Concept* (New York: Praeger Publishers, 1975), 28.
7. Smedley, *Race in North America*, 169.
8. See chapter 1, "Some Theoretical Considerations," in *Race in North America*.
9. Smedley, *Race in North America*, 27–29.
10. Mario Barrera, *Race and Class in the Southwest* (Notre Dame: University of Notre Dame Press,1979). See chapter 7.
11. See chapter 1, "Institutional and Ideological Roots of Racism" in the seminal book *Institutional Racism in America*, edited by Louis Knowles and Kenneth Prewitt

(Englewood Cliffs, NJ: Prentice-Hall, 1969), for one of the original discussions of the term "institutional racism."

12. Virginia Cyrus, *Experiencing Race, Class, and Gender in the United States* (Mountain View, CA: Mayfield Publishing, 1993), 11–13.

13. See discussion in chapter 2, "Race and Racism," in Hacker, *Two Nations*.

14. Knowles and Prewitt, *Institutional Racism*, 1–7.

15. Knowles and Prewitt, *Institutional Racism*, 5.

16. David Wellman, *Portraits of White Racism* (New York: Cambridge University Press, 1977).

17. A thorough discussion of the history of racism can be found in the following books: Fredrickson, George M., *Racism: A Short History.* Princeton, NJ: Princeton University Press, 2002; Davis, Thomas J., *Race Relations in America: A Reference Guide with Primary Documents.* Westport, Conn: Greenwood Press, 2006.

18. Hacker, *Two Nations*.

19. Abby L. Ferber, *White Man Falling* (New York: Rowman & Littlefield, 1998), 9.

20. Much more detailed discussion of the origins of ideologies about race can be found in Theodore Allen's two-volume work, *The Invention of the White Race* (New York: Verso, 1994, 1997); and Ivan Hannaford, *Race: The History of an Idea in the West* (Baltimore, John Hopkins University Press, 1996).

21. George Lipsitz, *The Possessive Investment in Whiteness* (Philadelphia: Temple University Press, 1998).

22. See the introduction in Lipsitz, *Possessive Investment in Whiteness*.

23. Lamar Howard, *Texas Crossings: The Lone Star State and the American Far West, 1836–1986* (Austin: University of Texas Press, 1991), xiii.

24. Elaine Manglitz, "Challenging White Privilege in Adult Education: A Critical Review of the Literature," *Adult Education Quarterly* 53, no. 2 (February 2003): 119–134.

25. Lipsitz, *Possessive Investment in Whiteness*, 233.

2

Institutional Racism

A Theoretical Framework

PERSISTENCE OF RACISM

This book focuses on the social phenomenon of American racism; however, racism is an international phenomenon. In many countries, notably South Africa and the former Yugoslavia, racism is an intricate part of daily social exchange. The attention not too long ago to German racism toward Turks and Africans, which resulted in homes being burned and individuals injured, is one example. Another is the revelation that during World War II, the Japanese government allowed the military to force women of Korean ancestry to be used as "sex slaves." In some countries, race colors all interactions, from religion to politics. In the United States, we are socialized to view race and ethnicity as the ultimate determinant in social intercourse. While European countries used class as the determinant of a person's worth and thus how goods and services would be distributed throughout the society, the United States, due in part to its tragic beginnings using slave labor, took another path. Americans are not so much defined by class, at least openly. Here skin hues are used as the proxy for social class. And now we have terrorism to add to the mix. African Americans and Latinos have been protesting "racial profiling" for some time; now Arabs are also complaining of being singled out because of the color of their skin and their religion.

Why Racism Endures

With all the public discussion of the negative impact of racism, one often wonders why it endures. With more than thirty years of active public policy to dismantle legal barriers to equality and equity, how is it possible for racism not to wither and die under the bright lights of the civil rights movement? *It persists because it provides an avenue of advantage and profit for those who engage in individual racist actions. It persists because it provides a mechanism for constant privilege for the dominant group through institutional practices.* The notion that racism persists because of bigoted, ignorant persons who have had little contact with groups different from themselves is insupportable. Far too many Americans cling to the notion that once these bigots have an opportunity to meet and know a Latino/African American/Asian American, their attitude will change. This notion fits neatly into the American ethos of individual responsibility and thus is comforting. Consequently, the reasoning continues, racism will be overcome by education. It is assumed that education alone will change attitudes, reduce ignorance, produce positive feelings, make our society more equitable. Clearly, education and social interaction can change attitudes, and can reduce stereotypical biases. Such avenues are to be encouraged. However, the foundation of racism is privilege, and as history has shown, is not easily conquered by enlightenment alone.

Cultural Blindness and Deafness

Far too many whites shield themselves from the ugly and painful reality of racism through cultural blindness and cultural deafness. **Cultural blindness and deafness** relates to the unwillingness to acknowledge that racism is not simply the resistance of the few to equality for all, but the refusal to witness the imbedded inequality within the very social institutions that maintain the society. Speaking on the embarrassment of whites regarding racism, Pumla Gobodo-Madikizela in the *Los Angeles Times* commented: "The constant silencing and denial of that memory [of racism] is an attempt to master, to conquer and finally to crush history. . . . To embrace this history would be to threaten their sense of humanity. So it is better denied as something of the past. When it comes to the question of racism, very few people can confront it openly and truthfully."[1]

In the case of the beating of Rodney King, most Americans saw the action of the police as extreme, unjust, and probably inflicted because the suspect was African American. However, African Americans and Latinos have been complaining for decades of police brutality—complaints that have largely been ignored by American society. Did the King video force Americans to look at the awful truth, which they had hidden from themselves? And how do we account for the tragedy of victims of Hurricane Katrina? How could the city and state government along with the citizens themselves be so unaware of the depth of poverty and disenfranchisement of poor African Americans living among them? Further, there were many complaints by evacuees of mistreatment by the police in the Superdome and during their evacuation from New Orleans.

The disparity in the unemployment rates between whites and minorities is another example of cultural blindness. It is seen as the norm that the unemployment rate for blacks is twice, sometimes three times, as high as whites. This disparity can be justified through unfavorable stereotypes regarding the work ethic of African Americans. The high level of black infant mortality is viewed as a curiosity, but the fact that it is connected to poverty and race is not salient enough to change public policy. Too many Americans refuse to see the racism all around them and appear genuinely surprised by the high level of racial violence that sporadically occurs. Recent examples of this are the 1992 riots in Los Angeles and the Cincinnati inner city riot of 2001.

THE BETTER MODEL OF INSTITUTIONAL RACISM

The remainder of this chapter will lay the groundwork for the development and discussion of the essential elements that support and foster the persistence of institutional racism. Offered is a theoretical framework for understanding racism that explores the three key components: *Economic Privilege, Social Privilege*, and *Psychic Rewards*.

The Positive Uses of Racism

This text puts forth the thesis that racism serves some very "positive" uses for the dominant group. Gans, in an article thirty-five years ago, used the term "positive" to explain the how the wealthy gained from poverty.[2] The term "positive uses" functions in the same sense, for the term explains that there is profit and gain accrued by all in the dominant group through the maintenance of racism. The positive uses of racism are (1) economic privilege, (2) social privilege, and (3) psychic reward. When one looks at racism or poverty in this light, it is easier to understand why both have been so intractable.

Economic Privilege

There is hardly a clearer example of economic privilege accrued from institutional racism than the enslavement of Africans in America. The colonies legalized the enslavement of Africans who were either sold by other Africans or kidnapped by Europeans. From 1619 to 1865, over 13 million enslaved Africans came to the New World. Historians estimate that between 10 and 15 percent died along the route of the "Middle Passage."[3] What motivated this huge international trade in humans? The primary motive was profit. In the South, the growing of tobacco—the main crop of the early farms—was labor intensive, requiring a large number of field workers. The enslavement of large numbers of Africans increased the margin of profit for the plantation owners. As earlier stated, enslavement of the large numbers of Africans made it possible to cultivate more land, thereby increasing the margin of profit for plantation owners. The African slave trade can be considered one of the first examples of globalization.

Here we get to the heart of the Better model regarding the antecedents of institutional racism. There is the ongoing debate regarding which came first: hostility and stereotyping of the Africans as subhumans—making enslavement palatable, or the establishment of the slave trade that subsequently led non-Africans to view enslaved Africans as inferior human beings. It is the contention of this monograph that it is the latter. This claim has been discussed earlier in reviewing the concept of race as explored by Audrey Smedley.[4] The negative attitudes and the stereotyping of Africans were the methods used to *justify* the maintenance of the slave trade, but did not create the institution of slavery. Slavery was profitable for all those who engaged in it. Thus, there was fierce opposition by slaveholders to acknowledging the humanity of Africans, for doing so would have made it more difficult to justify slavery. This fierce resistance to freeing African Americans from slavery remained a hallmark of the South and parts of the North throughout the Civil War. After the emancipation of African Americans, the Jim Crow laws that were established were simply a continuation of the slave system without slaveowners. Jim Crow laws were statutes enacted after Reconstruction to restrict the rights of the Negro in all spheres of life. These laws in effect took away from negroes the right to vote and political and economic equity and equality. These laws endured until the 1960s and the advent of the civil rights movement.

Another example of racism being used for economic privilege can be seen in the plight of Indian tribes. Native Americans were systematically shoved off their land starting in the late 1600s to increase the land available for Europeans to homestead. In the beginning, settlers were content to farm the land systematically bought from the tribes. Over time, as more and more Europeans came to the colonies, more land was needed. The solution, Europeans decided, was not to buy it from the tribes but to take it by force. The continued need to acquire new land led to the final decision to force all Native Americans into reservations. These reservations were generally established in the least arable land in the most inhospitable territory. Through the use of racism, Europeans received an economic advantage by being able to homestead, with the hope of increasing their wealth. As the frontier was pushed westward, the government also increased its land holdings and political and international standing.

American history is replete with examples of minorities being relegated to the most unrewarding jobs or being pitted against whites to ensure a docile labor force. Such a labor force would more readily accept inferior or dangerous working conditions. Workers would be less likely to demand higher wages, fearing that they would be fired from their jobs. An example of the latter is the race riot in 1867 during which Irish and German immigrants burned down the black district of Detroit because the power elite led them to believe that blacks would take over their jobs, or lower the existing wage.[5] Clearly, whites would continue to be wary of blacks or any others who offered to work for less. This tension created a situation in which corporations used blacks and other minorities to scare whites into being more pliable for fear of being replaced. This historical conflict has been repeated again and again in U.S. history. For example, in Chicago in 1919, a concern over jobs kindled twenty-five race riots that year.[6]

The Two-Tier Labor System

The **two-tier system of labor** in America is a more current example of economic advantage gained through racism, although the system has been in existence since the beginning of the Industrial Revolution in America. This two-tier system in the labor market, which will be discussed more in Chapter 4, is an intricate component of the operation of economic and social stratification in American society. The system operates as a two-layered hierarchical system of job distribution, with those on top allocated the better jobs. It is structured to ensure that minorities and women, along with poor whites, are relegated to the most unrewarding, dangerous, dirty, cyclical jobs in the system—at the bottom. On the other hand, the majority of white males continue to hold the most lucrative labor positions—on the top. Jobs are even relegated by race and ethnicity. In California, Latinos pick the fruits and vegetables. When I ask my class, which is composed primarily of Latinos, "Who are the porters in our hotels, and the dishwashers, and busboys in our restaurants?" they respond, "We are!" A significant shift in California's workforce is the changeover that has occurred from African Americans to Latino janitors and other low-skilled workers. While African Americans have more seniority, and may be the supervisors, their numbers are being replaced by Latinos and to some extent Asians. Across America, jobs are now being relegated by national origins as well. There is an ongoing debate regarding the effect on the economy of the great influx of both illegal and illegal immigrants. Some economists state that immigrants are good for the economy because they take jobs that native-born citizens will not.[7] Others have stated that they lower the wages of the native born at the bottom of the economic ladder because they work for less or eliminate their job opportunity all together. The Center for Labor Market Studies at Northeastern University stated that between 2000 and 2004, jobs held by immigrants rose by 2 million while the number of employed native born fell by 958,000.[8] We will note in chapter 5 the Web of Institutional Racism—the interlocking of the social institutions to insure that the two-tier labor force remains intact.

The two-tier labor system was threatened by a drive led by the civil rights movement in the 1960s and 1970s to level the field so that employment would be based upon merit. Many feel that the fight against affirmative action waged in the 1990s by neo-conservatives, and which continues to this day, is due to the concern that minorities were increasingly in the position to compete head on with whites in some areas. In the prolonged restructuring of the American economy, some whites have felt that they are "losing jobs" unfairly to minorities and this feeling is quite evident in the national debate on immigration. In 1997, California passed an anti-affirmative action plan for higher education. It had the desired effect—there was nearly a 50 percent drop in minorities entering the prestigious Langley Law School in San Francisco. Further drops in minority enrollment at institutions of higher learning have been recorded. Some universities, University of California, Los Angeles, for example, is trying to reverse this trend by using other criteria to increase student diversity. Of course neo-conservatives will argue that this simply proves that minorities had been given unfair advantage over more qualified applicants, never acknowledging that children of alumni and endowment givers receive preferential treatment. At the same time, they conveniently overlook the fact that talented minority athletes are given special treatment, too.

Social Privilege

There is a strong ideology built over hundreds of years, which supports white skin privilege. **Ideology** is a system of beliefs or concepts about human life or culture. The social ideology in this case extols the virtue, one might say "rightness," of white supremacy. In America, this ideology can be traced back to the colonies when the white settlers justified their right to control the land and enforce their lifestyle over the Native Americans. Poor whites are as much a victim of this ideology as are racial minorities. The message to them is, "No matter what your economic lot in life, you are better than any minority person regardless of their talent or economic standing because you are white." This was very useful ploy in the antebellum South to suppress wages and keep white laborers in line, for poor whites in the South were exploited just as African Americans were by the plantation system. Only landowners were able to make economic and social policy decisions, for they occupied all the governing positions. Plantation owners were the ruling class and they manipulated both blacks and whites to ensure economic advantage.

The elite policy makers have been quite astute in gaining the support of poor and working-class whites in maintaining institutional racism. Poor whites have been beguiled into acquiescing with their own economic exploitation with the ploy of "white skin privilege." They have been used as the army on the front line fighting affirmative action, believing that minorities and non-white immigrants were undeserving and were stealing their jobs and economic standing—gaining status, which threatened their social position in American society. All the while, their jobs were diminishing due to the transfer of American businesses overseas. Many whites who still have not accepted the reality of the restructuring of the American economy and globalization support current anti-affirmative action legislation. The current ascendancy of white Evangelicals in the Republican Party appears to me as another ruse to use poor and working-class whites to cement the control of the elites over the minorities, who generally are Democrats.

Euro-Americans have grown up with the ideology that they are better because they are white and therefore their lives should be richer than minorities in every way. No minority should be better off than they, except for a few exceptional people such as athletes and entertainers. Consequently, as more minorities have vied with them for entry into college, well-paying jobs, and housing outside of the inner city, many looked for a scapegoat and found the "usual suspects"—the minorities. Although this attitude is muted in our society, it would seem that most really endorse the notion that it is right that there is "white skin privilege," which holds that whites deserve to be dominant. Individual and institutional racism is the result of this national conferment of social privilege on Euro-Americans.

Psychic Rewards

I first heard the term "psychic reward" in connection with a discussion about university professors' current salaries. Jerry Brown, then governor of California, was purported to have said that while the lower salaries were not commensurate with their training, they were suitable nevertheless because the profession offered psychic rewards that made up for the loss of income. I use this term in the same context. **Psychic reward** relates to satisfaction one experiences emotionally and spiritually from holding a favored position. Thus, whites in general, and poor and working-class whites in particular, experience much internal satisfaction from being white. While working-class and poor whites may have little economic security, they always have the advantage of psychic reward. Further, through all its social institutions, American society reinforces the notion that whites are superior to all other groups. One can readily see how intoxicating this feeling can be. Certainly, one is loath to give up a favored position. Because many stand to gain by keeping racism in place, there is insufficient will in the American society to rid itself of anything more than the uncomfortable overt signs of racism. Unfortunately, too many Americans are tolerant of racism, so long as its most blatant manifestations remain concealed. I view the present attack on affirmative action as evidence of the resistance to erasing this privilege, especially that of white male prerogative. It is also reminiscent of the resistance of males to the women's liberation movement back in the 1970s and 1980s. Many males resented the fact that women wanted to share in the rewards of well-paying skilled jobs that they had enjoyed exclusively, such as being law enforcement officers, fire fighters, long distance truck drivers, plumbers, electricians, or engineers. Corporations fought vigorously to deny women positions in the business world. This fight against women's opportunities is also a fight for male prerogative.

Explanation of the Better Model

Figure 2.1 illustrates how racism is created—its cause and effect. Notice that institutional racism is the center of the model. This placement conveys the point that institutional racism is more potent and more devastating than individual racism. In figure 2.1 economic privilege is ranked higher than social privilege and psychic reward. All three contribute to the creation and the persistence of racism. As noted earlier, this theoretical framework refutes the prevailing theory of racism as being based on bias and prejudice (attitudes and feelings). My model puts forth the notion that the desire for economic privilege has fueled racism. Social privilege and psychic reward play a much less important role. For example, in early days of the develop-

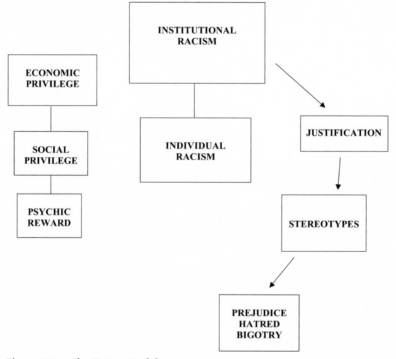

Figure 2.1.   The Better Model

ment of the American colonies, to justify the economic exploitation of Africans and Native Americans, it was expedient to link their enforced servitude by claiming that these people were inferior, dangerous, heathens, and defilers of white women. This justification has been encased in negative stereotypes that support and encourage prejudice, hatred, bigotry, and even genocide.

INDIVIDUAL RACISM

Individual racism relates to visible and often blatant individual actions that exploit and subjugate members of disadvantaged groups. Instances of personal racism require that the person perpetrating the act be in a power position in order to enforce negative consequences on the targeted person. It is important to remember that feelings are not the same as behavior; racism is behavior. Much has been written about individual racism, those premeditated acts performed when one person attempts to undermine the rights and dignity of another, and in so doing is personally rewarded.[9]

For example, an apartment building owner acts racist when she refuses to rent to an Asian seeking an apartment or quotes a higher rent to discourage the applicant. Even if the Asian is allowed to rent the apartment at a higher cost, the owner has effectively disadvantaged the new tenant who now has to expend more of his income for housing. At the same time, the owner benefits by receiving more rent. If the Asian is denied that apartment, he or she is being disadvantaged, for the apartment seeker is denied access to housing which is readily available to a white person. Again, the owner benefits, in this case with the psychic reward of reinforced feelings of superiority. Or consider another scenario that of a Latino who is restricted to a lower paying job than his skills should demand by his white boss. Clearly, he is being exploited while the employer enriching himself. Historically, minorities have been paid less than whites while doing the same job. It has been stressed earlier that the cornerstone of institutional racism is economic advantage. Race and ethnicity continue to be used as measures to control and limit upward mobility in business and labor, while at the same time enhance the possibility of profits for the companies.

Disliking a specific minority person does not in itself constitute an act of racism. If the person is unable or unwilling to act out their negative feelings to the disadvantage of the minority person it is not racism, but bigotry. **Bigotry** is the state of mind in which the individual is obstinately and intolerantly devoted to their own opinions and prejudices. Thus, while negative feelings toward an individual because of his racial/ethnic background pollutes the air and can make his life uncomfortable, it is institutional racism which poisons the air for minorities, making it very difficult to exist, much less flourish. I must emphasize here that I am not suggesting that a negative feeling toward others because of their differences is acceptable—it is not. However, in my discussion I am distinguishing between the harmful effects of actions/ behavior over feelings/attitudes.

Stereotyping

An underpinning to racism is stereotyping. Stereotyping was defined earlier but bears further discussion. For example, to hold the view that all Asians are highly intelligent is to stereotype Asians. To suggest that all Asians are financially successful is off the mark, for there is much variation in income, from the Hmong—80 percent of whom are on welfare—to other recent immigrants. As regards to Asians, the stereotype is a positive one. However, it is just as damaging, for the individuals are not viewed as persons in their own right. The "model Asian" myth has often been used as a cudgel to beat back the honest demands of African Americans, Latinos, and Native Americans. In effect, the implication is that since Asians have made it, these other groups should also be able to.[10] It saddles each Asian with unrealistic, unfair expectations. The reality for Asian Americans is much different. Bagaza stated in *Newsweek* that despite having education and training to rival their white colleagues, Asian Americans have not achieved parity in status and salary. He goes on to say, "An Asian American is 60 percent more likely to hold a bachelor's degree than a white American but [still] makes a lower median salary ($37,040 versus $42,050)."[11]

We are more familiar with negative stereotypes. For example, "African Americans are lazy and don't want to work; Latino males are violent and will kill with little provocation; Jews are cheap and will try to swindle you out of your money; Poles are stupid." Stereotyping becomes a building block, which allows the individual to confer a range of negative behaviors upon a group. Thus, feelings of hostility and fear are supported and then justified. With these rationalized negative feelings, it is then possible to excuse differential treatment of persons from the targeted group. An example is the demeaning treatment of African Americans in the aftermath of Hurricane Katrina when officials did not deem it important to even give updates on services to the people inside the Superdome. The fact that thousands of the poor, mostly African Americans, were left stranded without adequate food and water for days reveals the depth of the negative attitude toward them. Another example is, "Native Americans are drunkards and lazy so it isn't necessary to ensure that their children get a good education, it would just be wasted on them anyway. They deserve to stay on the reservation; for they aren't going to do anything with opportunities given to them." The individual then uses the rationalization to justify the exploitation, which conveniently provides advantages to them at the expense of the targeted group member.

This discussion regarding racism has been belabored because of my concern that too many disparate feelings and actions are being labeled "racist" in our society. Without clear-cut terms that we can all agree on, there is little likelihood that we can further the crucial discourse on race relations in the United States.

PLAYING THE VICTIM

I will end this chapter with a caveat to people of color—it has been said, "Increasing knowledge brings increasing pain." As you become more knowledgeable about the workings of racism you may become depressed, extremely angry and frustrated, and feel powerless. I caution you not to allow these negative feelings to overtake you. Doing so will only increase your feelings of powerlessness. This is what I call "playing the victim." Someone said, "There are no victims." To a large extent I accept this. It may seem that the only thing to do is to give up and not struggle against such powerful opponents as institutional racism and oppression.

This is playing the victim, that is, acquiescing to the oppression, confirming that you have no control over your life and that the power of racism is so great that it is useless to fight it. Giving in and giving up is not an option, for there is no place to hide, except for those few who can "pass" for Anglo. However, there is still a huge internal price paid for even doing this.

Minorities also play the victim when they act out pathologically to racism with dire personal consequences. Critically harming a fellow employee for calling you a "nigger/wetback/chink" on the job, and subsequently losing the job and going to prison, is a form of playing the victim.

Buying into the deficit model is also playing the victim. Hayes-Bautista and Rodriquez state, "A deficiency-oriented approach to describing minorities may have once been helpful in the battle to overcome discriminatory barriers and promote programs to level the playing field, but it is today a purveyor of minority stereotypes."[12] Unfortunately, some members of minority groups, along with policy makers, have bought into this model. This has caused some minority persons not to perform to their highest potential, or hold themselves to the highest standard of performance. Instead, they expect for exceptions to be made for them.

Persons of color can and do abet the power of racism by playing the victim. This often is done to save oneself. African Americans had to pretend acceptance of subjugation to stay alive during the centuries of slavery. In some parts of the South today, blacks feel compelled to continue playing a subservient role to stay out of "harm's way." Living up to a stereotype of some inner city blacks has grossed millions for gangsta rap artists and some movie actors. However, there is the downside of playing the part, for it reinforces negative images which minorities are trying so hard to erase.

Awareness of acting out the victim role is crucial as the first step to gaining personal empowerment. This primer is written to provide the knowledge and skills necessary to combat racism.

GUILT

This treatise is meant for analysis by whites as well. Let us discuss the ramification of the book for whites. Some whites have made no effort to learn the history of minorities in America. Until recently, American education has made a mockery of the contributions of African Americans/Latinos/Asian Americans. This ignorance permits the prevalence of cultural blindness and deafness; the aftermath of Hurricane Katrina is a perfect example of historical ignorance leading to disaster for poor blacks. Further, it encourages the acceptance of stereotypes, and race ideology.

The majority of Euro-Americans do not recognize or acknowledge that they have a culture. This failure to acknowledge that American institutions are created and supported by Euro-American culture prevents us from coming to grips with institutional racism. Failure to see Euro-American values as the dominant culture reinforces cultural blindness and deafness.

Many in the dominant group harbor deeply felt anger and hostility toward minority group members, holding them responsible for all manner of personal misfortune. However, there are also a number of whites who accept the fact of racism, but are uncomfortable discussing race relations in any way. While wanting to own up to the historical racism in America, they nevertheless find it impossible for them to openly state any present-day culpability. This denial of present-day racism justifies resistance to affirmative action.

As the twentieth century closed, America wrestled with the anxiety created by President Clinton who hinted at the possibility that he would make a public apology to African Americans for over three hundred years of slavery. I attribute much of the reluctance of some whites to such a public apology as deep-seated, feelings of guilt—guilt that begs for denial and/or repression. Owning up to the embedded inequality toward racial minorities forces the re-examination of American mythology which includes rugged individuality, and America as an inherently just civilization—a meritorious society.

It is important to note that there has been some public acknowledgment recently in the form of a public apology by the U.S. Senate on June 13, 2005, for the acceptance of lynchings. There was no federal law against lynchings and states refused to prosecute whites who murdered blacks. "The U.S. House of Representatives, responding to pleas from presidents and civil rights groups, three times agreed to make the crime a federal offense. Each time, the measure died in the Senate at the hands of powerful southern lawmakers."[13]

Whites reading this book are encouraged to get in touch with these deep-seated feelings. At the same time there should be the realization that people of color never would have achieved the success experienced in the civil rights movement had there not been a large number of white allies. Allies who put their lives on the line in the South and in the North have furthered the cause of human rights. It should be remembered that all human rights advances recorded in this country have required the active support or at the least the acquiescence of a sizable portion of white Americans.

SUMMARY

Although there has been public denouncements of institutional racism, still it persists. This chapter explored its tenacity and the cultural underpinnings that maintain its existence. The focus of the chapter is the Better Model on Institutional Racism. This model suggests that the reasons for the persistence of racism are its "positive uses" to the dominant group. Each of the components of the model were examined: economic privilege, social privilege and psychic rewards. Figure 2.1 outlined the nature of institutional and individual racism, including its side effects: justification, stereotyping, prejudice, hatred, and bigotry.

KEY TERMS

bigotry. The state of mind in which the individual is obstinately and intolerantly devoted to their own opinions and prejudices.
cultural blindness and deafness. Relates to the unwillingness to acknowledge that racism is imbedded inequality within the all social institutions that maintain the society.
ideology. A system of beliefs or concepts about human life or culture.
psychic reward. The satisfaction one experiences emotionally and spiritually from holding a favored position.
two-tier labor system. A two-layered hierarchical system of job distribution, with those on top are allocated the better jobs.

GROUP ACTIVITIES

1. Describe an occasion when you felt you were being treated differently from others because of your racial/ethnic group membership.
2. Identify one example of individual racism and one example of institutional racism
3. Find a current newspaper article that exemplifies individual racism. Discuss within your study group whether a person can be damaged more by individual racism than institutional racism.

STUDY QUESTIONS

1. Explain the difference between individual racism and institutional racism.

2. What is the importance of bigotry, bias, and prejudice to the understanding of racism?
3. Why has racism endured in the United States for more than three hundred years?
4. How is it possible to maintain institutional racism without individual actions?
5. Explain the term "nebulous." What is the importance of this term to institutional racism?
6. Define the term, "cultural blindness."
7. Give an example of a positive stereotype.
8. Why is justification an important component of the Better Model?

NOTES

1. Pumla Gobodo-Madikizela, "White People Just Don't Get It About Racism Culture," *Los Angeles Times*, July 12, 1999. Gobdo-Madikizela is the Jean and Joseph Sullivan Peace Fellow at the Bunting Institute of Radcliffe University.

2. Herbert J. Gans, "The Positive Functions of Poverty," *American Journal of Sociology* 78, no. 2: 75–289 (1972).

3. Hugh Thomas, *The Slave Trade* (New York: Simon & Schuster, 1997).

4. Audrey Smedley, *Race in North America* (Boulder, CO: Westview Press, 1999).

5. *Historical Annals of the African American Museum of History*, Detroit, Michigan, December 2000.

6. Anthony Platt, ed., *The Politics of Riot Commissions* (New York: Collier, 1971).

7. Tyler Cowen and Daniel Rothschild, "Unskilled Doesn't Mean Unnecessary," *Los Angeles Times*, May 15, 2006.

8. David Bacon, "Black/Migrant Rivalry for Jobs Can Be Eased," *Los Angeles Times*, August 22, 2004.

9. Paul Kivel, *Uprooting Racism* (Philadelphia: New Society Publishers, 1995); Herbert Hill and James Jones, Jr., eds., *Race in America* (Madison: University of Wisconsin Press, 1993); Michael Tonry, *Malign Neglect* (New York: Oxford University Press, 1995).

10. Ronald Takaki, *From Different Shores* (New York: Oxford University Press, 1987).

11. Angelo Bagaza, "I Don't Count as 'Diversity,'" *Newsweek*, February 8, 1999.

12. D. Hayes-Bautista and G. Rodriguez, "Killing Minorities Softly with Words Intended to Be Helpful," *Los Angeles Times*, April 15, 1997.

13. Avis Thomas-Lester, "An Apology for 'America's Holocaust,'" *Washington Post*, June 20, 2005.

3

Institutional Racism Dissected:
Part A

Few issues in American life have been as intransigent as race. In every century race has presented the nation its greatest paradoxes, challenges, and opportunities, calling into question time and again the principle of equality on which it was founded.

—Joyce Ladner[1]

THE POTENCY OF SOCIAL INSTITUTIONS

While much has been written about individual acts of racism, comparatively little less has been written about institutional racism. Individual violent acts of racism, such as the 1999 drive-by random shooting of Jews and African Americans in the Chicago area by an alleged white supremacist, or the 2004 shooting of children at a Jewish day care center in the suburbs of Los Angeles, again by an alleged white supremacist, received more attention than the continued disparity in the employment rates between whites and nonwhites of similar background and skill. Not enough has been written about institutional practices that are covertly racist, and often concealed. To understand the potency or power of institutional racism, one must first understand the function of American institutions.

All societies have similar social institutions. Whether a Western postindustrial technological society like the United States or a small agricultural society like Sudan, the society must have a system for educating its young. The educational system determines what knowledge is worth learning and what is spurious. The educational system is a social institution. All societies have a system of business and labor. The system determines what is to be produced, how it is to be produced, and by whom, and on whose behalf the products will be created. Legal and political institutions in all societies determine what laws will govern the inhabitants, how and by whom these laws will be enforced, and who will be prosecuted for which infractions. All of these systems that help a society to function are social institutions. As we will see in the case study of Hurricane Katrina, the system governing New Orleans set in motion the disaster.

Social Institutions Defined

A social institution is a social arrangement through which collective action is taken to maintain and perpetuate the society and its culture. Major American social institutions include the family, education, business and labor, health care, housing, religion, welfare, law enforcement, and politics. These same social institutions operate in all societies. To ensure that social institutions operate well, each society establishes formal and informal rules, that is, policies, practices, and procedures within them. These rules, which emanate from social institutions, are regularly modified to meet the ends or will of the society at any given time. In American society this can be done formally by the enactment and modification of laws. Informally, institutional changes are made over time through advancement in scientific knowledge, technological progression, the introduction of new ideas from other cultures, or innovation by popular culture.

Social institutions have the power to reward and punish their citizens. They reward by providing a good education for some and punish by foreclosing educational opportunities to others. Business and labor entities determine the qualifications required for each job. These entities also determine how much a person will earn for performing the job. The elites of this segment determine which jobs will have high status and which will be given very low status. The justice system (law and order) through its federal and state penal codes determine what personal actions will be punishable and to what extent. There was considerable debate for a time between conservatives and liberals regarding the disparity in the sentencing for the use of powder cocaine versus crack cocaine. Some civil rights groups suggest that racism is at play because powder cocaine more commonly used by whites draws a lighter prison sentence for possession than crack cocaine which is the form of the drug used most often by minorities.

Social institutions also reward individuals and groups as well by the way goods and services are distributed. For example, American corporations are able to gain favorable subsidies from the government while workers—whose labor sustains corporations—find that without union pressure, such profits gained are not shared with them. The implosion of energy giant ENRON, and communications giant WORLDCOM are examples of the corporation's elite benefiting at the expense of lower-level workers. Social institutions determine who will receive appropriate training and useful skills, quality health care, adequate housing, political influence, living wages, social standing, and the promise of a secure future for self and children. Unfortunately, one finds that race, ethnicity, gender, and social class heavily influence how goods and services are distributed.

American social institutions were established for purposes generally unrelated to matters of race; often the social systems created by the British were copied in part or in total into American society. These systems were intended neither to perpetuate inequality nor to ease it. On the matter of race, they began as **"race neutral."** The systems were race neutral in the sense that race and ethnicity played no part in their original development. However, practices and procedures within these social institutions have intended and unintended consequences which this book examines. As explored in chapter 1, American society early on made decisions to enslave persons to insure an adequate, cheap labor force. This arrangement proved to be so lucrative that the Southern plantation owner was unwilling to relinquish it. On the contrary, the Southern states expanded it into permanent enslavement of slaves' offspring. It is important to emphasize that enslavement did not occur by chance; it was a deliberate action reinforced over hundreds of years through slave revolts, abolitionist movements, and international disagreements. Racism began to insure a permanent and abundant labor force. However, to maintain slavery it became necessary to taint or compromise other social institutions. This resulted in racism becoming embedded in all U.S. institutions. Policies, practices, and procedures were subverted as needed to support the practice of lifetime enslavement.

Racism Embedded in Social Institutions

How did racism become embedded in all our institutions? We have learned that race ideology was used extensively to justify enslavement. This ideology stated that Africans and Native Americans were inferior to Europeans. To fortify this belief, it was necessary to establish a complicated social system that relied heavily on separation, isolation, and unequal rewards from the social institutions. If enslaved Africans and Native Americans were allowed to live in the same manner as whites there would be no way to enforce slavery. Therefore there was always a need to reinforce support of slavery by showing that Africans and Indians were inferior. Separation in housing naturally followed from the decision to establish widespread slavery. The slaves had to be watched constantly to prevent sabotage, uprisings, the murder of whites, and escapes. For this reason, closely guarded separate areas were crucial. Spatially separated slave quarters were institutionalized on Southern plantations.

Refusing opportunities for education to those enslaved was a natural next step. Knowledgeable people resist subjugation. The only schooling sanctioned for slaves was "Bible-learning." Christian indoctrination during this period taught that segregation was God's will and mandated that servants should be submissive to their masters. The next step involved blocking access to the judicial system. People of color were not allowed to testify against whites in court. Nonwhites had no rights that had to be honored by whites. Over time, each of the existing social institutions established one set of distinct practices and procedures for Europeans and another for all others. Each of these practices of separation was enacted into law or embedded into the culture. Both Europeans and non-Europeans were forced to abide by these laws or be punished. Thus, we see each social institution being subverted to maintain and justify enslavement for Africans. For Indian tribes, the same process of separate practices and procedures operated within the social institutions ensued. Eventually, Native Americans were barred from entering European settlements. The judicial system was subverted again and again to confiscate Native American land. Policies, practices, and procedures were crafted that made it possible to move Indian tribes easily from desirable land. These judicial policies were designed to give the advantage to white settlers and to ensure that the Indian tribes would be unable to live on the land under any circumstance.

Most persons are aware of the power of a political system, the public decision-making mechanism of most industrial societies. For nearly a hundred years after the Civil War, the South was able to maintain policies and procedures within the legal and judicial system, which prevented African Americans from voting, along with a host of other legal restrictions. These were called **Jim Crow laws.** In the 1800s in California, persons of Chinese ancestry were not allowed to testify against whites in court. They were not allowed to own land or become naturalized citizens regardless of the length of time they had lived in America.[2] Imagine what it meant to deny a person the right to own land. In an agricultural society, it meant that a person could not rise above being a laborer on someone else's property. It also took away their chance for upward mobility by being able to invest in a home. By requiring Chinese to be tenants, laws kept minorities at the mercy of the landlord. These policies were all calculated to ensure Anglo supremacy.

So far we have been discussing how institutions in 1700s and 1800s transformed to accommodate unequal distribution of goods and services. Now let us look at the power of essential institutions in American society today. The health care system can marshal goods, services, and talents to maximize the level of medical services provided to persons. The health care system as a social institution determines the policies, practices, and procedures that demarcate the type of health care that will be available, specifically who may provide health care in the field, and at what cost. Consider how much influence the health care system has over your personal health.

In the North, political institutions have regularly gerrymandered districts to dilute the vote of urban minorities. In California, Mexican American pressure groups forced the development of new guidelines for political representation after the 1990 census. These groups demanded fairer redistricting to increase the chances that Latinos, the largest minority in the state, could overcome racism in the political system. Because of the threat of a class action suit by the Mexican American Legal Defense Fund (MALDEF), Latinos now have a better chance of electing a person from their own ethnic group to represent them.

In October 2001, MALDEF revisited this issue by suing the state of California over its plan for redistricting required by the 2000 census. Again, MALDEF claimed that the proposed redistricting exploits them. So what do the above institutional practices and procedures tell us? In each instance, the dominant group stood to gain through the inequitable practices of each particular institution. The dominant group was more likely to be able to manipulate policies in their favor. When one group—whether the majority or the minority of the society—has managed to both define the rewards of the system and unfairly control who will succeed, the society indeed has forfeited its claim to being an equitable and meritorious one. When the population is multiracial but the members of only one racial grouping control the pathways to success for all racial and ethnic groups, then indeed the society is racist. As Euro-American society continues the process of understanding its own racism, it will need to understand its myopic view of success that is built solely on an Anglo model. No society will distribute goods and services in a perfectly equitable manner. However, no society should use race, ethnicity, gender, sexual orientation, or place of origin as a gauge to determine who will be rewarded and who will be penalized.

Racism is deeply embedded in our society through our social institutions. American institutions are heavily oriented to White, Anglo-Saxon, Protestant (WASP) values and its accompanying lifestyle; this is the dominant culture and lifestyle that permeates all of American society. This is not to suggest that there is anything inherently wrong in this cultural orientation. What must be called into question is the implication that only WASP culture can be viewed as exemplary in American society. The greatness of the United States has often been used to champion people who have been subjugated. American troops sent to Somalia, Haiti, and Kosovo in the 1990s attest to this country's concern for weaker and oppressed people. However, when other Americans are poorly treated because they do not adhere fully to the dominant cultural, social injustice is operating. Policies, practices and procedures in American institutions tend to favor the dominant culture of this society. When the term "mainstream" is used, it denotes conformity to "Anglo/WASP" standards. Many of these standards have been the back-bone to the formation of the richest, most powerful country in the world. However, when those standards are used to unfairly limit the opportunities of nonwhites, then one is dealing with racism.

The Invisible Hand of Racism

While institutional racism no longer has the status of law, it persists. This is due, not so much to the actions of frightened and/or bigoted persons, but rather because of well-meaning citizens who are merely carrying out "busi-ness as usual." It is too often exacerbated by the actions of unsuspecting re-formers. Detecting an individual culprit who is responsible for institutional racism is very difficult, even when one is able to determine the existence of racism itself. Who is to say who is responsible for the high rate of incarcer-ation of black and Latino males? Who is responsible for the 50 percent dropout rate of Latinos from high school? Who is responsible for the high unemployment of black males or the high rate of female-headed house-holds in the African American community? *The power of institutional racism is that no one person must act to maintain it.*

Institutional racism can function without much active individual assis-tance; a person need only follow the established racist policies and prac-tices. Until the 1970s, fire departments across the country had a policy of requiring that their firefighters be of a certain height and weight, for exam-ple a minimum of five feet, ten inches and healthy weight approximate to the person's height. The ruling effectively reduced the number of Latinos, and Asians. It was unnecessary for a fire department to state that it did not hire persons from these groups, for the rules automatically reduced their chances to qualify. On the face of it, the fire department could argue that it did not discriminate against Asians and Latinos. The height and weight re-quirements were considered necessary to do the job of carrying heavy water hoses and to rescue persons from buildings. However, one need only refer to Hong Kong and other parts of Southeast Asia to realize the deceptive na-ture of this reasoning. These countries have skyscrapers and their firefight-ers are as capable as American firefighters but few of them would meet the weight and height requirements stated above. The Los Angeles Police De-partment had a ruling that cadets needed to scale a seven-foot wall to pass the physical strength requirement. This policy effectively limited the num-ber of women who made it through the police academy. It was unnecessary for the department to state that they did not want women on the police force, because women could not generally meet the physical requirements. However, in the 1980s, women's groups discovered and publicized the fact that policemen never had to scale seven-foot walls, because the legal height for all walls in Los Angeles was six feet.

The thoughtful person will come to the same conclusion as the President's Commission on Civil Disorders nearly thirty years ago: "What white Americans have never fully understood—but what the Negro can never forget—is that white society is deeply implicated in the ghetto. White institutions created it, white institutions maintain it, and white society condones it."[3] Thus, the "minority problem" is really a "white problem." The crucial issue is whether whites can be self-critical. Throughout our history, Euro-Americans have found ways to justify racist policies and procedures, and this continues today. It is the unwillingness to look at our slave history and the genocide against Indian tribes, which allows us to continue our cultural blindness and deafness. It is this inability or unwillingness to be self-critical which prevents the ending of racism. Only when we deal honestly with white culpability can we erase injustice and inequality based on race and ethnic membership.

The Multicultural Nature of Racism

It has been a glaring omission that we do not look at the problem of institutional racism from a multicultural viewpoint. America has had a morbid fascination for social research that contrasts the fates of blacks and whites. However, American racism is not a black and white affair, and never was. The racism that culminated in the near genocide of Native Americans, as well as the documented legally sanctioned inequities toward Asians, attests to this. The multiracial component of the 1992 Los Angeles Riot is the most recent validation that racism is a more encompassing phenomenon. This riot proved to be the deadliest in the twentieth century, with a death toll of forty-five; it was also the most costly in U.S. history with an estimated $1 billion in insured losses.[4] Latinos were the largest group arrested during the uprising; young white activists stormed the Superior Court Building minutes after the King verdict to protest the "not guilty" ruling against the white police officers involved in the incident. Latinos beat whites; Latinos were beaten by African Americans. African Americans and Latinos assaulted Koreans, and Korean stores were looted and burned by both groups. Koreans brought out guns and shot back. Though white Americans have gained much by promulgating racism, America need not continue to be racist. We have the power to change the patterns, policies, and procedures within of our social institutions. And change them we must or we will continue to suffer cyclical race riots in our urban areas, each more explosive and destructive than the one before. The sections "The Hidden Face of Institutional Racism" will show graphically how social institutions have developed, intentionally or not, a system of exchange that ensures white skin privilege and maintains inequality in American society.

The Power of Institutional Racism

Institutional racism is powerful due to many factors. For one, the clout of institutional racism comes from the reality that it is a norm in American society. A **norm** is a widely accepted practice, procedure, or custom. Institutional racism is normal, expected action; it is not a pattern that is considered unusual or out of place. It has the false value of tradition. Second, America has maintained racial stratification. Racial stratification is the process of arranging the society into classes, or graded statuses, by race; most societies have some form of **social stratification**. America, as shown earlier, uses race ideology as one of the means to stratify the society. Over the hundreds of years of practice, racial separation and inequality has taken on the mantel of normalcy.

Third, as we have learned, institutional racism is financially lucrative. It provides unearned privileges to those considered to be white. Fourth, it bolsters the ego of those favored by the system, giving those privileged the psychological advantage of feeling good about themselves. One the other hand, it is expected and assumed that minorities should have and will have lesser social status and fewer of the privileges of American citizenship. Consequently, there is widespread surprise when a Latino or Native American is noted for high achievement in fields such as medicine, physics, and engineering. It is not expected that members of minority groups would be capable of excelling in certain fields. This societal expectation and acceptance that minority groups are not on a par with whites reinforces the power of racism throughout American society, and becomes a self-fulfilling prophecy.

In low-income communities, minority students have not been encouraged, as they should be, to aspire to be astronauts, engineers, or mathematicians. Since minorities are disproportionately poor, the numbers of them who move into these fields are low. This reinforces the belief of their inability to succeed in these fields. The end result is a perpetuation of race ideology. It is important to note that this attitude is lessening as meritocracy spreads, albeit slowly, throughout American society. **Meritocracy** is a system in which the talented are chosen and moved ahead on the basis of their achievement. The practice of meritocracy is most visible in sports, where race or ethnicity is given less consideration when choosing athletes for sports teams. Consequently, we see more minorities in athletics. Black males are disproportionately represented in professional basketball and football and Latinos in baseball where skill and not skin color, more likely rules.

The Nebulous Quality of Institutional Racism

The nebulous quality of institutional racism suggests the need for in-depth study of the phenomenon. Nebula means a mist or cloud; like a mist or a vapor, institutional racism cannot be seen, and often goes undetected. Racism is nebulous because it moves surreptitiously throughout our social institutions hardly making a ripple unless you are the recipient of its harsh treatment. Thus bureaucrats and citizens alike can plead ignorance of its existence. Unlike individual or personal racism, there is no one person to identify as the guilty party. Institutional racism does not need individual acts of hostility to perpetuate itself. Most importantly, racism within American institutions is normative, that is, racist patterns operate as ordinary forms of behavior and bureaucracy.

Chapter 1 provided an overview of how institutional racism functions. This chapter will now examine this phenomenon in greater detail. It was pointed out that social institutions generally maintain a neutral stance on race issues. However, patterns and policies may unintentionally or intentionally establish inequality. In the next section of this chapter and the following two chapters I analyze several major social institutions: housing, education, employment, law enforcement, politics, and public welfare.

THE HIDDEN FACE OF INSTITUTIONAL RACISM: HOUSING AND EDUCATION

This section dissects institutional racism by providing current examples of policies, practices, and procedures within housing and education. These policies perpetuate inequality by using race and ethnicity as a barriers to full participation in American society.

Housing

Housing is a crucial element of upward mobility for Americans. Where one lives helps define one's status in the socioeconomic structure of the society. Where a person lives determines one's ability to share in the goods and services offered in American society. Throughout the history of the United States, the distribution of housing has been a crucial enabler in maintaining inequality between racial and ethnic groups. In early colonial days, Native Americans were eventually barred from living in or near the European settlements. After racial slavery was established, strict separation of living quarters isolated the Africans. Further housing separation reinforced social stratification for rich as well as poor whites by forcing the Africans to reside in the most inferior housing available. When Chinese workers came to this country in the 1880s, separation of living quarters was strictly enforced; thus we now have "Chinatowns" throughout the United States. As the frontiers of America were pushed westward, Native Americans were systematically pushed off their ancestral land. Eventually they were herded into the most undesirable sections of the West, areas that would be known as Indian reservations.

After slavery legally ended, racism and racial ideology continued and was strengthened by Jim Crow laws and social practices. For Indians, African Americans, and Chinese Americans, housing continued as a form of apartheid. **Apartheid** is legally sanctioned racial segregation. Housing practices were constructed to keep members of targeted groups in their designated lower exploited social status, through spatial isolation.

Anthony Downs, a senior fellow in the Brookings Economic Studies Program, discusses three reasons for inner city slums, populated with minorities and the poor that are so characteristic of today's American metropolitan areas. The first is the policy of requiring all new housing to meet quality standards that are so high that the poor are effectively priced out of the market for new homes. Second is the policy of fragmented control by many small municipalities that establish procedures to maintain an exclusionary living space. The third cause of inner-core poverty concentrations is racial segregation in housing markets. According to Downs, "Repeated and recent studies of Realtor and homeowner behavior prove that racial discrimination is still widespread in housing transactions."[5]

John Powell, the executive director of the Institute on Race and Poverty at the University of Minnesota, has done extensive study of discriminatory housing patterns. He stated in 1998 that current housing apartheid "was constructed and is perpetuated through governmental housing and transportation policies, institutional practices, and private behavior."[6] This has changed little, for the Federal Reserve Report released in 2006 confirms continued inequity. The report states that blacks and Hispanic pay more for mortgages; it represents a tax on being nonwhite. The Fed's analysis of 2005 home lending data found that African American and Hispanic borrowers paid a higher than typical interest rate. Specifically, 54 percent of African Americans and 46 percent of Hispanics paid higher interest rates, while 17 percent of whites paid more on their home mortgages.[7] In the 1940s and 1950s, the Federal Housing Administration (FHA) had an explicit policy against granting mortgages for homes in predominately minority or racially integrated neighborhoods. Further, FHA preferred to finance new construction rather than the purchase of existing homes. This had the effect of paying whites to leave the city, while it confined blacks and immigrants to the central city. Cities, over time, lost a large percentage of their tax base derived from the middle class. This fiscal state has continued and has contributed to the disinvestment in the inner cities. Urban renewal efforts contributed to decline as blighted areas were torn down, but new housing was not constructed to be the needs of low-income residents. Local government policies and practices have also supported spatial segregation by exclusionary zoning, that is, requiring large numbers of minimum lot sizes or banning multifamily housing. This has made it impossible for the poor to buy homes.[8]

The continued decline of inner-city communities was accelerated by the social changes of the 1960s. It took the pressure of the civil rights movement to outlaw restrictive covenants. **Restrictive covenants** were laws enacted in cities aimed mainly at preventing racial minorities from moving into houses on blocks where whites were the majority of the homeowners. These laws were taken out of property deeds in 1964 in California, freeing many from de facto segregation. Large numbers of middle-class black families then moved away from the old and deteriorating neighborhoods into housing in working-class and middle-class white communities. Once there they found themselves isolated again. Whites stopped moving into neighborhoods that had near one-third or one-fourth blacks. There was also the practice of block busting engineered by unscrupulous real estate brokers. **Block busting** occurred when brokers entered neighborhoods that were experiencing modest integration and scared the remaining white residents with reports that many more blacks were planning to move in. The brokers cautioned these homeowners that their homes would lose value soon, and urged them to sell immediately. Middle-income African Americans, eager to leave the squalid conditions of the inner cities, paid the higher prices demanded by the brokers to improve their living conditions. Real estate brokers were able to profit in two ways: buying homes from whites below the market value in some instances and selling the same houses to blacks at inflated prices. Thus, we view another example of institutional and individual racism producing economic advantage for certain groups.

From 1970 to 1990, the number of people living in neighborhoods of high poverty—where the poverty rate is 40 percent or more—nearly doubled from 4.1 million to 8 million.[9] The reality of concentrated poverty is primarily an urban and racial circumstance, as TV viewers noted in the aftermath of Hurricane Katrina. More than half of public housing is located in high-poverty neighborhoods; only 7 percent in low-poor areas, that is communities with less than 10 percent of the overall population of poor people.[10] The shame of concentrated poverty areas must be placed on federal housing policy that has fostered housing the poor in this fashion.

There is no need to go to the past to find examples of apartheid. Shortly after the 1992 Los Angeles Riot, the Christopher Commission found that there was widespread redlining of minority communities.[11] **Redlining** is the practice of refusing bank loans to residents from targeted areas. Thus, many inner-city dwellers who might otherwise have qualified were unable to procure loans to upgrade or repair their property. Banks responded that bank officials perceived all inner city dwellers to be poor loan risks. While these residents may have had savings account at the bank, and a good credit history—qualities banks look for when awarding loans—loans were not forthcoming. Instead, inner-city bank branches sent their funds to suburban branches to provide loans to the suburban homeowners. In effect, inner-city dwellers were subsidizing homeowners in the suburbs. Block busting, redlining, and protective covenants are practices that maintain institutional racism in housing. See figure 3.1 for a historical review of housing discrimination and the struggle of African Americans to gain decent housing.

The Economic Value in Maintaining Segregated Housing

A low-income minority community can and often does serve as a conduit for wealth for both legal and illegal enterprises. The thesis of this book is that institutional racism pays off. This phenomenon can be examined in the ways that wealth operates within low-income minority communities even though the community rarely receives any benefits from the legal or illegal transactions. Poor minority communities are used to house illegal activities that would not be tolerated in middle-class areas, such as gambling houses, street prostitution, bordellos, street drug sales, and gun sales. Similarly, legal enterprises also abound here that would not be tolerated in middle-class communities: check-cashing stores, abundant liquor stores, overcrowded housing units, poorly maintained multi-unit buildings, swap meets, porno shops, and pawn shops. Huge sums of money illegally and legally flow through low-income communities, but do not circulate within in the community to enrich its inhabitants. The wealth generated by activities in the community quickly exits to enhance non-residents. Figure 3.2 graphically shows how the flow of money through the community.

Remedies to Spatial Racism

Homeownership is a crucial component to ending segregated living areas in America. Under the Clinton administration changes were made to help minorities become homeowners. As Ronald Brownstein reported in the *Los Angeles Times*, "Bank regulators have breathed the first real life into enforcement of the Community Reinvestment Act, a twenty year old statute mean to combat 'redlining' by requiring banks to serve their low-income communities."[12] Fannie Mae and Freddie Mac, the giant federally chartered corporations, have done much to increase the chances that minorities can purchase homes. These corporations buy mortgages from lenders and bundle them into securities that allow lenders the funds to lend more. In 1992, Congress mandated that Fannie Mae and Freddie Mac increase their purchases of mortgages for low-income and medium-income borrowers. This has lead to a dramatic increase in minority homeownership. Further,

African Americans	**Racism**
African Americans (AA) concentrated in South. Live in fringe areas of cities with poor access or denial to public services, e.g., hospitals, colleges, transportation, etc.	Rigidly enforced system of housing segregation throughout U.S. All minorities are more or less restricted in where they may live.

Restriction of AA to least desirable living areas maintaining economic inequality, steering by Realtors, zoning laws, and restrictive covenants.

Movement of millions of AA from South to North (the Great Migration) beginning in 1915.

1934 creation of FHA, which denied loans in non-segregated areas; redlining; lending institutions follow FHA lead.

AA who have risen in economic status attempt to buy decent housing outside ghetto areas.

Protest for decent housing in slum areas.

Policy of only token integration in public housing. 1949 development of urban renewal that removed AA and returned central/downtown area to middle-class whites. Denial of home improvement loans in red-lined areas.

AA demand government assistance. 1947 formation of a national Negro real estate association.

1945: official FHA segregation policy changed.

Nonenforcement of laws. Violence occurs as AA attempt to buy in white middle-class areas.

1948: Supreme Court ruling outlaw use of restrictive covenants.

During 1960s hundreds of fair housing laws passed.

Flight by whites to the suburbs.

Block busting by white Realtors; exorbitant prices placed on housing for AA. Rapid expansion of AA into previously all-white areas from 1950s through 1970s. City decreases public services.

Some whites refuse to sell to AA. Some sell at extremely high prices. Lowering of property values.

In 1990s, increased concentration and isolation of minorities in the inner cities.

Continued resistance to integration; continued flight to suburbs by white residents and businesses greatly depletes city tax base.

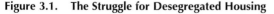

Figure 3.1.   The Struggle for Desegregated Housing

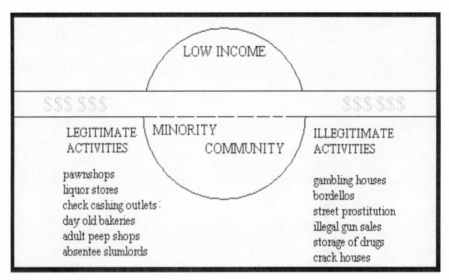

Figure 3.2.   The Minority Community as a Conduit

Brownstein states, "When President Clinton took office in 1993, 42 percent of African Americans and 39 percent of Latinos owned their own home. By spring 1999, those figures had jumped to 46 percent of blacks and 46.2 percent of Latinos."[13] Obviously, increased homeownership in minority communities helps to create a more positive community atmosphere. However, it does not alter isolation in those communities from the larger affluent communities. The increase in loans to medium-income minorities probably will increase the numbers of minorities who can purchase homes in better-maintained communities. The Bush administration has not seen this as a priority and thus there is little action in the current administration to monitor or improve this process.

Regionalism is often put forward as the way to end the economic and political disparity caused by an outer ring of suburbs peopled mostly by whites and inner cities populated mostly by minorities and the poor. *Regionalism would bring together the resources of both areas to benefit the area as a whole.* Powell also asserts that previous plans promoting regionalism have failed because some white segregationists and minority groups prefer **in-place strategies**.[14] In the past, segregationists resisted all plans to move minorities to the suburbs. Instead they promoted moving resources and opportunities to the inner city. In-place strategies sometimes gain support from minorities, but for different reasons. African Americans have worried about the outflow of the black middle class to the suburbs. Some felt that this would dilute the political power gained through block voting. **Block voting** refers to the majority of residents of a particular racial/ethnic group in a political district voting for the same candidate or issues. Some minority groups have been concerned about maintaining the strong cultural roots of inner city communities. Powell suggests that the needs of whites and minorities could be met through a strategy called "federated regionalism." This arrangement would integrate regional policymaking with local governance, that is, tax base sharing. He cites the Minnesota's Twin Cities plan as one successful model. "It shares the regional tax base without compromising local interests. Each city controls the tax rate for its residents, thereby maintaining authority and discretion over local issues."[15]

Education

Fifty years after *Brown v. Board of Education*, inequities in our public education system are widespread. For all the millions of dollars that have been directed at inner-city schools for either enrichment or bilingual education, the disparity between wealthy school districts and poorer ones is profound. It is instructional to give a historical perceptive to this inequity by using Los Angeles as a model.

Two commissions, twenty years apart, concluded that little had changed in the inequality of public education. The McCone Commission was formed to investigate the occurrence of the 1965 riots, and to make suggestions regarding preventive strategies for the future. Nearly nineteen years later, the Los Angeles County and City Human Relations Commissions sponsored public hearings. The purpose of the hearings was "to focus on the problems identified by the McCone Commission, provide analysis of current problems in South Central Los Angeles and most importantly, attempt to elicit solutions for current problems."[16] The Commission reported that there continued to be inequities in education between advantaged and disadvantaged schools. Schools in low-income communities suffered from disparities in teacher qualifications, double sessions, inadequate cafeterias and library facilities, uninspired course offerings, and deteriorating school plants. Federal funding was found to be inadequate compared to the situation. Throughout the hearings, it was noted that the problems listed in 1965 were essentially unchanged.

The litany of the disparities between schools based upon class differences is not new information. It is important, however, because it reveals the persistence of policies and practices that subjugate minorities to social and economic equality in America. While past failures of the public school system to educate its minority children are important to keep in mind, current reports are even more troubling. They document that the nation has continued to provide inadequate education to its poor and minority students and has returned to widespread segregation of the schools. The Department of Education reconfirmed in 2004 through its National Assessment of Education

Progress tests that low-income African American and Latino students in the largest school district in California, Los Angeles, still receive radically inferior educations.[17]

It is generally acknowledged that throughout the country, schools are more segregated now than they were before the famous 1954 Supreme Court ruling that confirmed the unconstitutionality of segregated schools. In *Brown v. the Topeka Board of Education*, the ruling undermined the social legitimacy of government-sanctioned educational inequality. It overturned the 1896 Supreme Court ruling that approved "separate but equal" public facilities for blacks. However, the majority of whites refused to abide by this ruling, resisting at every turn in both the North and the South. There was such blatant noncompliance that the Supreme Court was forced in 1968 and 1971 to compel school districts to move affirmatively toward integration with busing plans, if necessary.[18]

This created an era of widespread white resistance, sometimes violent resistance, to busing. An attempt was made to break the cycle of violence and the stonewalling of white parents inside the city by erasing the boundaries between the metropolitan area and the suburbs. This made it possible to view the city and the outer ring as one school district. However in the 1974 case of *Milliken v. Bradley II*, involving students in the Detroit area, the Supreme Court ruled that there could be no legal mandate of busing between cities and their suburbs just to meet integration of the schools.[19] This decision has proven to be the death knell for metropolitan school integration and it accelerated the resettling of minority inner cities ringed by predominately white suburbs discussed earlier. The white flight from the cities was the procedure used to resist school integration; whites realized that they could avoid integration by simply moving away.

Desegregation

While there was continued white resistance in the North and South, it should be remembered that court-ordered desegregation did succeed. Desegregated schools did not eliminate racism in the curriculum, and in personnel practices, but it did improved opportunities for a good education in grades K through 12. Desegregation also increased the numbers of minorities in college. More minorities are taking the SAT exams; more Latinos are entering colleges. The results of longitudinal research completed in 2004, verified that the effects have been positive.[20]

Desegregation was a good idea and marked the start of revolutionary thinking about how the educational system in America should operate. However, today many parents feel that this is a different time, and that it demands different solutions. Many minority parents object to the notion that only a school integrated with whites is capable of providing good educational standards. They have demanded that their neighborhood schools be upgraded, rejecting the notion that busing is the only way to provide their children with a quality education. Gary Orfield, a scholar on the history of school desegregation, suggests that integration on a multicultural basis with an infusion of the middle-class mainstream offered a wiser course of action.[21] Institutions of any sort that serve only the poor are apt to be highly ineffective. Thus, schools with a majority population of poor minority population will generally not fare well. Why is this so? Because such schools will most likely have aged physical plants, and a smaller share of tax dollars to buy books, computers, and enrichment activities. Hence, the schools will not attract highly skilled teachers who are the foundation of any educational system.

Consider what the state of inner-city schools would be if there was not a constant spotlight on its functioning. Money alone will not repair the harm done by institutional racism in our schools; however, the more we are aware of its invisible functioning, the better we can prepare to overcome it.

Resegregation

Schools that were highly segregated thirty years ago are still segregated; and as before they are segregated by race, ethnicity, and class. They have been rapidly resegregated in the North and the South.[22] Several studies have reviewed education in America in connection with the fifty-year commemoration of the *Brown* decision. These studies lament that resegregation has continued unabated. One report examined a decade of data from the time of the Supreme Court's 1991 *"Dowell"* decision, which authorized a return to neighborhood schools, even if that would create segregation, through 2001–2002.[23] The report found that resegregation was most evident in the South; however it was apparent throughout the country. Whites are the most segregated group, attending schools that are generally 80 percent white. During the 1990s, the number of African American students in majority white schools decreased by 13 percent to a level lower than any year since 1968. The report states, "Rural and small town school districts are the most integrated for both black and Latino children. Except in the South and Southwest, most white students have little contact with minority students. Asians in contrast are the most integrated."[24] Inner cities of large metropolitan areas are the epicenter of segregation. Segregation for Latino students is most severe in the Northeast, and in California and Texas. One reason for the increase in segregation of Latino students is the tremendous increase in the number and proportion of Latino students in most of the areas in which they have been concentrated during the past two decades. It is now understood that there was no serious sustained national effort to desegregate outside of the South. The South carried the brunt of court mandates because of its history of apartheid; however, the concentration on the South allowed the North and the West to evade the edict. Thus, the practice of white flight in the North confounded the process of integration.

A newspaper article described how one northern city created a unique system that evaded true integration of the public schools. In Rockford, Illinois, black and white children attended the same school but were assigned to different classrooms. In several of this city's schools, black and white kids ate at separate lunchtimes. There was a tracking system in place wherein whites went into honors and college-prep classes; minorities, even some who scored in the 99th percentile in testing, were mostly consigned to the slow-learner sections. Code words and special programs were used throughout the North to maintain inferior education for minority children. During the busing era of the 1970s and 1980s, in many cities only minorities faced mandatory busing, with long hours of commuting added to the school day. Anglo students were only bused if they choose to attend certain magnet school programs near the inner cities. Even this was rare and most of the "integration" was accomplished by busing minority children. These transportation patterns tended to disadvantage minority children while it enhanced the education of whites. White children were provided with enrichment classes as an incentive to keep them in the "integrated school" while minority children were generally not admitted to these programs.

Adding to the resegregation of the public schools is the ongoing failure to confront the effects of widespread institutional racism on the funding of public education. Across the country, the aging white majority has been less inclined to support funding for public schools and universities for non-white young at levels as high as those provided to primarily white youth. The lower financial support blocked the opportunities previously available for the young of modest means to pull up out of poverty. Statistics illustrate the strong association between crime and poverty. Young minorities in the inner city are more likely to be doomed to a life of poverty and violent crime because they are being blocked from receiving a good education.[25] It is important to note that there appears to be a turnabout regarding public education for the new millennium. During the late 1990s, many states put education at the top of their political agenda. The Bush administration initiated a program, "No Child Left Behind," with much fanfare. However, educators now say that not enough money has been put into this program to ensure its success. Many states are seeking increased funding for academic improvements though raising taxes, or through bond initiatives.

The battle to preserve desegregation in schools is constantly challenged. Now for the first time in a decade, the Supreme Court will review the legacy of a landmark: the *Brown v. Board of Education* decision of 1954 that declared unconstitutional the racial segregation of public schools.[26] Lawyers will debate before the Court in a pair of cases, whether school boards may use racial guidelines to assign students. The argument before the Court is the legality of voluntary desegregation. The outcome, which will not be known for months, could affect hundreds of school systems across the nation.

Testing and Academic Achievement

Beyond the issue of desegregation or disparity in the quality of education is the issue of testing and its effects on academic achievement and job acquisition. From kindergarten on, children are tested. Our society places great value on tests. Most Americans have taken any number of attitude tests, achievement tests, and intelligence tests before high school graduation. The test scores often follow us the rest of our lives and influence major decisions regarding our lifestyles. Students take tests to determine class placement, and whether enrichment or remediation classes will be included. Psychological tests may also be given in certain situations to determine a young person's state of mental health. Tests are necessary. In a complex society like the United States, there must be efficient and cost-effective methods to match ability with responsibility. We would be foolish to expect anything other than continued reliance on tests as a means to screen, select, and eliminate. School administrators and teachers provide their students with a quality education rely on tests for determining which students have what abilities. As a means to that end, intelligence tests have been considered "race neutral." However, these tests are often racist. "Neutral and objective tests" that are administered for one purpose but lead directly to racist outcomes is one of the key institutional practices in American society that is keeping our society mired in racial discord. Intelligence tests are not necessarily objective or neutral. These tests often have disastrous outcomes for minority children.

For example, educational researchers determined that the accountability requirements of the No Child Left Behind Act (NCLB) of 2001 place poor and minority in jeopardy. This is because the policy relies on "mean proficiency scores and require all subgroups to meet the same goals for accountability."[27]

Mark Goldberg, an educational researcher summarized the problem succinctly in the following 2005 report:

Compared to 2004 issues concerning NCLB, this year's issues in play are even more complex. First, much more media attention has been paid to testing. Second, objections to various aspects of testing have increased dramatically. Third, many cities and states, even parents in some cases, have found interesting, creative ways to circumvent the tests or their results. Finally, the U.S. Department of Education compromised on some NCLB requirements and is pressured to back down even more.[28]

Standardized testing continues to put poor and minority children in jeopardy and this is because most tests have been created by whites and were standardized on whites. Consequently, the tests assume a white middle-class frame of reference, vocabulary, and a set of abilities best obtained in a white middle-class home. Due to segregation, poor whites and racial/ethnic groups develop a different lifestyle, which incorporates a different vocabulary and reference points. Jencks and Phillips acknowledge that there is a white-black test gap and propose that there are probably several reasons for this gap.[29] In his book, *Racial Bias in Testing*, Jencks concludes with the following observation on testing:

> It seems fair to say that the invention of standardized tests has harmed blacks as a group [I would add poor whites and Latinos], both because of labeling bias and because of selection system bias. This does not mean the test themselves are flawed. The skill differences that the tests measure are real, and these skills have real consequences both at school and at work. But inability to measure the other predictors of performance, on which blacks seem to be far less disadvantaged, poses a huge social problem.[30]

The authors suggest that along with test bias are the effects of family background, parental schooling, income, and competency of teachers. They argue that narrowing the gap would do more to move the country to racial parity than any other political alternative. Often, the results of the standardized tests are to place poor whites and minority children in slow learners classes. The practice of tracking students can have long-lasting, detrimental results. For those persons intent on denigrating nonwhite groups, the gap in test scores can be used to reinforce their ideological position.

Remedies for Racism in Education

Housing vouchers, not school vouchers, may have a more lasting effect in upgrading the education of poor minority students. Low-income families use housing vouchers to secure access to communities outside of the inner cities. Larry Cuban, a professor of education at Stanford University, has suggested this alternative.[31] He stated that the problem of failing schools should be reframed to look beyond the school for the problem, and instead admit the culpability of the surrounding community with its overabundance of crime and unemployment. Cuban believes that the use of housing vouchers first launched by Jack Kemp, then Secretary of Housing and Urban Development during the Reagan administration, should receive greater funding. The movement to more diverse middle-class communities would provide access to better housing, schools, and job opportunities. Cuban states, "Over the course of 18 years, [across the country] nearly 6,000 families moved to apartments in neighborhoods known for their fierce opposition to African Americans [families] moving in, and there was no white backlash."[32]

As more and more working-class minorities move into the suburbs, balance by race and class must be built into all policies, practices and procedures in those communities. Administrators and parents must be vigilant in rooting out new pockets of school segregation as living patterns adapt to with demographic changes. Becoming more aware of the invisible hold that racism has on public schools is a crucial step for minorities in combating educational inequality. Jencks and Phillips recommend basic changes for schools that may affect the test score gap: smaller classrooms, testing to ensure competency of teachers, improving parenting skills, and improving cognitive skills of all students starting with preschool programs. They were skeptical, however, that their recommendations would be endorsed by society as a whole.[33] A hopeful sign is that California and other states are increasing funding to reduce class sizes.

Requiring students to take at least one "ethnic studies" course could contribute to answering the question, "How can we become more personally aware of racism in the schools?" Presently, more colleges and universities are requiring students to increase their understanding of racial and ethnic diversity. This requirement hopefully will sensitize future teachers who are now college students. There also have been some fledgling steps by groups of whites to tackle "whiteness and privilege." In a newspaper article, Lamb described one of these community-based groups examining racism in a new way with the purpose of achieving a just, multiracial society.[34] Whites must pick up the gauntlet and fight racism if there is to be lasting change. There is a growing number of white social science scholars who are tackling the problem of white privilege and this brings another dimension to the struggle for justice.[35]

A federal watchdog agency to oversee test makers is a novel idea put forth by Stanford professor Larry Cuban in a *Los Angeles Times* article.[36] According to Cuban, standardized tests have grown in use in public schools as a means to hold educational systems accountable for the academic success of their students. Cuban suggested a federal watchdog of these tests, much like the Securities Exchange Commission that oversees the financial dealings of the stock market.

As state government, parents, and the public have increased their criticism of the schools, schools are under more pressure to demonstrate improved student achievement through higher test scores. This increased pressure has led to a few reports of unsavory practices by some schools. Cuban states that Austin, Texas, Rhode Island, and elsewhere there was been reports of test tampering by teachers and administrators. He suggested a federal agency monitor these standardized tests and also perform several other functions:

- Assure the public that forcing students to repeat a grade because of a low score will enhance their academic achievement
- Force states and districts that use tests for unintended purposes to cease such practices
- Ferret out the reasons why minorities and poor children in general are the mostly likely to have to repeat grades
- Force schools to explain why minority students are tracked into less demanding classes
- Require test makers to provide a truth-in-test label that could be made available to schools, parents, and other interested parties
- Examine standardized tests for cultural bias and ensure that biased test content is changed

This proposed federal agency would provide a much-needed national oversight that could reduce inequality in the schools. Admittedly, there is not a great deal of support for yet another layer of bureaucracy. However, given the crucial role of education to equity and equality, it is much needed.

SUMMARY

To truly understand the nebulous workings of institutional racism in America, it is necessary to understand the importance of social institutions in a society. Social institutions are the structures that maintain all aspects of the society. This chapter begins the process of examining how their policies, practices, and procedures, which may appear to be race neutral, sustain racial inequality. The mask of race neutrality is removed for the social institutions of housing and education and the policies, practices, and procedures within them are examined. The chapter ends with suggested remedies to the racism uncovered.

KEY TERMS

apartheid. Legal racial segregation, most recent national example is the practice of apartheid in South Africa by whites against blacks and coloreds which included Asian and mixed race persons.

block busting. The practice of real estate brokers who panic whites into selling their property quickly and often below market value because non-whites are rumored to be moving into the area.

block voting. A majority of residents in a political district voting for the same candidate or issues.

in-place strategies. Housing term that refers to policies that foster minorities remaining in inner-city communities.

Jim Crow laws. Laws and procedures enacted in the South after slavery was abolished to maintain inequality and inequity for African Americans.

meritocracy. A system in which the talented are chosen and moved ahead based on their achievement.

norm. A sociological term that refers to a widespread practice, procedure, or custom. A norm is accepted as the regular state of activity, accepted individual behavior.

protective covenant. A document signed by a prospective homebuyer not to sell his home in the future to a nonwhite person.

race neutral. Policies, practices, and procedures that do not consider race or ethnicity.

redlining. The practice of refusing bank loans to residents from targeted areas. In effect, the bank draws a red line around a particular area. Persons in that area are refused loans regardless of their credit history.

restrictive covenants. A practice, now outlawed, of having new residents in a community sign a formal and binding agreement not to sell their home to Jews, or racial/ethnic minorities. This was a widespread practice from 1930 to 1965.

social stratification. The process of arranging the society into classes, or graded statuses.

GROUP ACTIVITY

1. Discuss within your activity group additional examples of the "invisibility" of racism in schools and in communities.
2. Within your study group develop a historical chart of the progression of racism in the institution of education. (See figure 3.1 on housing)
3. Bring to class a recent newspaper clipping that exemplifies institutional racism in housing or education.
4. Discuss whether "No Child Left Behind" has been successful.

STUDY QUESTIONS

1. Explain how institutional racism flows through social institutions.

2. Why would inner city minorities object to members of their group migrating to the suburbs?
3. Define "regionalism." How would regionalism improve the quality of life for minority groups?
4. What is redlining? How are minorities disadvantaged by it? Who gains the advantage? Why?
5. Did desegregation of public schools help minorities? In what ways?
6. Why are standardized tests, such as I.Q. tests, not neutral or objective?
7. Why is it better for poor children to be integrated into classes with middle-class children?
8. Discuss the importance of resegregation.

NOTES

1. Joyce Ladner, "A New Civil Rights Agenda," *Brookings Review* 17, no.1 (Spring 2000).
2. See the thorough discussion of Chinese in America in chapter 8, "Searching for Gold Mountain," in Ronald Takaki, *A Different Mirror: A History of Multicultural America* (New York: Little, Brown, 1993).
3. Report of the National Advisory Commission on Civil Disorders, 1968, vii.
4. Los Angeles Times Staff, *Understanding the Riots* (Los Angeles Times, 1992), 130.
5. Anthony Downs, "How America's Cities Are Growing," *Brookings Review* 16, no. 4 (Fall 1998).
6. John Powell, "Race and Space," *Brookings Review* 16, no. 4 (Fall, 1998): 21.
7. Report from the Federal Reserve Board, Associated Press, September 8, 2006.
8. Powell, "Race and Space."
9. Bruce Katz, "Enough of the Small Stuff! Toward a New Urban Agenda," *Brookings Review*, 18, no. 3, 7–11. (2000).
10. Katz, "Enough of the Small Stuff."
11. Independent Commission on the Los Angeles Police Department, *Report of the Independent Commission on the Los Angeles Police Department.* Los Angeles City Council, 1991.
12. Ronald Brownstein, "Minorities' Home Ownership Booms Under Clinton but Still Lags Behind Whites," *Los Angeles Times*, May 31, 1999.
13. Brownstein, "Minorities' Home Ownership."
14. Powell, "Race and Space."
15. Powell, "Race and Space," 21.
16. Human Relations Commission, *The State of Race Relations in Los Angeles*, Fall 1985.
17. Gary Blash, "Far Along Yet Far From Equal," *Los Angeles Times*, January 11, 2004.
18. See detailed discussion regarding this area in chapter 10, "School Desegregation After Two Generations: Race, Schools, and Opportunity in Urban Society," in

Herbert Hill and James Jones, *Race In America* (Madison: University of Wisconsin Press, 1993).

19. Hill and Jones, *Race in America*.

20. Thomas Pettigrew, "Justice Deferred a half Century After the Brown Board of Education," *American Psychologist* 59, no. 6 (September, 2004).

21. Gary Orfield and Chungmei Lee, "*Brown* at 50: King's Dream or *Plessy's* Nightmare?" Civil Rights Projects, Harvard University, 2004.

22. Jonathan Kozol, "Confections of Apartheid Continue in Our Schools," *Educational Digest* 71, no. 6 (February 2006).

23. Orfield and Lee, "*Brown* at 50."

24. Orfield and Lee, "*Brown* at 50."

25. Mike A. Males, "The Scapegoat Generation: America's War on Adolescents," *Journal of Psychohistory* 25, no. 2 (Fall 1997).

26. David Savage, "Cases Retread *Brown v. Board of Education* Steps," *Los Angeles Times*, December 4, 2006.

27. James S. Kim and Gail Sunderman, "Measuring Academic Proficiency Under the No Child Left Behind Act: Implications for Educational Equity," *Educational Researcher* 34, no. 8 (November 2005).

28. Mark Goldberg, "Losing Students to High-Stakes Testing," *Educational Digest* 70, no. 7 (March 2005).

29. See Christopher Jencks and Meridith Phillips, eds., *The Black-White Test Score Gap* (Washington, DC.: Brookings Institution Press, 1998). Several scholars provide detailed analysis of the several issues that may relate to the test score gap.

30. Jencks and Phillips, *Test Score Gap*, 84.

31. Larry Cuban, "Housing, Not School, Vouchers Are Best Remedy for Failing Schools," *Los Angeles Times*, January 31, 1999.

32. Cuban, "Housing, Not School."

33. See Jencks and Phillips, specifically their conclusion in their introduction, 43–47.

34. David Lamb, "Workshop on Whiteness Explores Unearned Rights," *Los Angeles Times*, November 19, 1996.

35. Two books that exemplify this are Paul Kivel, *Uprooting Racism: How White People Can Work for Racial Justice* (Philadelphia: New Society Publishers, 1996) and George Lipsitz, *The Possessive Investment in Whiteness* (Philadelphia: Temple University Press, 1998).

36. Larry Cuban, "Needed: Watchdog for Standardized Test Makers," *Los Angeles Times*, December 12, 1999.

4

Institutional Racism Dissected: Part B

THE HIDDEN FACE OF INSTITUTIONAL RACISM: EMPLOYMENT AND LAW ENFORCEMENT

> If there is any one key to the systematic privilege that undergrids a racial capi-
> talist society, it is the special advantage of the white population in the labor
> market.
>
> —Robert Blauner, *Race Oppression in America*, 1972

Employment and Its Importance for Equality

One of the most potent hallmarks of institutional racism is the organization and distribution of jobs in America. Examples abound of employment bias against minorities, women, and the disabled. In the past, there
were legal structures that prevented minorities from gaining certain types of
jobs. In the West, railroad companies and gold mine owners had policies
and practices that exploited Chinese workers and prevented them from rising above common laborers. As Ching-Yung Lee chronicles, "The California
Foreign Miner's Tax Law of 1853 allowed for the collection of taxes almost
exclusively from Chinese miners between 1853 and 1870. During the first
four years of its enforcement, Chinese miners paid 50 percent of the total
revenues obtained from working in the gold mines. During the next thirteen years, the rate was increased to 98 percent."[1] The Webb-Henry Act of
1913 prohibited land ownership and limited to three years the leasing
rights of aliens ineligible for citizenship. This act effectively limited business opportunities for Chinese and Japanese residents.[2] Enterprising Chinese found that the only businesses available to them were laundry and

cooking in the Old West. Early Japanese settlers found the rigid policies and procedures regarding employment so heinous that many opted for farming rather than attempting to gain employment within the existing Anglo workforce or ownership of a business.

Ethnic minorities were systematically barred from the fruits of the Industrial Revolution. Legal and public policy actions were taken in the 1870s to reduce the Chinese competition for jobs. The Naturalization Act of 1870 excluded Chinese from citizenship and curtailed the entry of laborers' wives. In the northern states, industrial plant administrators joined with unions controlled by European immigrants in refusing to share the jobs, except for the most menial ones. Racism in the North barricaded the avenue for Southern blacks to escape the harsh oppression of the South.[3] Had the formerly enslaved African Americans been able to enter the industrialized jobs of the North at the turn of the century, maybe the country would not have needed the civil rights movement a century later. Native Americans also were excluded from most industrial activities, as they were relegated to reservations in the Southwest. Northern industrialists and labor unions, Southern plantation owners, and southwest ranch owners conspired to profit from the labor of African Americans, Latinos, Native Americans, and Asians in the two-tier labor market.

The "Great Migration" of 1910 to1920—so named for the thousands of black farm workers and "sharecroppers" who migrated from the South— was launched by the invitation extended by the industrialists who needed workers; albeit for the most menial jobs. African Americans only were permitted into Northern industrial jobs in any numbers due to World War I; this was because European immigration was greatly reduced due to the war. Even though the African Americans had been encouraged to come north, job discrimination was widespread. While the leftists in the labor movement at the time struggled mightily to force fair working conditions and preached communalism, they were loath to examine the racism in American labor unions. Asa Philip Randolph, a prominent civil rights leader, so despaired over job discrimination in the North at the onset of World War II that he began to plan in 1940 and 1941 for a nationwide mass protest. This only occurred after pleas to President Franklin D. Roosevelt failed to bring results. Only after President Roosevelt was finally convinced that a black protest march on Washington would occur did he capitulate and sign the famous Executive Order No. 8802—the Fair Employment Practices Act— that banned discrimination by national defense contractors.[4]

The Two-Tier Labor Market

To better understand how job discrimination was operationalized, let's discuss the two-tier labor market that disproportionately disadvantages mi-

High percentage
of white males;
some females; some
minorities

| **UPPER TIER** |
| CEO; highly paid professionals |
| Or corporate jobs |
| High level of technically skilled persons |
| (high level of security of job; high social status |
| associated with the job) |

High percentage
of minorities,
females, and
poor whites

| **LOWER TIER** |
| Clerical and semi-skilled workers |
| Nonskill labor jobs: maids, janitors, busboys, |
| farm workers |
| (cyclical jobs, dirty work, dangerous jobs, often no benefits |
| paid; undesirable jobs) |

Figure 4.1. The Two-Tier Labor Market

nority groups in America (see figure 4.1). The term refers to a double layer system that allocates jobs not solely by skill, talent, and initiative, but also includes gender, race, and class in its consideration. The outcome is that women and minorities are relegated to the most unsatisfactory jobs. Minorities are more likely to be hired to do dirty work, to work in a dangerous environment, or to perform a job that pays substandard wages. They are often the last hired and the first fired; their jobs are more likely to be seasonal and pay no benefits. However, the lower tier jobs support upper tier employment and are essential to the well-being of persons in the upper tier.

Table 4.1 shows that whites males are nearly three times more likely to be a manager or other type of official as a minority male and four times more likely than a minority female. White males are nearly twice as likely to have professional status as minority males. Minority males hold only 6 percent of craft worker position or skilled jobs, while white males hold more than twice that at 14.9 percent. In the lower tier, a minority male is slightly more than twice as likely to be a laborer as a white male. Females, both white and minority, are poorly represented in managerial positions, however females fare better than minority males in obtaining professional jobs. Females and minority males occupy more positions as service workers than do white males. Steinberg suggests that this labor condition be labeled "occupational apartheid." He explains, "Apartheid is a racial division of labor, a system of occupational segregation that relegates most blacks to work in the least desirable job sectors or that excludes them from the job market altogether."[5] It is puzzling that information in the format of table 4.1 has not been reproduced since 1998 by the Equal Employment Commission.

The foundation of upward mobility and the challenge to subordinate status in American society rests on the division of labor and the compensation for that labor—*the social institution of employment*. The two-tier labor market

Table 4.1 Occupational Employment in Private Industry by Race/Ethnic Group/Sex and by Industry, United States, 1998 (data for the State of Hawaii are not included)

	Officials/Managers	Professionals	Technicians	Office/Clerical	Craft Workers	Operatives	Laborers	Service Managers
				Occupation Distribution				
White								
Male	16.0	16.4	6.8	4.8	14.9	17.8	7.0	6.2
Female	8.7	19.4	6.2	25.4	2.2	8.0	4.6	11.1
Minority								
Male	6.0	9.0	5.1	6.4	6.4	22.7	15.8	16.4
Female	4.0	10.9	5.1	23.5	2.2	12.1	9.1	19.5

From the U.S. Equal Employment Commission

or occupational apartheid splinters the notion of America as a meritocracy. A meritocracy is a system in which the talented or skilled are chosen and moved ahead on the basis of their achievement. The majority of Americans strongly believe that the United States is, for the most part, a meritocracy. However, studies have shown that this is not the case. Maldonado points out in a 2005 dissertation that race becomes a factor in employers' stated assessments of the desirability and ability of workers.[6] Even as employers state that they are color-blind in hiring, their evaluation of the ability of workers is heavily influenced by the employees' race and/or ethnicity. Thus, race and skill is combined in the final hiring process. Maldonado agrees with the author in not seeing this as a matter of individual racism, but as the normal outcome of the racialized structure of our society. A 1991 study by the Urban Institute highlighted the totally unequal experience of equally qualified white and black young men when they sought employment. The researcher sent white and black college students who were identical in almost all characteristics except race, to answer classified job ads in Chicago and Washington, D.C. White males received three times as many offers as equally qualified black males. Over the years, this experiment has been repeated many times with the same unfortunate results. Further, Asian Americans, although high academic achievers, are not immune to racism.[7] College educated Asian Americans earn almost 11 percent less than whites with college degrees, according to U.S. census data.

Employment Discrimination

Numerous workplace discrimination suits initiated by minority groups have been filed in both the public and private sector. This has occurred over the past sixty years as minorities gained this right within the courts. In 1990, two years before the Los Angeles riots, the U.S. census revealed that unemployment was running a staggering 26 percent in Watts, more than three times the rate of the rest of Los Angeles. This came as no surprise to social scientists, who have been documenting for several decades the reality that black unemployment is generally three to four times as high as the general population at any given time.[8] The reality of this long-term disparity in employment rates for whites and blacks and by extension Latinos illuminates that racist outcomes in employment are accepted as the norm. Even after the extended economic boom during the latter part of 1999 and into 2000, the disparity in employment rates between whites and minorities was discouraging. U.S. census data of 2000 reported that nearly 44 percent of the homeless in America are African Americans, while they represent less than 14 percent of the total population.

Steinberg maintains that social scientists treated job discrimination as a byproduct of racial prejudice and therefore focused on rooting out prejudice rather than addressing job discrimination head on. More important, he states that these researchers refused to take note, least of all, examine discrimination as a source of economic gain. Even leftists or Marxists who had spearheaded the development of labor unions and seemed to have the highest level of awareness of economic exploitation were loath to examine the racism in American labor unions, which perpetuated the two-tier labor market.[9] Euro-Americans, who dominated the unions, gained by keeping union jobs and the economic stability that came with them for themselves, thus reinforcing the two-tier labor market and economic privilege for whites.

Social scientists document that the nature of racism in the workplace is changing. It is becoming more subtle as blatant racism becomes less acceptable. It is no longer "cool" in most parts of society to make racist jokes, to voice racial prejudices, and it is now illegal to overtly discriminate in employment. However, social scientists continue to document that racism in the workplace is just as widespread but less overt.[10] Deitch et al. suggest that the subtle forms of individual racism allow individuals to hold racist views and practice racism while at the same time strengthening such views with nonracially based rationales (e.g., beliefs in prevalence of equal opportunity and individual mobility), thus maintaining a view of themselves as nonprejudiced.[11] That is, white employers verbalized a desire for diversity in the workplace, however the statistics prove that actions do not follow words. Jennifer Pierce poses a different way of viewing continued racism in the workplace, "racing for innocence," which she describes as a subtle practice that functions simultaneously to disavow accountability for racist practices at the same time that everyday racism is practiced.[12] For example, offering lukewarm mentoring to minorities while giving extensive support to newly hired white employees; isolating or reducing social contact with minorities on the job; giving a minority person an assignment without providing adequate support to complete the task. When the minority person fails and/or leaves the corporation, the whites say that the person was incompetent or didn't seem to fit in.

Many white middle-class Americans consider affirmative action to be unfair because it allegedly establishes a racial preference in hiring. Yet studies show that middle-class whites exhibit racial preferences in all parts of their lives. Whites choose to live in predominantly white neighborhoods, work in white-dominated occupations, and, if able to accomplish this without detection, hire whites rather than minorities. You will remember our earlier discussion of the deliberate practice of whites to maintain the value and power of whiteness.

Black Workers and Immigration

Another issue that must be addressed in a discussion of employment bias is the connection between black workers and immigration. We have noted in this segment the link between European immigrants and African American workers before World War I. This historical connection must be examined afresh in today's economy. The issue is further exacerbated by the current political debate about what is to be done about the growing illegal immigration. The reality is that immigrants are again taking the jobs that may have gone to American workers. Many of the jobs are subminimum wage and relegats the native worker and the immigrant to unsatisfactory lower-tier jobs. The two groups are in fierce competition with each other, neither fully realizing that they are both being barred from the fruits of American capitalism. The present immigration policy amounts to a form of disinvestment in American workers. This is graphically shown in the federal ruling that allows American corporation to import highly skilled foreign workers because there are insufficient numbers of Americans available. Some progressive and conservative groups are coming forward of late pressuring the federal government to implement laws that would require corporations to put more effort into training American workers. Under this present system, corporations are profiting greatly by either outsourcing jobs overseas or bringing in undocumented workers to the United States to work below the minimum wage with no health benefits and no job security. Fair labor practices would reduce the perpetual gap between income levels among whites and minority groups.

Some immigrant groups have a legitimate right to seek jobs here, such as Mexicans, who had their lands stolen from them. The American creed supports immigration, and it has been found that immigration is generally good for the country. However, all low-income workers—natives, immigrants, and their children—suffer from uncontrolled immigration. This is because all persons at the lower rung of the economic ladder have their wages suppressed when immigrants work for subminimum wages. This is especially true for the undocumented worker who is victimized and feels powerless to fight back. Aside from the issue of unskilled workers, another question that needs to be asked is why haven't American corporations encouraged the training of American citizens rather than bringing in highly educated foreigners? I would suggest that the power elite of this country are exploiting even well-trained migrants, reducing the possibility of young well-trained minority workers from entering the upper tier of the labor force. At present, low-income and middle-class American workers are being shut out of employment due to outsourcing of skilled job and illegal hiring of low-skill workers. It is only when minority communities explode, as occurred in the 1992 Los Angeles riots, that the country is compelled to give thought to the sorry conditions of the inner cities and the middle class.

Employers state that they hire the undocumented workers because Americans are unable or unwilling to do the jobs.[13] It's a myth that Americans won't do hard work. The truth is that Americans will not suffer indignities and unfairness that is heaped upon some groups of migrants. The present uncontrolled immigration is producing a political backlash against all Latinos that only increases unwarranted ill feelings. Even though President Bush signed a bill in 2006 to build a 700-mile fence on the 1,951-milelong Mexican border, there are few who believe this will solve the problem.

Remedies to Racism in Employment

Enlightened immigrant policy must reflect the creed of America to aid "the huddled masses seeking to be free" while it also takes into account the legitimate interest of native workers, especially those on the bottom rung of the economic ladder. Immigration policy must be made a part of a comprehensive human resource development plan that is committed to the improvement of employment opportunities and wages of marginal workers.

Affirmative action has had the most enduring, though inconsistent, effect on employment apartheid to date. The most potent cure for racism in employment today continues to be affirmative action. The white backlash of the 1980s and 1990s actually affirms the efficacy of the affirmative action legislation. **White backlash** refers to acts of concerted resistance or social disapproval of policies, practices, and procedures, which are perceived to benefit minorities at the expense of whites. In California, Proposition 209, dubbed "the civil rights initiative," was an example of white backlash as it was a desperate desire to restore the old order. Proposition 209 continues to have serious repercussion not only on fairness in hiring, but also on increase hostile attitudes of minority groups toward the government and the power elite.

Affirmative action guidelines did have positive effects on the leveling the playing field during the 1970s and 1980s. Thus it generated a sustained counterattack during the late 1990s. As more minorities challenged with middle-class white America for decent jobs and an opportunity for a seat in the classrooms of higher education, white America felt threatened and demanded restrictions on this leveling effect. However, it must be acknowledged that affirmative action has not worked as well as it might. This is because of the constant attempts by employers to neutralize the mandate by finding loopholes. Robert Lehr opines that the social institutions of politics and law enforcement that should protect human rights are controlled mostly by the white heterosexual, upper-middle class male population that institutionalized racism originally benefited.[14] It is ironic, Lehr concludes, after reviewing court cases challenging affirmative action, that this method of overcoming the effect of racism should rest so heavily on these institutions. Politics and law enforcement have their own political agenda that does not necessarily reflect liberty and justice for all, as we will note when we look at law enforcement later on.

James E. Jones, Jr., provides a working definition of this social policy. **Affirmative action** relates to "public or private actions or programs that provide or seek to provide opportunities or other benefits to persons on the basis of, among other things, their membership in a specified group or groups."[15] In 1961, President Lyndon Johnson set up the first formal institutional mechanism to overturn employment discrimination with his executive order mandating all federal contractors to practice nondiscrimination. Affirmative action is rooted in the principle of equity or fairness emanating from ancient Anglo-American law. America retained the English system of common law that was structured to provide fairness through flexibility when it was not be present in court proceedings.[16] Affirmative action is a corrective process when legal action or the adjudication process has taken place. It has two components: (1) to give "make-whole relief" to the identified victim of the defendant's misconduct, and (2) to provide prospective relief that focuses on the misdeed of the defendant. The second component is legislative or executive action. Both components are meant to remedy a situation that is deemed socially unacceptable. Affirmative action programs in employment require a good-faith effort on the part of the employer to reach objectives and goals. They do not ask for the impossible, nor do they mandate quotas. **Quotas** relate to a system that requires a fixed number of minorities and women and provides for sanctions to enforce compliance. Affirmative action guidelines *do not* require the hiring of unqualified persons.

Why are minorities and women urged to forget past inequities and pretend that they have no consequence for today's morass of inequality? American Jews are clear on the need to "never forget" the Holocaust. Their motto is informative, for it reminds us that we must take the measure of the past's influence on the possibilities of the future. The litany of present abuses in the business and labor cited above attest to the prevalence of racism in the workplace. We continue to need affirmative action or some other imbedded institutional response to our society's penchant to use race and ethnicity as a means to bar the opportunities of minorities while at the same time enriching favored groups. The reality is that America has never willingly dealt with the legacy of slavery that established employment apartheid, until forced to do so.

Law Enforcement

> Show me your courts and jails, and I will tell you the state of your country.
> —Charles Dickens

Ramifications of Present Policies

Although it is the wealthiest country, the United States incarcerates its poor, its uneducated, its addicted, its undisciplined, while many other countries provide treatment, mental hospitals, and community outreach programs. Our bankrupted drug war, the growing gap between the "haves" and the "have nots," and institutional racism have seriously burdened our country with a huge bill to finance the longest sentences in the industrial world. In doing so, the country has increased the enmity that young minorities feel toward the society. We have moved from moderate rehabilitation to excessive punishment and minimal rehabilitation. The double standard of law enforcement is endemic and long-standing in American society. Historically, Native Americans, Africans, and later Chinese, Japanese, and Latinos had no rights before the justice system that white Americans were obliged to acknowledge. White Americans established policies and procedures within the social system that abrogated those rights. This has resulted in a justice system that unfairly favors police and prosecutors—the establishment. The current racism within the system is glaring when one analyzes the data regarding who receive the death penalty. Studies have shown that blacks and other minorities are more likely to receive the death penalty than whites, and that the death penalty is given more often when the victim is white. This is an issue that has been at the top of the agenda of civil and human rights groups. These groups have protested loudly that the numbers show that the system is skewed against minorities. In 1994, Congressman Edwards of California introduced in the House a bill, the Racial Justice Act, HR 4017, which would have allowed a defendant to prove by statistical evidence that racial bias took place in the sentencing. However, the Senate voted down this bill.

There should be no argument regarding the importance of citizens giving respect to those who administer those laws. However, if large segments of the community are at the least cynical and at most hostile to law enforcement, you run the risk of creating a general atmosphere of lawlessness. One example is during the 1930s when citizens largely refused to accept the edict that drinking alcohol was a crime. The refusal by otherwise law-abiding citizens to obey that law contributed to the development of notorious gangs and the Mafia. These groups provided alcohol and other illegal activities, thus creating a generally disdain of justice and promoting widespread lawlessness. Lawlessness could become the normal state if the minorities lose all faith in the criminal justice system.

Law Enforcement and American Minorities

The residents of inner cities often view the police, the courts, and the jails as agents of control that lack a commitment to fairness and justice. Harsh punishment reminiscent of Southern slavery is more often the case in adjudicating crime and punishment for minorities. The disparity in treatment has had a ripple effect, impacting not only those who are personally involved in the "justice system," but the family and the quality of life in minority communities. Supreme Court Justice Anthony Kennedy in 2004 lamented that the justice system is broken as he recounted that nationwide, more than 40 percent of the prison population consists of African American inmates.[17] In some cities, more than 50 percent of young African American men are under the supervision of the criminal justice system. Based on trends, a black male born in 2001 has a 1 in 3 chance of being imprisoned during his lifetime, while the chances for a Latino male are 1 in 6, and for a white male, 1 in 17.[18] The total number of inmates rose 35 percent from 1995 to 2005, but their racial composition was little changed.[19] How much does this influence the increase in female-headed families, in the increase in out-of-wedlock births? How important to the possibility of marriage for minority females is the reality of a disproportionate number of males incarcerated? The number of black families headed by single females more than doubled between 1970 and 1987, and it continues to rise today, so that the majority of black babies are born to single mothers.

The following section on institutional racism will focus on four areas of egregious policies and practices within the law enforcement, which belie the term "criminal justice system." They are police criminality, the three-strike law, the disparity in sentencing for cocaine use and cocaine sales, and the California Gang Violence and Juvenile Crime Prevention Act (Proposition 21).

Police Criminality

The Rodney King beating that was aired repeatedly throughout the nation and the world is the most notorious example of police brutality, and it lead to widespread rioting in 1992 in Los Angeles and other parts of the country. The cost exceeded $5 billion over the next five years to rebuild riot-torn communities in Los Angeles. Excessive force by police has been at the heart of many of the violent inner-city uprisings. The 1965 Watts riot, again in Los Angeles, was caused by the shooting death of Leonard Dedwyler, who was stopped for speeding while taking his pregnant wife to the hospital. There were three riots in Miami in the 1980s, each precipitated by police shootings or beatings of African Americans. In June 2003, segments of the black community of Benton Harbor, Michigan, rioted over the killing of a black motorcyclist who crashed while fleeing a white police officer.[20] Several times a year, every year, there is a news report of an African American being shot or mistreated by local police.

The outgrowth of the Rodney King beating was the creation of the independent commission on the Los Angeles Police Department, known as the Christopher Commission, because its chair was Warren Christopher, former Secretary of State in the Clinton administration. The Commission's examination of personnel reports and computer messages sent to and from patrol cars substantiated the existence of a significant number of officers with a propensity toward violent actions against suspects. Officers frequently used the communication system to express their eagerness to be involved in shooting incidents.[21] The problem of excessive force is accentuated by racism because there is informal acceptance of differential treatment toward minorities embedded in police policies and procedures. Those the commission found racist include verbal harassment, detainment based on racial/ethnic profiling, employing unnecessarily invasive or humiliating tactics, and using excessive force.

Community unrest from Los Angeles to New York has occurred because minorities have reacted to what they perceived as excessive police force and/or brutality. The issue of police brutality and criminality is endemic across the nation. One of the most sensational of these incidents was the barbaric sodomizing with a broom handle of Abner Louima, an African American in Brooklyn. Louima was arrested, handcuffed, beaten, and dragged into the precinct house bathroom. There he was assaulted by a white police officer, while other police officers looked on or left the area pretending nothing was happening. The offending officer later pleaded guilty. Another incident involved a twenty-two-year-old African immigrant, Amadou Diallo, who was shot nineteen times in his apartment lobby in Harlem despite the fact the he was unarmed and had no criminal record. The police stated that they thought he was going for a gun when he reached in his back pocket for his wallet to provide identification. There is also the death of a nineteen-year-old African American female, Tyisha Miller, of Riverside County in Southern California. She was shot twelve times by three white officers and one Latino officer when she was startled awake in her locked car with a gun in her lap. She was waiting for her family to come and help her with her disabled car. Finally, there is incident of a fifty-four-year-old homeless, mentally ill African American woman who was shot to death by a policeman because she menaced him with a screwdriver, she was only five feet, one inch tall and weighed 130 lbs. All of these incidents occurred from 1997 to 1999, and this is only an abbreviated list of such actions by cops in this time period. In 2000, Chicago was examining accusations that the city police department has tortured more than sixty persons to gain confessions; some of those who are now in prison are being reviewed for possible retrial. In October 2006, a citizen videotaped a LAPD officer striking a handcuffed Latino five times in the face; this incident is being investigated.

The perception of minorities is that the police do not have to respect their rights. Again and again they see people in their communities treated unfairly by the police and nothing is done. Often minority members believe they have to prove they are innocent, not that the criminal justice system has to prove they are guilty. Consequently, young minority males have little respect for the police or the courts. As we continue to examine police corruption, we will see that their vision of policies, practices, and procedures in the criminal justice system is vindicated.

Our examination of police misconduct focuses on the Los Angeles City Police Department (LAPD) because of the breadth of misconduct within the department and its effect on low-income bicultural minority communities. The charges against LAPD Rampart Division, in 2000, read like a cheap detective novel but unfortunately are true. Rampart, a district of Los Angeles, is the home of a large number of legal and illegal immigrants, mostly from Central America and Mexico. Rampart is a glaring example of how policies, practices, and procedures can go awry and create a social system that operates secretly to exploit minorities for self-aggrandizement. These are the facts: corrupt cops planting rock cocaine on unsuspecting victims; officers selling stolen drugs to drug dealers rather than arresting them; cops kidnapping gang members, stripping them of their clothes and dropping them in a rival gang area; cops shooting a man and then allowing him to bleed to death while they invent a scenario to justify the shooting; cops awarding each other plaques, with highest honors going to those who not only wound but kill; allegations that the police routinely plant evidence, such as a gun or drugs on a presumed gang member. The only persons I am sure will not be astounded by these particulars are residents of low-income minority communities, for they have been complaining and having mass protests for years against police criminality.

These revelations of LAPD misdeeds came to light because of testimony from a former police officer, Rafael Perez, a member of a special gang suppression unit. Perez was caught stealing drugs from the police station, and agreed to reveal the illegal activities committed by his colleagues for a reduced sentence. This broke the "blue wall of silence"—a creed within big city police forces that says no policemen ever snitches on a fellow officer. The social and economic cost of these revelations on the city has been staggering. The city attorney states that the city's liability in cases arising from the scandal will rise to $125 million, maybe more. More than seventy officers were investigated and hundreds of prosecutions must be reviewed.[22] The Chief of Police called for the dismissal of ninety-nine defendants in fifty-seven cases. Anti-gang injunctions were suspended, but recently were reinstated. Twenty thousand to 25,000 cases will have to be re-examined by the Public Defender's Office to determine if defendants received a fair trial.

Twenty officers have been suspended or fired, and forty convictions of purported gang members were overturned because of tainted evidence and officer perjury. The unraveling of practices within LAPD was the most extensive case of police abuse in the history of the city and perhaps the nation. By December 2000, LAPD had paid out 30 million dollars for the year for police misconduct. The relevance to our examination of these institutional misdeeds is that all of the victims are either Latino or African American.

Along with the above abuses, the Immigration and Naturalization Service (INS) alleged that LAPD Rampart Division anti-gang unit set up Latinos to be deported and coerced INS to deny citizenship to others. It is my thesis that such widespread abuse is directly linked to the acceptance and support of institutional racism.

In 2000, Los Angeles entered into a settlement with the U.S. Justice Department after the agency concluded the LAPD had engaged in a pattern of civil rights violations. A federal monitor was assigned after the Rampart scandal to evaluate how well the department is moving toward its goal of substantial compliance with reform measurements. There have been some improvements in the operations of LAPD; however incidents of excessive force and racial profiling still dog the department. Five years after the consent degree was signed with the U.S. Justice Department, many of the items targeted for reform have not been completed.

Racism and the Justice System

Racism is pervasive throughout the criminal justice system. Although the Christopher Commission set in motion wide-ranging reforms of LAPD, it is now apparent that the wide-ranging abuses of Rampart were occurring at the same time the reforms were being put into place. For years, police criminality has been allowed. It is not surprising that corrupt cops at Rampart would have had every confidence that their actions would go undetected and if detected, unpunished by LAPD Internal Affairs, the district attorney;s office, and the courts. For a comparison of problems identified by the Christopher Commission in 1991 and the LAPD Board of Inquiry, an internal report of 1999, see figure 4.2.

Using the Rampart debacle, we can see evidence of practices of racism up and down the law enforcement system. It has been suggested that the district attorney's office relied on the testimony of officers and their evidence even though they often had doubts about their truthfulness. Stated in a different way, minority persons have less standing and are stereotyped within the courtroom. Others suggested that the prosecutor's desire for convictions that would lead to their own promotions cause them to look the other way. I would add that minority members were seen as less worthy of justice. Charles Lindner, past president of the Los Angeles Criminal Bar Association, alleged that the district attorney's office has fostered a culture of mistrust between prosecutors and defense attorneys. Deputy district attorneys are trained and encouraged to have a near-paranoid distrust of defense counsel. The district attorney has access to the one eyewitness whose version often varies substantially from the police officer: the defendant. But prosecutors simply cannot accept that a defendant could be telling the truth.[23]

In 1991, the Christopher Commission issued its landmark report on excessive force, racial bias, and other problems. The Commission was formed to respond to the Rodney King beating. In the wake of the 1999 Rampart scandal, an LAPD Board of Inquiry issued its own study of the corruption case. Some of the problems raised are strikingly similar to those revealed in the Christopher Commission report.

CHRISTOPHER COMMISSION	BOARD OF INQUIRY
CODE OF SILENCE	
"Perhaps the greatest single barrier to the effective investigation and adjudication of complaints is the officers' unwritten code of silence. An officer does not provide adverse information against a fellow officer."	"None of the employees interviewed recognized any particular trend toward code of silence, which is certainly ironic, to say the least, given what we now know regarding events at Rampart."
RECOGNIZING PROBLEM OFFICERS	
"The failure to control these [problem] officers is a management issue that is at the heart of the problem. The documents and data that we have analyzed have all been available to the department; indeed, most of this data came from that source. The LAPD's failure to analyze and act upon this revealing information evidences a significant breakdown in the management and leadership of the department."	"Time and again, the board found clear patterns of misconduct that went undetected. Nowhere was this more apparent than in the investigation of personnel complaints by the Rampart community. Regardless of the source, complainants all seemed to be viewed as recalcitrant and their allegations were not taken seriously by some of the investigations. Equally significant was the failure of management to recognize those clear patterns and correct the behavior of the officers involved."
HIRING PRACTICES	
"The LAPD 'pays too little attention to a candidate's history of violence.' Experts agree that the best predictor of future behavior is previous behavior. Thus, the background investigation offers the best hope of screening out violence-prone applicants."	"Pre-employment data on four of the profiled [Rampart] officers raises serious issues regarding their initial employment with the department. Criminal records, inability to manage personal finances, histories of violent behavior and narcotics involvement are all factors that should have precluded their employment as police officers. . . . So, as painful as it may be, we must recognize that this problem has not been solved."
PERFORMANCE EVALUATION	
"Personnel evaluation reports...often paint unduly favorable pictures of officers who appear to have significant problems in their use of excessive force."	"The fact is that our personnel evaluations have little or no credibility at any level in the organization, and that must be corrected."

Sources: Christopher Commission and Board of Inquiry Reports

Figure 4.2.   Issues in the Los Angeles Police Department

Judges are also players in this tragic drama, for they have a constitutional duty to protect the defendants' constitutional rights. In the last fifteen years or more, judges appointed by the governor have been conservatives and "tough on crime." During all these years, the judges must have had some suspicions about officers' testimony and evidence. Nevertheless, they accepted it and ignored the pleas of poor minority males that the officers were framing them. It is suggested that state court judges may accept police fabrications because they do not want "technicalities" such as the fourth, fifth, and sixth Amendments of the U.S. Constitution interfering with the apprehension and imprisonment of "bad guys", i.e., minorities. Lindner further states,

> In too many cases, the judge is the *de facto* prosecutor because the deputy district attorney is either so inexperienced or inept that he or she needs a little help. So the judge steps in and questions the officer testifying, strengthens dubious parts of the story and withdraws after bolstering the cop's testimony. With the singular exception of the court's most senior jurist, judges never take over cross examination to hammer at a cop for what seems a questionable story.[24]

Defense attorneys find that complaining to the judge about officer perjury and abuse gets them nowhere, for the defendants themselves are viewed as unworthy. The LAPD has enjoyed much independence. Originally, this was to shield the officers from political control; it was thought this freedom would prevent police corruption, but this has not proven to be the case.

Finally, the Los Angeles Police Commission, the citizen review board appointed by the Mayor and approved by the city council, failed to provide proper oversight and identified too closely with the department they were supposedly monitoring. The U.S. Justice Department and the FBI opened investigations into the Rampart scandal. As mentioned earlier, the Justice Department entered into a federal consent decree to finally force the city toward true police reforms.

Remedies for Police Criminality

The Justice Department required an outside monitor to report on the progress of reforms and put forth the following remedies for LAPD; however, they may be a prescription for many big city police departments:

- Revamping internal police investigations and increasing of powers and more independence to the department's civilian oversight
- Expanding the LAPD's internal affairs division
- Upgrading its computerized system for tracking officers
- Creating new training programs
- Enhancing civilian leadership for auditing and publicly reporting on the LAPD's performance

Other remedies I suggest are the following:

- Increase the number of minorities and women in all areas of the criminal justice system
- End the excessive sentences for relatively minor crimes
- Increase funding for after-school programs for pre-teens and teenagers
- Increase funding for summer job programs for teens in low-income communities
- Provide more training for the trainers in the Police Academy
- The Police Inspector General must be given greater power to oversee the police department
- Stop the intimidation of judges who on occasion doubt police credibility and who are thereafter falsely accused of being "soft on crime"
- Each state should mandate that all interrogations and confessions be tape recorded[25]
- The prevailing political climate of "tough on crime" fosters fear in elected officials who support a more humane system, and this climate must be ended
- The president should establish a national commission on police criminality to investigate the national implications, just as the Kerner Commission was created to deal with uprisings in black communities in the 1960s and 1970s

The Three-Strikes Law

To combat the widespread incidence of brutal murders being committed by former felons, California enacted the much debated *three-strikes law*. This statute, which was endorsed by 72 percent of California voters in 1994, states that any criminal with a serious or violent prior felony would automatically have his sentenced doubled for a second conviction. On a third felony conviction, offenders would be incarcerated for twenty-five years to life. What appeared to be a good idea to some has now come under heavy attack, especially by human rights groups. Three-strikes policies now operate in nearly twenty states, although California stands out because of the breadth of its legislation. Because any felony in the state qualifies as a third strike (or for enhanced prison terms under its second strike provisions), more than 15,000 offenders were sentenced to prison under the law in just two years.[26]

Proponents of this law suggest that it has contributed to crime reduction. However, they may be confusing cause with effect. California's crime has declined for the two years after the enactment of this legislation, but it is also true that the crime rate was declining for the two-year period prior to the enactment of the law. In fact, there has been an overall decline in the crime rate throughout the country since 1992.[27] Those who support the law argue that is has a positive effect and that there is a need to build additional prisons. Those who oppose the law contend that not only is it immoral, and economically infeasible, but that it is heavily biased against poor minorities. Some community groups suggest that the law is too harsh, and that judges should have sentencing discretion. They point to its consequences for petty crimes, such as shoplifting food, and being caught with small amounts of marijuana.

Criminologist Larry Siegel states in his book *Criminology* that the three-strikes legislation expands the racial disparity that already exists in sentencing. He claims that under the law African Americans face an increased risk of being sentenced.[28] The incarceration rate is 44 to 1 for blacks versus whites, clear evidence that Siegel's conclusion is true. While investigating the pros and cons of introducing a three-strikes law in Britain, the Prison Reform Trust, a British pressure group, found that 43 percent of California's "three-strikes" offenders were black, although blacks make up only 20 percent of felony arrests. Whites, who make up less than 25 percent of "three-strikes" cases, account for 33 percent of felony arrests.[29] Stated differently, while whites represent one-third of felony arrests, only one-fourth of whites are sentenced under the three-strikes law. Because the statute is used extensively in drug possession cases, it appears to target minorities. The statistics regarding drug use and incarceration gives credence to this suspicion. Consider: there are 13 million drug abusers in the United States: 77 percent are white; 15 percent are African American; 8 percent are Latino. However, African Americans comprise 41 percent of all those arrested on drug charges.[30] A 2006 Boston study reconfirms the racial disparity; of the one thousand people treated in 2004 by a network of residential treatment centers in Boston, 62 percent were white, 22 percent were black, and 11 percent were Hispanic.[31]

A policy analysis of the law by Van Loben Sels Foundation, *Three Strikes: The New Apartheid*, found that 85 percent of those sent to state prison under the law are sent for nonviolent offenses. The authors reported that while blacks make up 7 percent of California's population and constitute 23 percent of felony arrests, they represent 31 percent of the prison population and 43 percent of "three-strikes" defendants sent to state prison.[32] Four of every ten young black males in California are under some form of criminal justice jurisdiction. These figures belie the axiom that justice is blind. What the figures confirm is a high level of negative differential treatment of minority groups.

In 2004, California voters narrowly defeated a ballot initiative that would have softened the three-strikes law by qualifying an offense as a third strike only if the act was a serious or violent. There was an intense eleventh-hour fear campaign which stopped the approval of this change. The initiative would have force resentencing for as many as 4,100 felons now serving twenty-five years-to-life terms.

Proposition 21

Mike Males, a scholar in social ecology, states that no other Western nation puts juveniles to death. However, the United States has executed 300 juveniles since 1979—125 of them age sixteen or younger, and nearly all of them African American.[33] Minority youth are leading the statistics of arrests for violent crimes. These questions are not being asked: How much of the violent crime behavior is associated with poverty and lack of opportunities for this segment of the population? How much is associated with the policies and patterns that lock minorities out of the system? There seems to be a continuing desire to demonize adolescents, especially minority teens, as inherently evil regardless of scientific study, which strongly support the effects of poverty on youth behavior. Since the demonization of youth has played so well for politicians, we have continued to enact harsh punishment to the exclusion of opening paths of opportunity for them.

In recent years, our society has been fixated on juvenile crime, primarily due to the sensationalized school killings of young students by other teenage students. This section will concentrate on a policy enacted by California to illustrate how policies, practices, and procedures within a social institution can have a devastating effect on minorities. California has one of the highest youth incarceration rates, 549 per 100,000 as compared to 368 per 100,000 for the nation as a whole. It houses 12.6 percent of juveniles, and accounts for 18 percent of juveniles in custody. Minority youth are particular impacted, with African American youth more than six times as likely to be incarcerated as white youth.[34]

In March 2000, the "Gang Violence and Juvenile Crime Prevention Act," known as Proposition 21, was passed with 62 percent of voters supporting it. The bill was sponsored by the former governor Pete Wilson, along with California's District Attorneys Association and the State Sheriffs' Association. It is one example of how state legislatures continue to expand laws regarding juvenile waivers to adult courts. Proposition 21 was proposed as a deterrent to the high profile violent acts committed by gang members and juvenile criminals. Current California laws have two methods of transferring juvenile offenders to adult court. First, the judicial waiver involves a fitness hearing before a judge. Second, SB334 provides for automatic prosecution in adult court for a youth sixteen years and older accused of murder, specified sex crimes, or aggravated kidnapping, provided the minor previously committed any felony when age fourteen or older. Proposition 21 increases the circumstances under which a juvenile offender can be sent directly to the adult criminal court system. It requires youth age 14 and older to be tried in adult court for specified violent crimes, allowing prosecutors, without judicial review, to directly file cases in adult court for several categories of juveniles charged with certain serious offenses.

Proposition 21 includes gang-related offenses such as gang related extortion, witness/victim intimidation, and home robberies, labeling them as "violent" felonies. Other crimes such as carjacking, shooting at an inhabited dwelling, and drive-by shootings are punishable by life in prison. Proposition 21 also includes a three strikes law. Under its three strikes provision, a number of offenses are added to the list of "serious" or "violent" felonies. If a juvenile is charged with these offenses, the youth cannot plea bargain to a lesser charge. Also, most of these crimes would be subject to current law, requiring at least 85 percent of the juvenile's time be served before being released.

Many groups, especially within low-income communities, protested the law before its enactment. Several questions emanated from the protests: Are existing laws working? Are tougher laws truly needed? Is prevention or better enforcement a more desirable alternative?

The provisions have had a significant impact on minority juvenile offenders, for it raises the number incarcerated or supervised by the criminal justice system. Research has demonstrated a pattern of differential processing of minorities at various stages of the juvenile justice system.[35] Two of the most comprehensive reports to date, completed since the implementation of Proposition 21, claim that at every stage of the nation's system of crime and punishment—from arrest through plea bargaining to sentencing—black and brown Americans get tougher treatment than whites. The studies call attention to a number of troubling statistics. Among first-time offenders charged with the same crime, young minority group members are six times as likely to be locked up as are young whites. As earlier stated whites are more likely to use drugs, yet nearly two-thirds of those convicted of drug offenses are black; between 1985 and 1995, the rate of Latino incarceration nationwide more than tripled.[36] Latinos are the fastest-growing group of imprisoned Americans. Current reports on the crime justice system generally support the above data, suggesting that the political policy of being tough on crime is having a devastating effect on minority communities, which increasingly are feeling hopeless and powerless. The Leadership Council on Civil Rights report states that the aftermath of Proposition 21 will be ruinous on minority youth given the demonstrable incongruity in juvenile justice. The race crime gap has widened even as the crimes rates have decreased, probably due to the strong anti-crime sentiment across the nation that has fostered the new laws.

The figures above show the ongoing patterns, practices, and procedures within the social institution of criminal justice to be unequal, unfair, and racist. The data discussed above plainly shows that minorities continue to be treated disproportionately harshly. Such treatment greatly reduces the possibility of their partaking in the American dream. Early in their lives, many poor minority children are singled out and placed into the criminal justice system, thus reducing any possibility of them being able to compete for a good education, and a high-paying career. The consequences of Proposition 21 are staggering. A reasonable argument can be made that today's poor minority youth are an endangered species.

A current example of perceived unequal justice targeting young black males is the series of incidents that occurred in Jena, Louisiana. On August 31, 2006, a black student at the local high school asked a school official if he could sit under the large tree situated on the campus. The school administrator immediately said that he could sit anywhere on the campus that he wanted. The black student along with some of his black friends did so. The next day three nooses were found hanging from the tree. Traditionally, the tree was perceived by all students as a designated whites-only area. In a 2007 CNN interview, the black youth implied that he knew this and wanted to confront the segregation. The black community was incensed; some stating that it was a symbol of intimidation to keep blacks in their place and a throwback to the Jim Crow era of lynchings. The three white boys who hung the nooses were quickly identified; their immediate expulsion for a week was overturned when their parents complained to the school board. They were suspended instead and returned to school the next week. Blacks in the town were outraged that the punishment for the white students was so light. From then on the tension in Jena escalated from the school to the small rural town, population approximately three thousand—85 percent white and 13 percent black. Confrontations between black and white residents occurred. Adding to the tensions in the town was the incident of a white youth confronting a group of black youth at a local store with a shotgun because he felt threatened by them. The black youth wrestled the gun from him. The police charged the black youth with battery and stealing the shotgun; no charges were brought on the white youth.

In December 2006, an incident occurred that gave birth to "the Jena 6," which, on September 21, 2007, produced the largest mass protest rally led by African Americans the country had seen since the Civil Rights Movement. Six black teenagers reportedly beat and kicked a white male student, knocking him unconscious. Five of the students were initially charged with attempted second-degree murder and conspiracy to commit second-degree murder. Five of the youth were to be tried as adults; this charge was subsequently reduced to battery and conspiracy and they are now to be tried as juveniles. The conviction by an all-white jury for aggravated second-degree battery and conspiracy was overturned by an Appeals Court for the only youth tried because he was illegally tried as an adult rather than a juvenile. He was sixteen years old at the time of the beating.

There is much complexity to this case and it is being referenced here not to suggest that the black youth should not be punished but to highlight the earlier discussion of the frequent severity of sentences against black youth. The mass march, numbering twenty thousand to forty thousand was a protest against the severity of the charges and their perception of unequal justice. Black and Latino youth are often given sentences six times more severe than white youth. Publicity about the Jena 6 was propelled by black bloggers, African American students using the internet, and black talk show hosts, not the mainstream media, which didn't pick up the story until months later. It is believed by most in the black community that the mass outpourings of concern led to the reduction in sentence for the black youth. African Americans in Jena state that there is on-going racism in the town. White residents state that they are not racist. Clearly, the two racial groups have contradictory views of life in Jena.

Finally, one must also wonder how much economic gain plays into the problem. Throughout this book, I have emphasized the importance of economic gain in perpetuating racist institutions. In examining the juvenile justice system, it is clear that many careers rely on continuing to incarcerate large numbers of youth in the criminal justice system. Prison guards, social workers, probation officers, municipal and state police all owe their jobs due to the ballooning of the criminal justice system. Since that system primarily entraps young African Americans and Latinos, white America can be deluded into believing that it is the proclivity of minorities to engage in criminal behavior, thereby justifying the need for the harsh system. In addition, those who benefit from the current system, the white majority, may feel less emotionally concerned about these young people from a different class and a different culture.[37]

Remedies for Youth Incarceration

The level of violent gang activity seems to rise and fall over time. Experts in the field are unsure about the reason for the cyclical nature of the violence. Certainly the society must be protected from violent youth. However, can we step back and examine prevention rather than incarceration as a remedy for antisocial behavior? Here are some tried-and-true solutions that have decreased juvenile delinquency in the past:

- Mobilize a gang truce in the community. This was successfully accomplished by the rival gangs: the Crips and the Bloods after the 1992 Los Angeles riots.
- Increase the amount of federal dollars made available to low-income communities for job training.
- Restore and increase federal and state funds for summer jobs for teens.

- Increase funding for intervention programs.
- Increase funding of social research on intervention of juvenile delinquency.

Eugene F. River III, the founding director of the Boston-based National Ten-Point Leadership Foundation, offers a sensible remedy that he calls "The 3 M's." In the 1990s, Boston succeeded in reducing youth crime by emphasizing community-based preventive strategies that involved three components: monitoring, mentoring, and ministering.

- *Monitoring.* This entails strict monitoring of the whereabouts and behavior of juveniles and young adults on probation. The procedure was to visit the homes of ten to fifteen youth offenders in teams two to three times a week. With clergy and street workers, the teams also stopped at public areas where youths congregate. The program strictly enforced curfew and other area restrictions. Most probationers received drug treatment, counseling, and help with finding jobs.
- *Mentoring.* A recent federal report estimated that 1.5 million children, about half of whom are children of color, have one or both parents in prison. Studies have show that these children are more likely to suffer lifelong illiteracy, substance abuse, imprisonment, and premature death. Thus putting caring adult mentors into their lives is a logical approach to producing change. Black churches in Boston took up the task of monitoring these children.
- *Ministering.* Studies have shown that for a portion of lawbreakers, religious involvement and holistic ministering programs can reduce drug use and violent behavior. Thus the Boston program uses ministers and other church members to work directly with youth with the hope of increasing their academic success, and escape from poverty.

The Boston faith-based experiment has achieved some success; Rivers states that while the state as a whole experienced a 14 percent increase in the number of probationers arrested, Boston's poorest high-crime neighborhood had a 9 percent decrease. Inspired by the Boston model, probationer recidivism rates statewide has fallen by nearly 20 percent.[38]

This approach of faith-based prevention is spreading to other communities as well. In South Central Los Angeles, I have met with the Los Angeles Metropolitan Churches (LAMC), which have a program similar to the one in Boston. So far they have gotten moral and financial support from the state district attorney, the Los Angeles County Probation Department, the Los Angeles Unified School District, and the Social Work Department at my university, California State University at Los Angeles.

SUMMARY

The examination of institutional racism in this chapter focuses on its covert nature in two major social institutions: employment and law enforcement. The chapter examines the policies within the job market and discovers a long history of denying minorities equal opportunity to earn a living, with job discrimination cutting across all of the racial and ethnic groups. There is discussion of the two-tier labor market and how it assists in the maintenance of economic inequality by relegating minorities to the more undesirable jobs. The use of immigrants throughout history to ensure minority exploitation is also discussed. One remedy that is suggested is ensuring strong support at all levels of affirmative action. It has had the most impact on job discrimination in the past and is still the most potent cure to the two-tier labor market. The other social institution studied for evidence of hidden racism was law enforcement. Examined were the criminal behavior of some law enforcement personnel, the three-strikes law, and Proposition 21. Throughout the criminal justice system, evidence exists of harsh, differential treatment of minorities that reinforce a system of racial inequality. Remedies for police criminality and youth incarceration are discussed.

KEY TERMS

affirmative action. Public or private actions or programs that provide or seek to provide opportunities or other benefits to persons on the basis of, among other things, their membership in a specified group or groups.

enlightened immigrant policy. Openness to immigrants while taking into account the legitimate interests of native workers.

quotas. A system that requires a fixed number of minorities and women and provides for sanctions to enforce compliance.

white backlash. Acts of concerted resistance or social disapproval of policies, practices, and procedures which are perceived to benefit minorities at the expense of whites.

GROUP ACTIVITIES

1. Discuss other examples of white backlash in American society.
2. Bring to the group a newspaper article depicting a current example of racism in the workplace.
3. Discuss the ramifications of the Rampart scandal to Latino immigrant communities.

4. Should the criminal justice system have a different role within immigrant Asian communities?
5. Has gang violence subsided in your city this year?

STUDY QUESTIONS

1. In what ways were minorities barred from employment during the early stages of the Industrial Revolution?
2. Why does upward mobility rest on the division and compensation for one's labor?
3. Each person in the group should give a reason why social scientists refused to examine employment discrimination.
4. Explore the various methods used by business and labor to deny jobs to minorities, or prevent their retention.
5. How has Proposition 21 affected minority communities?
6. Who stands to gain by the ballooning of incarceration of juveniles?
7. What has been the role of the following segments in the Rampart scandal: the police, the judges, the public defender, and the district attorney?
8. Why are minorities overrepresented in the criminal justice system?
9. Who gains by the high level of incarceration of adults?

NOTES

1. See chapter 7, "Organizing in the Chinese American Community," in Rivera and Erlich, *Community Organizing in a Diverse Society* (Boston: Allyn and Bacon, 1998).

2. See chapter 8, "The Japanese American Community and Community Organizations," in Rivera and Erlich, *Community Organizing*.

3. For a more thorough discussion of this historical phase, see chapter 9, "Occupational Apartheid and the Myth of the Black Middle Class," in Steinberg, *Turning Back: The Retreat from Racial Justice in American Thought and Policy* (Boston: Beacon Press, 1995), 80.

4. Bradford Chambers, *Chronicles of Black Protest* (New York: New American Library, 1968).

5. Stephen Steinberg, *Turning Back: The Retreat from Racial Justice in American Thought and Policy* (Boston: Beacon Press, 1995), 80.

6. Marilyn Maldonado, "Harvesting the Fruits of Color Blindness: Racial Ideology in Employers' Discourse and Everyday Production of Racial Inequality in Agricultural Work," *Dissertation Abstracts International A* 66, no. 2, 773-A- 774A (August 2005).

7. U.S. Commission on Civil Rights, *Civil Rights Issues Facing Asian-Americans in 1990s* (Washington, DC: 1992).

8. James Blackwell, "Looking for the Working Class," *New Society* 61 (September 1982).

9. Steinberg, *Turning Back.*

10. See Elizabeth Deitch et al., "Subtle Yet Significant: The Existence and Impact of Everyday Racial Discrimination," *Human Relations* 56, no. 11 (November 2003).

11. Deitch et al., "Subtle Yet Significant," 1301.

12. Jennifer Pierce, Racing for Innocence: "Whiteness Corporate Culture, and the Backlash Against Affirmative Action," *Qualitative Sociology* 26, no. 1, 53–70 (2003).

13. For more discussion of black workers and immigration, see David Bacon, "Immigration Reform: Uniting Black and Immigrants," *ColorLines* (Winter 2004–2005).

14. Robert Lehr, "A Brief Critical Look at Affirmative Action," *Social Work Perspectives* 4, no. 1 (1993).

15. James Jones, Jr., "Rise and Fall of Affirmative Action," in Herbert Hill and James Jones, eds., *Race in America* (Madison: University of Wisconsin Press, 1993).

16. For detailed discussion of the history and development of affirmative action, read chapter 12 in *Race in America.*

17. Henry Weinstein, "Justice System Is 'Broken,' Lawyers Say," *Los Angeles Times,* June 24, 2004.

18. Weinstein, "Justice System."

19. Mima Mohammed, "U.S. Prison Numbers Up 35% in 10 Years," *Los Angeles Times,* December 1, 2006.

20. Eric Slater, "Town Is on Edge After Rioting," *Los Angeles Times,* June 19, 2003.

21. Independent Commission on the Los Angeles Police Department, *Summary* (Los Angeles, 1991), 5.

22. Editorial, "Getting to the Bottom and the Top," *Los Angeles Times,* February 11, 2000.

23. Charles L. Lindner, "The System Has Become Dysfunctional," *Los Angeles Times,* March 19, 2000, M1.

24. Lindner, "System Has Become Dysfunctional," M6.

25. For more detail, see Henry Weinstein, "Illinois Poised to Set Taped Interrogation Rule," *Los Angeles Times,* July 17, 2003.

26. Marc Mauer, *The Crisis of the Young African American Male and the Criminal Justice System* (Washington, DC: U.S. Commission on Civil Rights, 1999), 15–16.

27. Mauer, Ibid, *The Crisis of the Young African Americal Male,* 10.

28. Larry J. Siegel, *Criminology* (New York: West/Wadsworth, 1998).

29. Dyan Machan, "Habitation, No Rehabilitation," *Forbes* 90 (1998): 90.

30. Report from the National Institute of Drug Abuse, 1990.

31. Michael Levenson, "Drug Tally Shoots Down a Racial Myth; Whites Top City's Rising Toll From Abuse," *Boston Globe,* March 25, 2006.

32. C. Davis, C. Estes, and V. Schiraldi, *Three Strikes: The New Apartheid* (San Francisco: Van Loben Sels Foundation, 1996).

33. Mike A. Males, *The Color of Justice: An Analysis of Juvenile Adult Court Transfers in California* (San Francisco: Justice Policy Institute, 2000).

34. California Budget Project, *Will Proposition 21, The Gang Violence and Juvenile Crime Prevention Act, Decrease Juvenile Crime in California?* (2000).

35. C. Pope and W. Feyerherm, "Minorities and the Juvenile Justice System," Final Report (Washington, DC: U.S. Department of Justice, 1991). Also see other reports from the same source for 1993 and 1995.

36. The new reports were compiled in 2000 by two umbrella public policy groups: the Washington, DC–based Leadership Council on Civil Rights, a fifty-year-old group that represents 185 human rights organizations, and Building Blocks for Youth, a liberal group of child and legal advocacy organizations focused on helping minority juvenile offenders.

37. Special thanks to my students Kenya R. Roberson, Alejandro Torres, and Lusine Abasyan who did the research for this section on law enforcement.

38. Eugene Rivers, "The 3 M's Help Keep Youth Violence at Bay," *Los Angeles Times*, October 2, 2000, B7.

5

Institutional Racism Dissected: Part C

People of all races and ethnicities with liberal and conservative views often have strong, sometimes emotional differences of opinion regarding many social welfare issues; welfare reform and child welfare are of prime concern.

Shirley Better

THE HIDDEN FACE OF RACISM:
SOCIAL WELFARE AND CHILD WELFARE

Social Welfare and Its Importance to the Study of Racism

Social welfare policy in the context of this book refers to human services that provide benefits to people to assist them in meeting basic life needs, such as employment, income, food, housing, health care, and interpersonal relationships. The largest social welfare program of this kind is the **Social Security Act** created in 1935, in response to the Great Depression. This program sought to provide both monetary assistance and nonmonetary aid such as subsidized housing, food stamps, free medical care, and social services to the needy. The program was targeted to the elderly, the disabled, dependent children, and former workers and their dependents. The program was far reaching, supporting eligible recipients from birth to death. As some minorities in America, specifically Native Americans, African Americans, and Latinos, are disproportionally poor, their numbers are significantly higher in governmental programs—public welfare programs. Thus the policies, practices, and procedures of this mammoth social institution affect the lives of one-third of American minorities and approximately 10 percent of the white population.

91

Definition of Social Welfare Racism

Social welfare racism relates to policies, practices, and procedures that operate within the various sections of public and private helping agencies and organizations so as to consistently penalize, disadvantage, and exploit individuals who are members of nonwhite groups. In reviewing the development of public welfare policy throughout American history, a salient reality is that African Americans have been used as the touchstone. A touchstone is the test or criterion for determining the quality or genuineness of a thing. In social welfare African Americans have been the ultimate other; and they have been used by both sides of the welfare debate, liberals and conservatives, to determine what must be done for and about the poor. Thus, in this reality, racism has become the covert and mighty determinant of the quality of life for all of America's poor. Even though the overwhelming numbers of the identified poor are white, Latinos and African Americans are still used as the government's yardstick for determining how to reduce the burden of caring for the poor. Thus, social welfare policy, as a framework for action, is always tinged with racism.

Our present-day Social Security program is the overarching basis for all our governmental programs that address poverty. The model for the Social Security program was the Elizabethan Poor Laws of 1601 that was developed in England. These statues codified all existing policies as they related to meeting the needs of the poor; it also was the first such law which gave the government the major responsibility for meeting the needs of the poor.Unfortunately, the American colonies also brought with them the prevailing English attitudes regarding the poor; that there are "worthy" and unworthy" poor people. The **worthy poor** were young children, widows, the aged, and the disabled. The **unworthy poor** were those who the community believed had brought their misfortune upon themselves. Those who were deemed unworthy were not accorded the same benefits and were often chided and stigmatized, if not mistreated. With that background in mind, let us examine the pervasiveness of racism in the formulation of public welfare policies; policies and practices that throughout American history have been shaped with people of color in mind, and very specifically African Americans.

Historical Examination of Racism in Public Welfare Policies

Figure 5.1 provides a graphic display of how public welfare policy, practices, and procedures were shaped to control, penalize, and exploit a targeted group, African Americans. Americans want to believe that public welfare programs are essentially benevolent and caring and simply ineffective and bureaucratic in its delivery of social services to people of color. However, as we review the policies we learn that there has been the conscious and unconscious manipulation of these policies to reinforce white skin

Public Welfare Policy	What it Provided	How Racism was Implemented	Effects on African Americans (AA) and other Nonwhites
The Mothers' Pension Movement	In 1911, successfully lobbied for state legislation that encouraged local government to assist poor children and their families	American society was heavily dominated by Jim Crow laws enacted to protect white supremacy. White attitudes toward blacks was hostile; African American (AA) stereotyped as lazy and immoral; thus not worthy of public aid.	1. AA mothers, even widows, were often seen as "unsavory and morally loose" and thus often ineligible for aid. 2. Often poor mothers were disqualified due to "unsuitable homes." 3. Some local governments had higher benefit level standards for white mothers than black mothers.
Aid to Dependent Children (ADC)	1935 Social Security Act provided financial aid and in-kind services to needy children	States were given much latitude to determine eligibility and type of aid to be received. Prevalence of "States Rights" especially in the South.

1930s and 1940s were dominated by Jim Crow laws, high levels of job discrimination. Racial disparities in all social institutions. | 1. In Mississippi, an unwritten quota of no more than 10% of blacks would be eligible. 2. Texas and New Mexico placed restrictions on poor Mexican children's eligibility. 3. Black mothers' removal from the rolls often corresponded with seasonal agricultural, other low-wage labor needs. 4. Studies found that, the higher the proportion of AA in a state's population, the less aid they received. |
| Aid to Families with Dependent Children (AFDC) | 1960s Modification of Social Security Act provided more comprehensive assistance in the form of cash payments, social services, and in-kind services. | White backlash of the 1970s and 1980s. Welfare cutbacks by Reagan. Updated stereotypes of welfare recipients–"Welfare Queens"

Charles Murray "Losing Ground" and Gilder. | 1. Reduction in welfare payments through failure to keep up with rising costs of living. 2. Increased stigma of the poor. 3. Increasing covert racism in the form of harassment, threats, intimidation. |

Figure 5.1.   A Graphic History of Public Welfare Racism

privilege and white supremacy. We will examine the historic shift from discriminatory practices within policy implementation prior to 1994 to a federal policy that leaves poor families without any legal entitlement or rights to public assistance.

Historical Implementation of Aid to Families with Dependent Children. Under the public welfare section, the worthy poor were the aged, the permanently and totally disabled, and the blind. However, the category labeled "Aid to Needy Children" was view with a jaundiced eye. Mothers who were widows were considered worthy. Those mothers who were separated, divorced, or never married were targeted by society for retribution. The categorical aid program was later renamed Aid to Families with Dependent Children (AFDC). As marriage decreased in America and children born out of wedlock increased, recipients in this program received the wrath of our society and were considered the "unworthy poor." Since dependent children are universally considered worthy of assistance, there has always been the conflict of wanting to punish the "unworthy mother" while protecting the children. This societal conflict continues today as we will see with the 1990s welfare reform.

Some will say that it is irrelevant how public welfare policy was implemented sixty years ago, or even twenty years ago. However, I suggest that a historical perceptive is essential in understanding current policy execution. Let us look at the more recent past implementation of AFDC. The welfare rolls increased dramatically in the 1960s. At the same time, liberal and civil rights groups legally challenged the unfair policies and practices of public welfare. For example, such groups protested the meager financial assistance given to these poor families. Further, they challenged the right of agency investigators' to visit a home unannounced and sometimes at night to determine if there was a boyfriend or a husband living with the family. In the early versions of AFDC, a mother was only eligible for assistance if she had no other means of support. Thus, poor couples often had separate to insure their children received food, shelter, and health care.

The 1960s ushered in much militancy by the poor and minority groups, which translated into political activism. The economic and political pressures spurred politicians and policy makers to come up with other ruses to hold down the expansion and cost of these programs. The new enactments appeared to be race neutral, but in effect disadvantaged the poor even more. Let's call the new policies, the "**new paternalism**." It was simply the most expedient method to use during the high level of black activism to continue to provide unequal services to minority groups. It took the guise of new and strict behavioral requirement that tended to come down heaviest on minority mothers. Be reminded that the attack on poor minority groups was not simply a matter of negative attitudes and feelings, though of course that played an important role; often not discussed is the economic profit, social status, and psychic reward to be gained by reinforcing a stratified society with whites on top. Through the 1980s and the early 1990s, welfare cost continued to climb and politicians and policy makers continued to rail against the increasing outlay. The debate became more strident as the makeup of the recipients was increasingly people of color.

Myths about Welfare Mothers and Immigrants.   More and more articles emphasized the myth that the face of welfare was an unmarried African American mother; this myth got widespread play. Ronald Reagan once referred to the "welfare queen" with the implication, not missed by anyone, that he was referring to a black woman. The importance of this negative depiction was that it justified the cuts in AFDC benefits. Psychologically these cuts were more acceptable when sufficient numbers of the taxpayers could be led to believe that the program was populated by lazy, immoral women of color. Another myth is that divorce and out-of-wedlock births are the primary cause of poverty. It was decided by some that single female-headed families were perpetuating poverty and causing the increase in taxes.[1] As stated earlier, single female heads of household had always been viewed as the "unworthy poor." There was a drumbeat of the myth lead by conservative policy makers that welfare caused or perpetuated poverty; however as we will learn even when welfare payments were reduced, poverty within this group did not decline.[2]

Charles Murray's book *Losing Ground* attempted to put a scholarly face on racism by providing empirical data to support the concept of a culture of poverty that reinforced dependency. However, Murray's own data undermined the argument that the poor make carefully reasoned economic decisions to seek public assistance. Several researchers examined Murray's data and determined that during the period studied—the 1970s—the real value of welfare payments was declining. Given Murray's reasoning there should have been fewer persons seeking welfare since its value was decreasing for more people.

Another myth employed to discredit welfare recipients was the notion that the provision of welfare to the poor promoted a constant cycle of illegitimacy and female-headed families. However, Marmor et al. quote the Children's Defense Fund, stating, "there is no data which reveal a connection between the upward trend in illegitimacy and either big increases or declines in the availability of cash assistance to the poor."[3] Of course, the truth doesn't matter, as long as taxpayers are willing to believe it. Unfortunately, there has always been a bias against poor people. An enduring myth of Americana states that anybody can make it in America. Thus, the poor are too often seen as lazy, shiftless, and undeserving. This coupled with the enduring racism against minority groups creates a contentious environment for positive social change.

A myth that is fueling the debate about immigration is the cultural notion about non-European immigrants. It is said that they are "more dependent" than the general American population, tend to be more criminally inclined, that they come to the United States in order to receive welfare, and that they do not contribute to the American economy. The hidden message is that these non-European immigrants are endangering the country's culture. Regarding undocumented immigrants being a drain on the economy, it must be remembered that they were never eligible for public welfare assistance outlined in the Social Security Act, only emergency health services. Documented immigrants were eligible for some monetary and nonmonetary assistance. It is true that as more immigrants came to this country, there were increased costs associated with emergency medical care and incarceration of those who broke the law. However, immigrants are found to be as law abiding as the native born.

The Current Version of Public Welfare Racism

During the 1990s even liberal politicians were falling over themselves to play the welfare race card as a way of winning votes. Bill Clinton, during his campaign for the presidency, had as a cornerstone of his campaign the promise that he would "end welfare as we know it." The president who was well liked by the African American community, often said to be the "first black president," signed into law in 1996 the most stringent reform ever in federal support to poor families—the **Personal Responsibility and Work Opportunity Reconciliation Act** (PRWOR). Note the naming of the bill. The myths regarding the poor and the racism against minority groups loom large in its title. The title suggests that the poor are irresponsible and unwilling to work. The demise of AFDC must be considered a key turning point in the manifestations of welfare racism. Any policy that severely restricts the life chances of poor people will be devastating for minority groups who are disproportionately poor.

What is the definition of poverty? Poverty can be defined in a number of ways: lack of health insurance, lack of adequate housing. However poverty is generally connected with lack of income. In this context, the poverty rate is the share of people living below the government's poverty line. The national poverty rate has remained relatively steady over the past thirty years, at between 12 and 14 percent. The Census Bureau sets the poverty threshold for the nation. In 2005, this was $22,951 for a family of four (around $9.50 an hour).[4] Each year, the threshold of poverty is adjusted for inflation. See figure 5.2.[5]

In 2004, Wider Opportunities for Women estimated the actual costs of basic family needs, including housing, food, child care, transportation, and health care, in ten communities. They found that on average, a parent with two children earning $12 an hour would only be able to pay for 72 percent of those necessities, assuming they receive no government help with the

12.9% of the population are classified as poor

Of those   23.6% are black
              7.7% are white

44% of the homeless are African American, 3.5 times more blacks than whites

Figure 5.2.   Poverty in America

items mentioned. To cover all their needs, they would need to earn $16 an hour, year-round.[6]

While federal and state assistance to the retired, disabled, and poor all came under the general umbrella of the Social Security Act of 1935, the Welfare Reform Act of 1996 targeted primarily one segment of welfare recipients—those who had previously qualified for AFDC. Under AFDC a parent was eligible for assistance as long as they had a dependent child and no source of income. The new legislation targeted this group with a new program, **"Temporary Aid to Needy Families"** (TANF). You will remember that many in this category were considered the "unworthy poor." In this new program, Congress gave the states the flexibility to design their own welfare replacement programs and issued to the states block grants to support the programs.

We have learned that housing and employment policies have conspired to reinforce social stratification. Earlier we discussed spatial apartheid in America that operates around housing. At the end of the twentieth century and now in the twenty-first century, many new and viable industries have moved to the suburbs situated in modern industrial parks. The poor and minority groups are housed in the inner city—far from these well paying, upwardly mobile jobs.[7] Some of those receiving welfare are poor because they do not have access to the education, the technical skills, the transportation, and the personal contacts to vie for these jobs. The negative outcomes of policies in our major social institutions have led to much of the poverty which public policies such as TANF are designed to address.

Let's focus on the current practices and procedures of TANF to discern the embedded racism. This newest version of the racial attack on racial and ethnic minorities operates the same way as racism in other social institutions. The policies are written to be race neutral; the practices embedded in the social institutions act out the racial disparity in such a way that is often invisible. This welfare reform policy emphasizes the goal of getting welfare recipients into jobs quickly and permanently off the welfare rolls. The majority of welfare mothers when polled state that they would prefer to work at a job which would allow them to pay for child care as well as other essentials, and not receive public welfare. However, TANF mandates work first at any job available. This precludes obtaining work that pays a living wage. "Welfare to Work" may be an acceptable concept but racism and bias against the poor have severely diluted its viability in leading welfare recipients out of poverty. Most welfare recipients do not have the education, training, or work experience to demand a job paying a living wage. To compound matters more, we have the macro issues of globalization, immigration, health costs, child care costs, and the economy's need for low-wage labor for unskilled service jobs. These economic and social realities must be addressed as well to make Welfare to Work viable for the poor.

Further, we must continue to address the inequity discovered in the policies, practices, and procedures of this vast bureaucracy. For example, the Applied Research Center cited an investigation conducted in 1999 by the Office for Civil Rights at the federal Department of Health and Human Services. It found several New York City welfare offices in violation of Title VI of the Civil Rights Act, due to their discriminatory practices toward limited English proficient clients. This type of discrimination is widespread and has been found in California, Florida, Idaho, and Texas.[8]

Other statewide examples of past welfare racism follow:

- In 1996, only thirty-six percent of families on the welfare rolls were white. Even as the overall size of the welfare rolls have dropped significantly since that year, whites have been leaving the fastest. Thus, impoverished people of color are left to carry the brunt of the negative outcomes of welfare reform policies.[9]
- Some researchers found that the welfare rolls of those states adopting strict sanctions are most likely to be disproportionately African American.[10]
- The use of diversion tactics to keep people from applying for welfare has been used by some states. For example New York City under Mayor Giuliani used this tactic extensively.[11] By aggressively denying thousands of people of color welfare payments, many felt too intimidated to apply for other forms of aid to which they were legally entitled, such as Food Stamps and Medicaid. It is important to note that at the time that these diversion strategies were used, the welfare rolls were 33 percent African American and 59 percent Latino in New York.

Public Welfare as We Know It.   There are several requirements in the TANF legislation that can be devastating for racial/ethnic minority groups. Let us look at a few:

First, there is a lifetime, five-year limit of eligibility. Recipients are required to find work within two years. For women with limited education and little or no job experience it is extremely difficult to even find a job. Jobs available to them pay the minimum wage, which makes it nearly impossible to meet living expenses and child care cost. These service jobs generally do not provide health coverage. Thus, mothers working at minimum wage service jobs find themselves in an awful dilemma. Ronald Haskins of the Brookings Institute, a conservative think tank, states it succinctly, "While it is accepted that economic growth can reduce poverty, we are finding that because of low and often declining wages at the bottom of the income distribution, economic growth is less effective than in the past at reducing poverty."[12] Racism, sexism, and bias against the poor further limit these women from getting jobs or being able to hold them. We can define poor minority women as being in "triple jeopardy."

Second, child care is crucial to any working mother. Most employed mothers of young children regardless of class would not be in the workforce if they did not have child care. Good-quality child care costs typically range from $4000 to $10,000 a year—but one-quarter of families with young children earn less than $25,000 a year.[13] States report that they can not adequately fund child care costs. Once the woman is fully employed at a minimum wage job and no longer eligible for governmental support, how is she to pay for adequate child care?

The neoconservatives felt vindicated when the welfare rolls decreased as PRWOR was first operationalized. By 2002, fewer than half of families with children poor enough to qualify for cash assistance got help from TANF, down from 52 percent just one year before, and steeply down from about 80 percent in the mid-1990s.[14] However, we now know some of the aftermath:

- Most poor women are working jobs that pay only minimal wage.
- Many of the jobs have turned out to be temporary.
- The number of poor families who are homeless is increasing.
- Poverty has not been reduced for this group even during the boom of the late 1990s.
- The wretchedness of their employment circumstances spills over into their homes, leading to more children being removed from their mothers for neglect.
- Poor families are getting by through the help of charities and shelters. Across the country food banks and shelters for the homeless cite the increased number of working families needing assistance to make it to the next payday.[15]

It is true that there has been a dramatic drop in the numbers of women and children receiving welfare since the enactment of TANF. Poverty has been reduced for a number of poor families. However, more than a decade later, poverty and racism continues to disadvantage minorities. Even the conservative Ronald Haskins of the Brookings Institute conceded, "there are several types of evidence that a number of mothers are in fact floundering."[16] He goes on to state that 40 percent of the mothers who leave welfare do not work regularly, raising some concerns; however the 30 percent who have not worked at all since leaving welfare raise even more serious concerns. New legislation was enacted by Congress in 2005 and signed by President Bush in 2006 to continue TANF, which would have expired except for continuing legislation for several years. One of the new provisions requires "all states to achieve the goal of engaging at least 50 percent of those receiving cash assistance in work and work-related activities designed to promote self-sufficiency."[17] Thus, welfare policies continue to produce inequality—further exploiting poor minorities.

Remedies to Make Welfare Reform Effective and Humane

The goal of welfare reform should be *to get people out of poverty, not off welfare*. Thus, changes in the legislation should include:

1. Enhancement of employment capacities of recipients: All recipients should be given the opportunity to attend programs that will improve their marketable skills. Programs should explore the usefulness of providing more opportunities for increased education and training in nontraditional jobs.
2. Requirement that all employer pay a living wage: Presently, most jobs that recipients get pay only minimum wage. The federal and state governments must lead the fight for a living wage.
3. Uniform guidelines to the states: Current legislation allows states to shape how the program will operate. This leads to disparities state by state in the types of programs available to improve economic conditions for recipients.
4. Include a standardized system of research: This would provide a universal system of data to determine the benefits and hazards of current legislation. Further, research needs to be outside government control so there can be impartial evaluation and monitoring of the program. The current system of collection of data makes it impossible to make inferences nationwide.

Child Welfare: The Importance of Family

The changes in social structure of American families have been charted by social scientists over the decades. Since the 1970s, there has been a decline in marriage. African Americans have had the most serious decline in marriage rates, most startling during the 1980s. Few will argue that family is not crucial to the well-being of children. The president of Joint Center for Political Studies in 1987 stated, "Families give children the basics of food, clothing, and shelter. The family shapes values and aspirations. It provides them with the support and encouragement they need in order to be successful."[18] However, more and more minority children are growing up outside their biological families, to their detriment and that of the community. Over several decades now, there has been an increase in the number of female-headed families in all races and ethnicities and across all classes. Conservative and liberal politicians along with ministers and social scientists suggest that this change in family structure is detrimental to children. There is little disagreement in our society that is would be best for children to be raised inside their biological family with stable and loving parents. Increasingly, minority children disproportionally are being raised in strangers' foster homes. After examining a large percentage of foster care children in 1998, it was determined that 42 percent of children and youth in child welfare programs met DSM-IV criteria for a mental disorder.[19] The child welfare system was created to ensure that all children were provided with a safe home and the essentials to thrive. In many ways, child welfare services is a vital program that is mandated to intervene as the surrogate parent when the biological family is unable to provide a safe and nurturing home. However, there is the flip side of child welfare that serves as a detriment to some of our children; this is the focus of this section on public welfare.

To begin, let's chart how the child moves through the system. The report of neglect or abuse can be reported by the health care system, law enforcement, school, neighbors, or other members of the community. The report is received by the designated local child welfare agency. An investigation is initiated by the child welfare agency, and if the abuse is substantiated several pathways can be chosen: foster care, home-based services, a referral to a family preservation program which will use social services to strengthen the family so that the child can return to the home, or permanency planning. In the latter path, the child may be placed for adoption; see figure 5.3.

Racial Disparity in Foster Care

Since the early 1980s, the number of foster children has gone up fivefold in California, and doubled in the county and the nation; nearly one in four children came into the **child welfare system**. In the 1990s, African American children represented the largest racial or ethnic group at 45 percent in public foster care.[20] However, policy analysts and agency administrators have stated repeatedly that children were unnecessarily being placed in foster care. In 1992, California's Little Hoover Commission cited experts who estimated that 35 percent to 70 percent of foster children in California should never

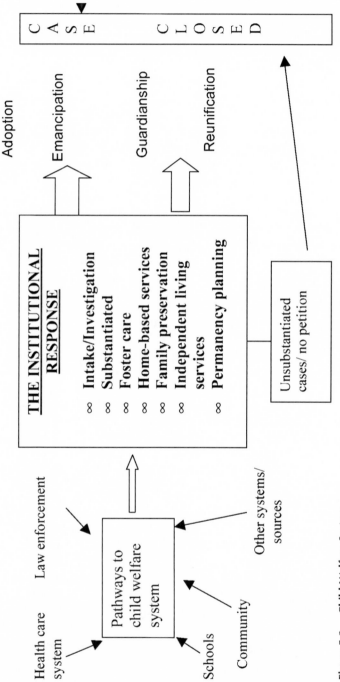

Figure 5.3. Child Welfare System

have been removed from their homes and have suffered deep psychological trauma as a result.[21] Recently, David Sanders, head of the Department of Children and Family Services for Los Angeles County, averred that the experts guess that up to 50 percent of the 75,000 children in the system and adoptive homes could have been left in their parents' care if appropriate services had been provided.[22] In recent years, I have been invited often to social service agencies to conduct workshops on racial disproportionality in child welfare. The concern is the disproportionate numbers of minority children, especially black children in the child welfare system. As we will learn throughout this chapter, much of the disproportionality is race specific. However, many professionals in the child welfare system insist on remedies that are color-blind. African American professionals in social services agencies have been leading activists groups in sounding the alarm.

The history of racism in child welfare is well documented. Orphaned and poor African American and Native American children were placed in alms houses, while white children were placed in adoptive homes. The early history of child welfare services set the tone for present-day disparities. Various policies and practices installed since then have not worked. The 1974 Child Prevention/Treatment Act and the Adoption Assistance and Child Welfare Act—all supposedly enacted to address the disparities—have not worked. The number of African American and Latino children in care continues to grow disproportionally. Much can be learned from the research of Dr. Ruth McRoy, professor at the University of Texas at Austin School of Social Work. See figure 5.4; the data is from Dr. McRoy's lecture at the University of Southern California in 2002.[23]

Economics and Child Welfare

The newspaper article "Foster Care Cash Cow" uncovers a startling reason for the overrepresentation of minority children in foster care.[24] As it turns out, the reason is in part economic! Remember my discussion earlier about the economic gain in institutional racism. There is money to be made in foster care. For example, Los Angeles County receives nearly $30,000 a year from federal and state government for each child placed in the system. This money is used to pay foster care parents, the professional staff, and the administration necessary to operate the program.[25] For some special-needs children, the county receives up to $150,000 annually. Anderson referred to this as "legal kidnapping to make a profit."[26]

So while there has been much pressure to reform the system by finding ways to keep children in their homes, there is a perversity involved. Public policy is shaped by money, and the county's $1.4 billion child welfare system relies heavily on federal funds geared toward children who are removed from their homes.[27] This funding stream has the effect

Of the U.S. child population under the age of 18:
  61% white (37% in care)
  17% Hispanic (15% in care)
  15% African American (38% in care)

For every 1,000 white children, 5 are in care
For every 1,000 black children, 21 are in care

700,000 come in contact with the child welfare system

542,000 children in foster care: black 38%; white 37%

Mean age of black children in care is 10.1 years
Mean length of time in care is 33 months

62% of children of color in care; in some places as many as 80–97% of the children in care are African American.

Figure 5.4.   Racial Disparity in Foster Care

of a negative incentive to take children from their homes, rather than finding ways to strengthen the family and maintain children within their biological family.

Recently, we have learned that a new approach to the overrepresentation of African American babies in foster care is to internationalize adoption. Some private adoption agencies, with the agreement of the mother, are arranging for black children to be adopted by Canadians. In justifying such a plan, American private adoption agencies stated that this arrangement, while providing a good home, would ensure that the children were less likely to experience racism. For any American social service agency to make such a statement is an indictment of our societal structure. This reasoning is reminiscent of the rationale for taking Native American children from their families and raising them in Indian Schools. I would suggest that the solution is to solve the problem of racism here, and there would be no need to export our children.

Racism in Child Welfare.   Currently, 42 percent of all children in foster care nationwide are black, even though black children constitute only 17 percent of the nation's youth. Dorothy Roberts states that in Southern California, where African Americans constitute 15 percent of the population, they are placed at a rate three times greater than their census proportion.

> *Correlates for out-of-home placement: poverty, racism, substance abuse, correctional system, differential attributions, and labeling bias*

Where blacks constitute less than 2 percent of the population, their placement soars to fifteen times their proportion of the population.[28] How could this be so? Social scientists hypothesize that visibility increases the chances of minority placement because agencies are more likely to investigate underrepresented groups, or because these groups lack social supports that could ward off investigation. The foster care system is currently designed to deal with the problems of poor minority families, primarily black families. Problems of white families are handled by separate and less disruptive mechanisms. Judges, social workers, probation officers, and lawyers have become so accustomed to the racial separation in our society that they are often numb to the implications of this in America. Luckily, minority professional groups are taking on a more activist role in sheltering children from the system.

Dr. McRoy, in her extensive study of racial disparities in child welfare, identified several factors listed above that appeared to have a causal relationship to children being placed in foster homes. She avers that racial discrimination has much to do with children being taken out of their homes and put in a stranger's home. "African American children are more likely to be removed from their parents all else being equal. Studies show that the actual incidence of child maltreatment among black families is no greater than the incidence among other groups. The problem is that all else is not equal because of the continuing legacy of racial discrimination."[29] Two of her other correlates relate strongly to racism: poverty, and differential attributions and labeling bias.

Poverty. We have discussed earlier my theory that economic advantage given to whites by maintaining differential employment opportunities reinforces both individual and institutional racism. Consequently, poverty is closely associated with racism. Black families are on two tracks. Seventy percent are healthy families, and 30 percent are poor. Conditions for many of the poor families have worsened in part because of the loss of manufacturing jobs and globalization. Another contributing factor to poverty for some minority families is the bias against hiring ex-felons. Remember the earlier discussion of racism in the criminal justice system. Since African Americans and Latinos are overrepresented in the prison system, their families are less financially stable as the fathers and mothers have more difficulty finding steady employment.

Most Latino and African American children are removed from their homes because of neglect, which often is simply poverty. The poor family is less likely to have the support to withstand calamity; consequently, it may fail to meet the needs of the family. New census data show 1.3 million children have fallen into poverty since 2000.[30] As earlier stated, the overrepresentation of poor children in foster care is felt to be due to greater monitoring of poor families (public hospitals as opposed to private doctors) and a higher incidence of reporting, rather than higher incidence of abuse.[31] While there are social services for drug abuse and physical abuse, ironically there are no services for just poverty.

Differential Attribution and Labeling Bias.   Another correlate that influences out-of-home placement is disdain for the groups who exhibit values and behavior that differ from mainstream America; these attributes are seen as deviant. **Differential attribution** is the practice of giving negative connotations to the behavior of a minority child while the same behavior in a white child would be seen in a less disapproving way, such as when a minority child exhibits anger and is viewed as dangerous and violent. However the same behavior in a white child might be viewed as mental distress, prompting a mental health referral. Minority groups who live in two cultures or may not have adapted to mainstream behavior are sometimes held in disdain. The differential attribution label is reminiscent of *race ideology* previously examined. Unspoken negative feelings seep into the professional evaluation of the home to the detriment of the minority family. Labeling bias relates to the practice of regularly categorizing behavior of minority children as negative and deviant, rather than culturally different.

Other Issues Contributing to the Overrepresentation of Minorities in Foster Care.   Too many professionals have shown a gross indifference to the bonds between parents of color and their children. This may be due to the increasing separation of our society into the "haves and have nots." This feeds into emotional separation, a lack of empathy for those from a different class or racial/ethnic group. Further, it appears that more intense training is needed to help professionals truly understand of the effects of poverty on family patterns. On the same note there is the persistent gulf between the material welfare of children of color and white children in America, which also encourages insensitivity.

Child Welfare Agency Response

I am not adverse to "parenting skills"; however, I am thoroughly dismayed by the naiveté, for want of a better word, as it relates to the response of the child welfare bureaucracy to the crisis in poor minority homes. What are child welfare agencies providing? They are providing parenting classes, individual therapy, and group therapy. It is as if poverty itself is a crime or at least a mental illness! Much data has been cited in this chapter that should leave little doubt that the root of the disproportionality in child wel-fare is largely racism and poverty. Yet what do our social service agencies get funded to do—parenting. What we have as a response is a classic example of "blaming the victim."

Parenting classes clearly indict the parents alone as being unable or un-willing to offer the necessary supports for their children. This is clearly not the true problem in every incidence. The lack of stable jobs paying a living wage is too often the culprit. As we have learned, poor families are more likely to be under scrutiny as they are more likely to frequent governmental funded services—county hospitals, public health facilities, and public hous-ing. Thus a reexamination was clearly called for. Fortunately many states are heeding the need for reform. These are retooling their programs and now initiating programs, such as "wrap-around services." As the term implies, these programs examine all the areas that need strengthening and ensure that those services are provided. For example, parents may referred to job training or encouraged to get their GED, drug abuse problems are referred to professional agencies, domestic violence is squarely addressed, families are helped to find adequate housing and health care services.

Another glaring weakness in agency response is the incorrect training in cultural competency; often the training encourages case workers to behave as if cultural differences do not matter, that they should be color-blind. It is obvious that insufficient attention has been given to teaching child welfare workers about the macrodynamics of poverty and racism. Too often these professionals are taught to accept that all social problems should be viewed as individual inadequacies. Thus, the problem can be solved only if the par-ents pull themselves up by their bootstraps. Providing training in cultural differences, and skills in combating societal barriers, which prevent many from leaving poverty, are not given sufficient importance.

The child welfare bureaucracy is so complex, even seasoned social workers are often at a loss in trying to navigate through it. There is much fragmentation of service delivery as each agency department tries to pro-tect its turf and ensure its continued funding. Too often various agencies have poor relationships, so that professional referrals are not executed in a timely fashion. The mental health system is also complex and bureau-cratic, and in too many instances children are referred for services but the parents are not. There are multiple pathways to treatment, with many families falling through the cracks. Too often human service providers are regulators rather than advocates for the poor and minority groups. Much of the professional training and individual sensitivity is over-whelmed by the predisposition toward counterproductive separation. The campaign to increase adoptions has hinged on the denigration of foster children's parents and kin, the speedy destruction of family bonds, and the rejection of family preservation as an important goal of child welfare practice. Advocates for positive change in child welfare are encouraged to refer often to www.childwelfare.gov for updates on private and governmental planning. Also, refer to www.childrensdefensefund .org for current activities in this area.

Remedies for Racism in Child Welfare

- Parenting classes need to be retooled to provide more in-depth learning for the trainers. There needs to be less blaming and providing more help to get the families out of poverty.
- Emphasize prevention: Provide more "front end" services to families. It is recognized that there is a built-in counterpoint of financial incentives to push foster care. Foster care parents and group homes for youth will often see the change as an attack on their earnings.
- Minority communities in conjunction with caring social work professionals and organizations must continue to raise awareness of the seriousness of the problem through collaborative endeavors.
- Poverty alone must not be used as the evaluation tool as to whether the home is adequate.
- Child welfare workers must be trained to view race, ethnicity, and poverty in a nonjudgmental way. This would first reduce out-of-home placement, and encourage the use of kinship care as the first out-of-home placement option.
- Wrap-around services must be used at the presenting problem level to keep children with their family. Further, the state must develop adequate support services for children leaving the system, so that they do not return to the system.
- Finally, to resolve implementation issues and ensure progress is made, child welfare efforts need to be continuously re-evaluated. This evaluation should be based on consistent data and rigorous analysis.[32]

SUMMARY

Public welfare is one of the most influential social institutions to the minority poor, as it is pervasive in their lives from birth to death. A review of its importance and how it has been used to reinforce poverty and control is illustrated in this chapter. Further, there is a review of the history of social welfare legislation and how it has reinforced inequality. The newest policy directed at the poor, TANF, has a devastating effect on single minority mothers. The chapter then moves to a close examination of how one area of child welfare, foster care, has disproportionately placed minority children into strangers' home, reinforcing the vulnerability of the family and the community.

KEY TERMS

child welfare system. Social service programs created to ensure that all children are provided with a safe home and the essentials to strive.

differential attribution. The practice of giving negative connotations to the behavior of a minority child while the same behavior in a white child would be seen in a less disapproving way.

new paternalism. Changes public welfare policies to hold down the expansion and cost of these programs. The new enactments appeared to be race neutral, but in effect disadvantaged the poor even more.

Personal Responsibility and Work Opportunity Reconciliation Act (PRWOR). Welfare reform enacted by Congress in 1994. Often called "The Welfare Reform Act."

Social Security Act of 1935. Federal and state assistance to the retired, disabled, and poor.

social welfare policy. Human services that provide benefits to people. These services assist them in meeting basic life needs, such as employment, income, food, housing, health care, and interpersonal relationships.

social welfare racism. Policies, practices, and procedures that operate within the various sections of public and private helping agencies and organizations so as to consistently penalize, disadvantage, and exploit individuals who are members of nonwhite groups.

Temporary Aid to Needy Families (TANF). Shortened label for 1994 welfare reform policy.

unworthy poor. Those who the community believe have brought their misfortune upon themselves.

worthy poor. Young children, widows, the aged, and the disabled.

GROUP ACTIVITIES

1. Bring to the group a current article related to poverty in America. Does the article support or differ with the text?
2. Discuss within the group ideas for meeting the needs of the poor minority groups.
3. What governmental policy would you suggest to meet the needs of low income minority children.

STUDY QUESTIONS

1. Explain the term "social welfare racism."
2. Explain the components that lead to the statement "social welfare policy is always tinged with racism."

3. Explain the term "new paternalism."
4. What methods were used by politicians to cut welfare benefits to the poor?
5. What were the myths used to discredit welfare recipients?
6. What do race neutral policies mean? Give an example.
7. List and explain three examples of current social welfare racism.
8. Discuss how money plays a part in foster care placement.
9. Explain the term "differential attributes." Why did the author suggest that it is similar to race ideology?

NOTES

1. See more detailed discussion in Patrick F. Fagan and Robert Rector, "The Effects of Divorce on America," Heritage Foundation paper, June 5, 2000.

2. Kenneth Neubeck and Noel Cazenave, "Welfare Racism: A Force in the Rise, Demise, and Aftermath of AFDC," *American Journal of Sociology*, 108, no. 3, 1153–54 (2000). Also, see their book *Welfare Racism: Playing the Race Card Against America's Poor*. (New York: Routledge, 2001).

3. "Myths That Explode Like Firecrackers," *Los Angeles Times*, May 2, 2000; Children's Defense Fund analyses of Census Current Population Survey 2001 data, in *Quality Child Care Helps Parents Work and Children Learn* (Children's Defense Fund 2002).

4. U.S. Census Bureau, Housing and Household Economic Statistics Division, August 2006.

5. Figures come from Ruth G. McRoy, *The Color of Child Welfare Policy: Racial Disparities in Child Welfare* (Austin: Center for Social Work Research, University of Texas, 2000).

6. Wider Opportunities for Women, "Coming up Short," 2004. http://wowonline .org/docs/dynamic-CITA-43.pdf.

7. See more detailed discussion of metropolitan housing issues in Center on Urban Poverty and Social Change, "Metropolitan Inequities and the Ecology of Work: Implications for Welfare Reform," *Social Service Review* 77, issue 7 (June, 2003).

8. Applied Research Center, *The False Foundations of Welfare Reform* (Oakland, CA: Applied Research Center, 2001).

9. Pamela Loprest, *Families Who Left Welfare* (Washington, DC: The Urban Institute, 1999).

10. Joe Soss, *Unwanted Claims: The Politics of Participation in the U.S. Welfare System* (Ann Arbor: University of Michigan Press, 2000).

11. Karen Houppert, "You're Not Entitled," *Nation*, October 25, 1999, 11–13.

12. Ronald Haskins, "Statement before the Committee on House Ways and Means," *Congressional Quarterly*, July 19, 2006.

13. Children's Defense Fund analyses of Census Current Population Survey 2001 data, in *Quality Child Care Helps Parents Work and Children Learn*, Children's Defense Fund, January 2003.

14. Administration for Children and Families, U.S. Department of Health and Human Services, *Change in Numbers of TANF Families and Recipients, 12/2002–12/2003*; Center on Budget and Policy Priorities, "Employment Rates for Single Mothers Fell Substantially During Recent Period of Labor Market Weakness," Washington, DC: June 22, 2004.

15. Diane Suchetka, "From Welfare to Work but Still Not Making It," *Cleveland Plain Dealer*, June 6, 2006.

16. See his full testimony in *Congressional Quarterly*, July 19, 2006.

17. Tommy Thompson, "Capitol Hill Hearing Testimony on Welfare Reform, House Ways and Means," *Congressional Quarterly*, July 19, 2006.

18. Margaret Simms, "The Changing Black Family: Implications for Children," in *Focus* (Washington, DC: Joint Center for Political Studies, 1988), 5.

19. U.S. Department of Health and Human Services, "Mental Health: Culture, Race, and Ethnicity," supplement to *Mental Health: A Report of the Surgeon General*, 2001, 62.

20. Health and Human Services, "Mental Health: Culture, Race, and Ethnicity."

21. Troy Anderson, "Perverse Incentive Factor Rewards County for Swelling System, Critics Say," *Daily News*, December 6, 2003.

22. Anderson, "Perverse Incentive Factor."

23. McRoy's lecture was based on her chapter, "Color of Child Welfare: Racial Disparities on Child Welfare Services" in *The Color of Social Policy*, K. Davis and T. Bent-Goodley, eds. (Washington, DC: Council on Social Work Education, 2004).

24. McRoy, *Color of Child Welfare Policy*.

25. McRoy, *Color of Child Welfare Policy*.

26. McRoy, *Color of Child Welfare Policy*.

27. Sue Fox, "Overhaul of Poster System Wins OK," *Los Angeles Times*, February 18, 2004.

28. Dorothy Roberts, *Shattered Bonds: The Color of Child Welfare* (New York: Basic Civitas Books, 2002).

29. McRoy, *Color of Child Welfare Policy*.

30. Children's Defense Fund, "New Census Data Show 1.3 Million Children Have Fallen into Poverty Since 2000." childrensdefense.org (accessed September 22, 2006).

31. From a paper presented by Toni Oliver, Director of Roots Adoption Agency in Atlanta, Georgia, 2003.

32. Richard Terzian, "Committed Management Is Needed to Reduce Abuse of Costly Foster Care Programs," *Cal-Tax Digest*, October 2002.

6

The Web of Institutional Racism

Up to this point, we have been reviewing the complexity of racism through the functioning of the major American social institutions. In chapter 2, we have reviewed how the practices, whether intentionally or not, often operate to disadvantage racial and ethnic minorities. We have examined the policies, practices, and procedures flowing through these institutions that reinforce and strengthen covert, culturally normative actions. These actions bind racism in place. The question that will come to mind is, "How can it be that our country has been unable to eradicate the vestiges of institutional racism?" Another question might be, "Why haven't the various minority groups been able to eliminate racism after so many centuries?"

To answer those questions, let us now explore a second theoretical framework. This theory suggest that major institutions over time have developed an exchange system wherein policies, practices, and procedures flow into other social institutions in such a way as to reinforce the binding effect of racist patterns on individuals and groups. Social institutions by their nature operate to support the functioning of the society as a whole. Picture social institutions as the spine of the society. The myriad social institutions function in a holistic way; they operate as a complete system. Thus, social institutions have an interlocking character and in this theoretical framework operate as a single unit. One could say that racist policies of one institution are supported and reinforced in the other closely related social institutions.

THE WEB EXPLAINED

The power of institutional racism and its invisible impact on life opportunities can be graphically illustrated. I have expanded the characteristics of Baron's theory on this social phenomenon, which he coined, "The Web of Urban Racism."[1] The term "Web of Institutional Racism" is substituted to suggest a more in-depth theoretical framework to explain this phenomenon (see figure 6.1). This theory suggests that there is an interlocking relationship between the major social institutions in America, an interweaving of covert racist policies, practices, and procedures, that conspires to retain minorities in disadvantaged positions within the society. The term "web" is used to denote the invisibility of the phenomenon.

What do you think of when the term "web" is mentioned? You probably envision a nearly invisible lacework or mesh-like weave that entangles the unsuspecting fly. You have noted how surprised you are when you find a large spider web in a place you have passed before. Sometimes after a rain the water settles on the web and if you look at the web from a certain angle you can see it. Or you have passed it when the sunshine hits it just right and you are amazed by its existence. The fly, ignorant of what looms ahead of him, is caught in this nearly invisible web. The fly struggles mightily to loosen itself. However, its vain struggle only results in tightening the transparent strings that hold it. One might say that if this fly is at all lucky and frees itself, it would be smarter the next time, and recognize the web and avoid it. Alas, scientists know that spiders of different species spin different designs. Consequently, the fly gains nothing from the former harrowing escape, because each invisible web is slightly different and provides little hint of its presence. The fly will be trapped again, although the fly has done nothing to deserve this fate. The fly is the victim of a force beyond its control.

This analogy is offered to dramatize how social institutions in America weave a pattern of policies and procedures that have negative outcomes for targeted, unsuspecting groups. The term "web" suggests invisible interlacing barriers that prevent minorities from partaking of the riches/rewards of American life. The concept implies that unsuspecting ethnic and racial minorities become ensnared in the "Web of Urban Racism." The theory suggests that social institutions through their built-in systems of actions entrap and reduce the chances of minorities. Figure 6.1 denotes the overlapping and interweaving of the major social institutions: Housing, Education, Employment, Social Welfare, and Politics that reinforce the imperceptible network of racism. There is a network exchange of urban racism. The new theory goes beyond poor blacks and well-off whites and shows how other ethnic groups along with poor whites are equally victimized.

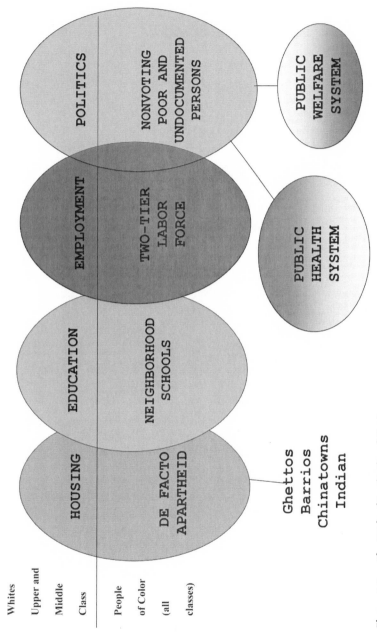

[Network of Policies and Practices of Racism]

Mutual Support Network

Whites
Upper and
Middle
Class

People
of Color
(all
classes)

HOUSING

EDUCATION

EMPLOYMENT

POLITICS

DE FACTO
APARTHEID

NEIGHBORHOOD
SCHOOLS

TWO-TIER
LABOR
FORCE

NONVOTING
POOR AND
UNDOCUMENTED
PERSONS

PUBLIC
HEALTH
SYSTEM

PUBLIC
WELFARE
SYSTEM

Ghettos
Barrios
Chinatowns
Indian

Figure 6.1. The Web of Institutional Racism

THE SAGA OF FRANKLIN AND JOSE

Let us develop a vignette to illustrate how the network operates by describing the lives of two hypothetical infants: one African American, the other Latino. Let's call the African American male, "Franklin," and the Latino male, "Jose." Both of these males are born healthy in every respect and they are both of above-average intelligence. The boys are born at the county hospital (knowing that they are born at a public hospital informs us that they are born into an impoverished or working-class family). We have learned in chapter 3 that goods and services meted out by our institutions are distributed inequitably, with minorities and the poor receiving the least desirable potions of those goods and services. We have noted earlier that there is a strong association between race and poverty.

Housing

Jose and Franklin leave the hospital and return to their poor or working-class neighborhood—Jose to a barrio and Franklin to a ghetto. Poor neighborhoods in America have an abundance of inadequate housing, high unemployment, high underemployment, poorly maintained streets, scarce public open space, and high levels of crime. As you can note in the figure, we have terms that denote low-income minority communities: barrios, ghettos, Chinatowns, Indian reservations. What all of these terms have in common is that they designate living areas/communities that are for the poor and minority groups.

Native Americans were forced to march hundreds of miles southwest to the barren lands of Arizona, New Mexico, and Nevada. All their lands in the original thirteen colonies were taken away from them. All the settlements they developed for themselves in the Midwest after they were pushed westward were taken away from them in fraudulent treaties. As we have noted earlier, Chinese did not live in "Chinatowns" because they preferred to, but rather because ownership of property was restricted. African Americans had much the same experience with neighborhood restrictions. From the earliest times, restrictive covenants, mentioned earlier, were used to prevent middle-class blacks from buying homes in middle-class white neighborhoods.

Living areas commonly designated for minorities were the undesirable places in the city to live. Residents live in these areas because they cannot afford to move out, or feel constrained to stay in the area out of fear. Earlier we illustrated how institutional racism maintains de facto apartheid in America. Most of our urban areas are highly segregated by race and class. However, it is the poor minorities who suffer the most negative aspects of urban living. The sociologist William J. Wilson hypothe-

sizes that poor whites are by and large invisible to the general society because they are disbursed through the community. However, Wilson suggests that the isolation of poor blacks, the truly disadvantaged, into restricted living spaces makes them not only more visible, but more
vulnerable to racist elements of our social institutions. More important,
Wilson suggests that this isolation from the black middle class and the
society in general contribute to the adaptation of a different lifestyle to
cope with unrelenting poverty and isolation.[2]

Figure 6.1 suggests that we have in America a living arrangement that could
be aptly labeled de facto apartheid. **De facto** means "in reality" or in this context "being in effect though not formally recognized." Apartheid is defined as
racial segregation. Most people think of this term in relation to the policies of
segregation and political and economic discrimination against non-Europeans
practiced in South Africa until 1992. **De facto apartheid** includes the reality of
segregation in housing that while illegal, nevertheless is being informally practiced. If we were to take a train ride in any major metropolitan city in the
United States we would witness this de facto apartheid in play. I ask my students to tell me how would they know, even if there were no people of the
street that they were in a community that might be labeled a barrio or a ghetto?
At first there is puzzled silence. Then a student might say, "There is graffiti!"
Then students begin to catch on. Out comes a litany of characteristics which
label the community: poorly maintained houses and apartment buildings, inadequate open space, trash in the streets, few shopping centers, lots of liquor
stores. Communities inhabited by poor whites would probably have the same
characteristics. However, as stated earlier, it is less likely that urban poor whites
live in concentration. Thus, Jose and Franklin, through no action of their own,
begin their lives disadvantaged because of the surroundings in which they live.
Both are exposed to results of inadequate living conditions, exposed to high
levels of violence, few planned recreational facilities, inadequate social services
in all forms, and poorly planned and financed municipal services. Socially,
they lack the abundance of role models that mainstream communities have.
Mainstream communities include successful persons who reinforce social
mores and are the role models. In many poor, minority communities, the middle class has moved away and young people have few adults to emulate. The
loss of the middle class also weakens existing social institutions, for the middle class often offer the leadership and financial support for community organization and social institutions.

The condition of the housing stock affects the overall status of any community. Thus, in the barrios, ghettos, and Chinatowns, the community is defined
by inadequate housing. Poor housing is the harbinger for the overall inadequacies in other areas of community life. What has not been discussed is the
profit/gain that the maintenance of such communities brings. There is a great
deal of wealth generated in low-income minority communities. Earlier, the

persistence of racism in America was explained as tightly associated with economic gain. The wealth that flows through and out of the ghettos and barrios is a good example of this. Many of these communities are conduits/pipelines for the wealth—wealth in the form of illicit activities such as gambling, prostitution, and the storing and distribution of illegal drugs that bring in billions of dollars to drug dealers internationally. Wealth is made through legal activities, such as the profits by absentee landlords gained by overpricing existing housing, or the selling of inferior products at unfair prices. Wealth is also generated by legal activities that are not present in middle-class neighborhoods—pawnshops, check cashing outlets, thrift stores, day-old bread outlets, secondhand furniture and appliance stores . . . the list is extensive. Maintaining these communities as "outposts" from mainstream America ensures the profits of many in the mainstream society.

Education

The educational norm in America is neighborhood schools. Most families of Middle America send their children to a local school, one within two miles or less of their home. Thus, the neighborhood in which you reside becomes crucial in the determination of the quality of your education. The quality of education, like housing, depends on what you are able to afford. Minorities restricted to certain living areas, often regardless of income, have their life chances curtailed by the quality of the schools in their neighborhood. **Life chances** refer to the opportunities available to a person, such as a good education, adequate health care, and a well-paying job. Jose and Franklin, our fictional young boys are both above average in intelligence, but due to their racial membership and class, they are not destined to receive the high-quality education that their intelligence would suggest. Through no actions of their own, they begin their life journey hampered by an interchange of rewards and punishments meted out by social institutions.

Education is a component of the Web of Institutional Racism. Even with the expenditures of millions of dollars to public schools in the inner cities, there continues to be stark disparities in the quality of education along class, race, and ethnic lines. Jose and Franklin move along uneventfully into the public school system—a system that in many inner cities lacks sufficient well-trained teachers, sufficient books, and computers for the classes. It is a system that exists within an often stark and violent environment.

Let us assume that Jose and Franklin are good students, they stay out of gangs, and they excel in the studies available to them. They move through the educational system doing better than society might expect of them. They are proud of themselves and their parents assume a bright future for them. Nobody has ever said to either boy that they would not be allowed to get the education they intellectually qualify for because of their racial membership. They may be only vaguely aware that their educational accomplishments are not on a par with students in the larger community. However, they do see around them the lack of hope in the faces of the adults. Some of their schoolmates have dropped out of school to get a job, because of out-of-wedlock pregnancy, gang or drug activities. Though Jose and Franklin are good students, they may be academically below students in middle- and upper-class school districts.

Let us say that they do not drop out of school, but in fact graduate from high school having done all those things they were told to do—making good grades, etc. Yet they are poorly prepared to compete in the job market. They have not had extensive time on the computer. They have not been involved in an intern program where they would be exposed to a professional work environment. They have no contacts in the white collar or professional work world. They have had no experience in the culture of the middle class, except their association with schoolteachers. Their inadequate education and ignorance of the work world is a direct outcome from living in an isolated low-income community. Racial/ethnic minority students have been the messages and actions that suggest that they are not worthy to receive the rewards available to the dominant group.

The interlocking of policies, practices, and procedures within and across several social institutions has converged invisibly to limit the share of goods and services available to our hypothetical pair. This has been accomplished with no specific individual doing anything special to our duo. No one in the schools has behaved negatively toward them. No one has said that because you are Latino, Native American, or African American you will be allotted an inferior education.

Employment

Jose and Franklin, now eighteen years old, go out into the job market, having done all the things the society states is necessary to gain adequate employment—they have stayed out of the gangs, have not been arrested, have graduated at the top of their high school class. They look for jobs. Both are disadvantaged because they do not have cars, but they are young and willing to take the bus. They look throughout their neighborhoods for a job. Nothing appears but low-paying jobs in fast-food restaurants. Their high school provided them with no training in computer literacy; the automobile training class was insufficient to qualify for a job. They are discouraged. There are several ways this scenario can now proceed:

1. The young men reluctantly take menial jobs at minimum wage and remain trapped in poverty. As they marry and have children, they begin the cycle of the web of urban racism for their children.

2. They realize they have somehow they been cheated, become disillusioned and alienated from the society, and take up the equal opportunity employer in the community—dealing drugs.
3. They take the available low-wage job, marry, and have children; but
   they ensure that their children will go to good schools and have a better chance than they had.
4. They draw upon inner strength, refuse to become discouraged, and
   apply for admission into the community college while they work the
   minimum wage job.

Politics

The last major social institution illustrated in the theory is politics. **Politics** is the art or science concerned with guiding or influencing governmental or public policy. **Policy** is any procedure or plan embracing the general
goals of a governmental body. How does politics affect our two protago-
nists? Governmental policy determines how much money is allocated for
public housing, for school lunch programs, and summer job programs for
inner city youth; and what types of public health services will be available
for the indigent or undocumented person. In California, public policy or
laws determined the differential sentences for those convicted of possession
of rock cocaine versus powder cocaine. Possession of rock cocaine draws a
much longer prison sentence than powder cocaine, even through each has
the same potency. Minorities are more likely to be arrested for the former.
California also devised the "three strikes law." Minorities are disproportionately arrested and convicted of felonies in America. Consequently, Jose
and Franklin have accomplished a formidable task by having avoided being
picked up by the police before graduating from high school. Many young
minority males find their life chances severely limited due to some youth-
ful infraction that will haunt them the rest of their lives. Some of these same
infractions in a middle-class white community would engender probation
or community service. Unfortunately, the pressure of poverty pushes too
many young people to commit felonies. The avenues of jobs in fast-food
restaurants are not as available for poor minority teenagers as they are for
white middle-class teens. All American teens want to participate in the
youth culture lifestyle; this leads poor teenagers to take risks, such as selling
crack, or robbing a liquor store. These criminal behaviors are not condoned;
however, the desire to participate fully in the youth culture is a tremendous
allure.

How politics are played out in our society affects everyone. California's
Proposition 209, if enacted, would have dealt a serious blow to undocumented persons. The state courts found sections of this proposition unconstitutional. One section of it would have denied an undocumented person

residency status as a college student, thus nearly tripling the fees to be paid. This would have applied even if the student had gone to school in the United States since kindergarten. Other legislative policies have reduced the amount of free health care available to nondocumented persons. Our health system, which like our education system is influenced by politics, metes out services within a market economy system—one receives the quality of health care one can afford. Rich people can receive excellent care; poor people receive the health care the government (the taxpayer) is willing to pay for from the General Fund. Because racial/ethnic minority groups are disproportionately poor in our society, they are more apt to be totally dependent on government edict to meet their health needs. The public welfare system, financed mostly by the federal government, (discussed extensively in chapter 5) is also governed by politics.

How the social institution of politics responds to the needs of minorities is greatly influenced by the attitudes and behaviors of the voting public. Politics, like every other social institution, has policies, practices, and procedures that operate in such a way as to disadvantage racial/ethnic minorities. The national and local elections of 2000 and 2006 illustrate the stress of mega-trends that affect American politics. The increase in immigration from Mexico, Central American countries, and parts of Asia, the changes in American culture due to increased diversity, and the changes to a global economy, are examples of these trends. They are affecting voting behavior in many areas of the United States. California is the harbinger of this trend; voters are whiter, more affluent, better educated than the majority of residents in many communities. Seventy percent of California voters in the 2006 election were white Anglos. Voters are also aging; two-thirds of the voters were over forty-five years old. This is in contrast to the growing diversity of the general population, which is more diverse, younger, and less affluent. This disconnect between the composition of voters and the composition of the general population could be called political apartheid. **Political apartheid** is the reality that the majority of the residents of an area are not the majority of the voters.

Poor people are less likely to vote than the middle class. Legal residents, persons who are not citizens but have been legally permitted to reside in the United States, and undocumented persons cannot vote. However, in some communities, especially those on the East and West Coasts, undocumented persons and legal residents may make up more than 50 percent of the population; their concerns may not be considered by the politician representing the district in which they reside. Some minorities have been able to influence political decision more than their numbers would suggest. Jews and African Americans are examples of disproportionate political clout. This was possible for these two groups because they voted as a block. Further, since they lived in geographically defined areas, they were often able to elect representatives from among their membership group. Latinos in California are fast approaching this status across the state. The large Latino population already heavily influences political outcomes in Southern California. Recently, Los Angeles elected its first Latino mayor in over one hundred years.

The Limitation of the Theory

It is important to point out the limitations of this theory of the Web of Institutional Racism. It is limited in a positive way, as there are many persons from low-income minority communities who do escape the Web's grasp. There are many individuals who manage, regardless of housing conditions, to achieve in school, go on to receive a college education, and succeed in a well-paid job, breaking out of the cycle. This suggests that individual effort, social support, family values, personal fortitude, and role models can make a difference in life chances. The importance of the Web Theory is to emphasize that the attention of Americans must be on ridding our country of racist social institutions. Until more resources are made available and the remedies suggested in each chapter are acted upon, the number of people who escape the web will remain at a constant and dismally low rate.

THE LIMITS OF BLACK, BROWN UNIVERSALITY

Although all American minorities have a certain commonality or shared life experience, it would be a mistake to take this commonality too far. Each minority group has its own unique history, customs, values, and culture. Among liberals there is the tendency of likening the problems and obstacles confronting Latinos to those facing black Americans. In education, the segregation is much more pronounced for Latino children; Latino segregation has steadily and unequivocally increased. Skerry states, "In 1970, a typical African American student attended a school with a white enrollment of 32 percent; in 1994 that enrollment was 33.9 percent white. For the Latino student, white enrollment over this same period was down, from 43 percent to 30.6 percent."[3] African Americans have been more willing than Latinos to bus their children to better schools outside the ghetto. The experience of Latinos has been different, as Latinos have been more willing to suffer double sessions and year-round schools to keep their children close to home. This has influenced how education is perceived and used by these two groups.

Skerry further proposes that Latinos view the barrio differently than blacks view the ghetto. Latinos see the barrio as the more or less desirable outcome of the pairing of economic necessities and individual preferences. The barrio may bear less of a stigma for Latinos than the ghetto does for African Americans. Latinos tend to move up and out once middle-class status is achieved. Middle-class African Americans tend to move into neighborhoods where their group dominates. Therefore, Latinos are more integrated in American neighborhoods than are African Americans. Probably the most telling evidence that racial isolation does not affect African Americans and Latinos alike is the rates of interracial marriage. In 1990, only 3 percent of African American marriages were interracial, while the rate for Latinos was ten times higher.

SUMMARY

The second theoretical concept, the Web of Institutional Racism, is explained through an allegory—a fable—to further illuminate the almost invisible workings of institutional racism within our social institutions. Jose and Franklin are meant to represent any poor minority child; these two are African American and Latino. However, they could very easily be Asian American or Native American. These two hypothetical children are taken through four social institutions during their normal childhood, and through no fault of their own, become tangled in the Web of Institutional Racism. Fortunately, the Web does not entangle all minority children, but in sufficient numbers to ensure disproportionate poverty for American minorities.

KEY TERMS

de facto. In Latin, means "in reality" or "being in effect though not formally recognized."

de facto apartheid. The reality of segregation in housing; while illegal, nevertheless is informally practiced.

life chances. The opportunities available to a person, such as a good education, adequate health care, and a well-paying job.

policy. Any procedure or plan embracing the general goals of a governmental body.

political apartheid. The reality that the majority of the residents of an area are not the majority of the voters.

politics. The art or science concerned with guiding or influencing governmental or public policy.

GROUP ACTIVITIES

1. Within the group discuss in turn your own experiences in high school. Do you find any parallels to the saga of Jose and Franklin?

2. Do you see any additional alternatives for the hypothetical duo after high school?

STUDY QUESTIONS

1. Explain how the Web of Institutional Racism explains the nebulous quality of racism.
2. What is the importance of housing to the fate of Jose and Franklin?
3. What is the normative policy with American education that fosters the Web?
4. How does politics contribute to the Web?
5. How are minorities disadvantaged by voting patterns?
6. Explain the term "life chances" as it relates to Franklin and Jose.
7. How does the interlacing of education and employment determine life chances?
8. In what ways is the theory limited?
9. Explain why the remedies for Latinos and African Americans may differ.

NOTES

1. The term "web of urban racism" was coined by Harold M. Baron in the appendix of Louis Knowles and Kenneth Prewitt, eds., *Institutional Racism in America* (Englewood Cliffs, NJ: Prentice-Hall, 1969).

2. William J. Wilson, *The Truly Disadvantaged* (Chicago: Chicago University Press, 1987).

3. Peter Skerry, "The Limits of Black, Brown Solidarity," *Los Angeles Times*, February 1, 1998.

Case Study: A Perfect Storm

The Aftermath of Hurricane Katrina

On August 29, 2005, Hurricane Katrina thundered in and blew away the veneer of racial equality and equity in the Big Easy. Was the human cost of Hurricane Katrina a matter of race? The majority of the persons seen on television were poor blacks. So, many say it was racism. No, some say the word is too harsh, and only inflames. The persons stranded were mostly poor people, white and black; so was it a matter of class? Actually, it was both. For race and class are tightly interwoven in American society, with racism being the forerunner of poverty for people of color. As we explore the aftermath of the hurricane, we will see a classic example of how institutional racism, set in place during the time of slavery, contributed to the calamity. Katrina caused an estimated $81.2 billion in damages and killed at least 1,836 people, making it the deadliest U.S. hurricane in nearly a century. The federal government's disorganized and slow reaction in bringing aid, particularly to desperate flood survivors in the city of New Orleans, led to a congressional investigation and the resignation of the head of the Federal Emergency Management Agency (FEMA), Michael Brown.[1] Katrina caused the country's largest mass migration since the Dust Bowl in the 1930s. As many as 150,000 evacuees still resided in Houston a year later. And a year and half later, nearly 80 percent of the evacuees are still disbursed throughout the United States.

COLONIAL AND ANTEBELLUM TIMES IN NEW ORLEANS

New Orleans followed the pattern of other parts of the South, creating the wealth of whites from the unpaid labor of African slaves. From the late 1700s

125

and early 1800s, thousands of Africans were brought into Louisiana Territory to work on the many plantations. The sugar boom of this time encouraged the importation of Africans as had the tobacco industry in the southeastern colonies. New Orleans became the foremost slave market for North America.[2] Slave labor was used not only in agriculture but on civic building projects, such as maintaining the levees, erecting public buildings, and expanding the city. Huge amounts of uncompensated black labor modernized New Orleans, ushering in a new era of city prominence.[3] By 1840 there were 23,448 slaves in increasingly diverse New Orleans and nearly 20,000 free people of color.[4] The free blacks were generally the children of the mixed unions of white men and enslaved black women. Persons of these unions were encouraged to see themselves as a distinct "third class," which assisted whites in maintaining control over the enslaved population as well as the mixed-race group. New Orleans came to be known for its long history of white-black sexual relationships; however, whites remained staunchly against any movement toward equality between whites and blacks.

CLASS AND RACE DURING RECONSTRUCTION

During Reconstruction, from the late 1860s to the 1880s, newly emancipated African Americans saw some improvement in their status and their access to New Orleans politics, public accommodations, and education. However, life was still very harsh for them as there were constant violent attempts "to keep them in their place." Some black professionals were able to advance, but in the main, blacks were kept in "near slavery" through sanctioned violence. Because of recurring depressions, unemployment was endemic; thus unions created by blacks were weak.[5] During this time, blacks argued vehemently for integration of the schools; whites argued just as intensely against the comingling, declaring in 1875 that "the compulsory admixture of children of all races, color, and condition in the schools, in the same rooms and on the same benches, is opposed to the principles of humanity, repugnant to the instincts of both races, and is not required by any provision of the laws or constitution of the State."[6] As throughout other parts of the South, white vigilantes roamed throughout the New Orleans area with impunity, meting out harsh treatments to African Americans who dared to resist white supremacy. Race riots and lynching were not uncommon.

NEW ORLEANS AND JIM CROW

By 1890 "separate but equal" statues were written into Louisiana state law, and Jim Crow was in full force in the area. Whites completely dominated all spheres of community life, effectively forcing blacks to remain in second-class status. Life was exceedingly harsh for blacks who were forced into sharecropping, which was much like slavery without the chains. Lynching was increasingly used to quell the upward strivings of African Americans who refused to accept the lower status without a struggle.

After World War II, whites began leaving urban New Orleans. As the city prospered it was able to drain the Jefferson Parish swamp and convert the land for suburbs. African Americans were barred from these new neighborhoods by economic constraints or the unscrupulous behavior of white realtors. Thus, spatial apartheid continued as a norm in the area. The consistently high level of white flight dramatically changed the demographics of urban New Orleans. Between 1950 and 2000, the city lost almost two-thirds of its white citizens. The city went from 37 percent to 67 percent black. Some public housing projects had been white-occupied during legal segregation, but when housing segregation was outlawed, [poor] whites left and blacks moved in.[7] New Orleans had always had one of the largest percentages of African Americans of any Southern city, however until recent decades it was not as racially segregated as some other cities its size.

CONTEMPORARY PRE-KATRINA NEW ORLEANS

Housing

By 2000, with the continuation of white flight, the city became more segregated than ever before, and the gap between the haves and have-nots was as great as any time since slavery.[8] Fifty percent of residents of New Orleans were renters in 2005. New Orleans was a tale of two districts: the Ninth Ward, and the French Quarter, where tourists visited the festive area with no awareness of the Ninth Ward and its destitution. The Ninth Ward had 74–100 percent of its population living below twice the poverty level ($35,000/yr income for a family of four) with over 88 percent of the residents being African American. On the other hand, the French Quarter had 0–21 percent living below the poverty line and residents who are primarily white (80+ percent).[9] The Ninth Ward was one of the poorest and the most storm-ravaged part of the city after Hurricane Katrina.

In the 1970s and 1980s the federal Housing and Urban Development Office (HUD) initiated a poorly planned policy of urban renewal by tearing down public housing in "blighted areas" with the goal of improving inner-city housing stock throughout the nation. However, large swatches of the inner-city areas were left as vacant lots with no improvement to be done for years; this was also the case for New Orleans. Seventy thousand units of public housing were removed and too often nothing was built in its place for low-income renters. Housing vouchers that had been instituted by HUD did allow many poor families to move into adequate housing, as their rent was subsidized by the federal government. However, with the election of Ronald Reagan, a conservative political ideology has dominated policy decisions. Housing vouchers have been severely reduced; presently some cities no longer provide new ones and the waiting list for those who have vouchers can be more than five years.[10] Current and past housing policies and practices set into motion the first of the dominoes that led to the disastrous Hurricane Katrina aftermath. Residents crowded into an unsafe living environment at the mercy of a horrendous storm are the first segment in the Web of Urban Institutional Racism that sustains racial inequality in America.

Education

Historically, public schools were underfunded in southern Louisiana because many Catholics sent their children to parochial schools, and resisted paying public school taxes. Well-to-do Protestants opened their own private schools. Thus, poor children were left to the poorly financed public schools. Mandated school desegregation did little for poor black children who were housed in the lower Ninth Ward. Attempts to integrate the schools were met with angry white mobs and hostile white politicians, showing New Orleans to be no different from other Southern cities in their demand to maintain white supremacy.

When Katrina hit, the city's public schools were in a failed condition. An accepted reality is that a quality education is a crucial requirement in America to rise out of poverty. However, New Orleans showed graphically its collusion in maintaining racial inequality by its failed public school system. Schools continued to be segregated by race and class throughout the 1970s, 1980s, and 1990s, so that even poor whites received a better education than poor blacks, for poor whites were less likely to live in areas of concentrated poverty. The neighborhood school concept mentioned earlier in this text was one of the invisible anchors holding blacks in second-class status. Louisiana ties with Arizona as having the highest school dropout rate (12 percent) in the nation. Over half of black ninth graders were projected to not graduate in four years.[11] Nearly two years after the hurricane, New Orleans continues to struggle to educate its poor minority children. After Katrina, the state took control of 85 percent of the public schools in the area, it then invited citizens to rebuild the schools and declared them "charter schools." Charter schools are independent and have the right to create their own curriculum, hire teachers, and administer the affairs of the schools. This all began with great hope; however, a year and a half later, many of the schools still did not have sufficient books and supplies, and school libraries were not stocked. Parents, teachers, and students are frustrated at the pace of renovation. Louisiana, a poor state with few resources to draw on, is struggling to rebuild its educational system. For now those black families who have returned find their children caught in the Web.

Employment

Due to the exodus of large corporations and manufacturing industries, tax revenues plummeted and unemployment rose. New Orleans had to turn to a more tourist-oriented economy to survive. The disappearance of low-skill unionized jobs hit poor blacks especially hard. They did not have the finances or the skills to move to a more promising area. However, the economic problem isn't unemployment, but low wages for workers of all races. By 1990 unemployment among black men was 11 percent—more than double the rate for whites—and those who were able to keep jobs were often poorly paid.[12] Service jobs, the core jobs in tourism, paid an average of only $8.30 per hour and represented 26 percent of all jobs in the area.

The above is typical of the two-tier labor market discussed earlier in this book. With a weak union and no increase in the national minimum wage in ten years, workers are at the mercy of the employers. Since 2001, the United States has lost 2.7 million manufacturing jobs. New Orleans' good jobs left long before that time, replaced by the restaurant and tourism industry that pays less, often with no health benefits. Medicaid covers poor children but few poor adults. The entanglement in the Web starts with the apartheid housing that isolates individuals and reduces their social contacts that would lead to connections that help them to find jobs. Thus, we find that four in ten black families were living in poverty.

Politics

Housing, education, and employment were the unstable dominoes that fell one into the other with Hurricane Katrina. Politics is the final social institution to be examined that contributed to the disaster. Political power has always been held primarily by the white elite, with a few chosen light-skinned blacks in New Orleans. Poor people are less likely to vote or to be involved in civic affairs. New Orleans had a large poor community out of the sight of the downtown hotels and the French Quarter, and apparently out of the minds of the politicians. During this conservative era dominated by Republicans, the poor were off the radar of the nation. Republicans have made little headway in gaining the black vote; consequently they have not catered to their needs. One the other hand, the Democrats take the black vote for granted, and feel that they can ignore their needs and still get their vote. Thus, politicians were barely aware of the existence of the poor or concerned about their fate.

When Katrina hit, two-thirds of New Orleans were black, and 28 percent white. It was the sixth-poorest large U.S. city. Despite many (mostly white) commentators' and onlookers' tendency to lay blame on residents' character or intelligence for not abiding by the mandatory evacuate notice, race and class conditions, likened to past racial oppression, were major determining factors in whether people were able to evacuate.[13] Because of prior inadequate political planning, the evacuation of New Orleans in advance of the hurricane created another disaster. Politicians failed to understand or to take into account that many residents of the lower Ninth Ward were too ill, too old, too young, and too poor to leave without specific assistance by city officials. The media revealed the difference between the races. Poor blacks outnumbered poor whites in being stranded in New Orleans and poor whites were clearly better off. Only 17 percent of poor whites lacked access to a car, while nearly 60 percent of poor blacks did.[14]

THE AFTERMATH OF HURRICANE KATRINA: A PERFECT EXAMPLE OF INSTITUTIONAL RACISM

Hurricane Katrina provides a vivid example of the urban web of institutional racism, a horror story compared to the saga of Jose and Franklin— but all too familiar just the same. The interconnection between the major social institutions of housing, education, employment, and politics led to the socioeconomic conditions of poor African American residents. The policies, practices, and procedures of these social institutions created the deplorable conditions that left so many stranded. The historical development of New Orleans detailed above shows how each of the social institutions contributed to the abandonment of the poor blacks of the lower Ninth Ward. First, African Americans were isolated in an area that everyone knew was a disaster zone waiting to happen. This area of spatial apartheid had an overabundance of inadequate housing and slum landlords and few amenities to enhance life chances. The educational policy of maintaining neighborhood schools led to the children being confined to failed, segregated schools. Thus, they either dropped out or graduated with few skills that would allow them to compete for good jobs. The equation of poor environment plus poor education equals poor job opportunities and poverty. Thus, we discover a high level of poverty in this area. Many of the residents of the Ninth Ward scraped by on incomes less than half the official poverty level.

With little money, no car, and family members too old or too ill to leave the city, we find thousands of citizens confined in the Super Dome, which some equated to living in a sewer. There, they languished for days with lit-

Network of Policies and Practices of Racism Exhibited in

New Orleans

WEB OF INSTITUTIONAL RACISM

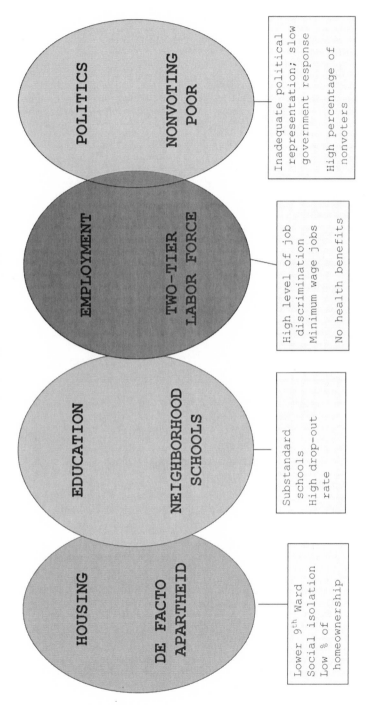

POLITICS

NONVOTING POOR

Inadequate political representation; slow government response

High percentage of nonvoters

EMPLOYMENT

TWO-TIER LABOR FORCE

High level of job discrimination
Minimum wage jobs
No health benefits

EDUCATION

NEIGHBORHOOD SCHOOLS

Substandard schools
High drop-out rate

HOUSING

DE FACTO APARTHEID

Lower 9th Ward
Social isolation
Low % of homeownership

tle food and water, feeling that they were prisoners being guarded by the police and National Guard who manned the exits. They were treated with dis-
respect by officers and viewed by the media as "looters" when they sought
food in the devastated supermarkets. Officials did not deem it necessary to
keep the evacuees appraised of the outside circumstances, or what was being done to rescue them. Some of the evacuees stated that they felt like they
were back in slavery as their families were dispersed throughout the country and their children taken from them and sent to different locations without their permission. One woman in the Super Dome stated, "It brought
back an ancient memory of being on an auction block."

The aftermath of Hurricane Katrina was a perfect example of the Web of
Institutional Racism (see figure below). As mentioned in the first chapter
of this text, the Kerner Commission was wrong; the aftermath revealed that
we are not moving toward being two nations, one black, one white, one
rich, one poor—separate and unequal. We are profoundly isolated into
separate worlds. Unfortunately, we Americans, crippled by cultural blindness and deafness, and racism, have to be forced to see the great racial divide with our own eyes to remember the above truth.

For additional in-depth analyses of the aftermath of Hurricane Katrina,
please refer to the following publications:

1. Manuel Pastor et al., *In The Wake of the Storm: Environment, Disaster,
   and Race After Katrina.* A Report from the the Russell Sage Foundation,
   New York, 2006.
2. Sundiata Keitha Cha-Jua, ed., "Hurricane Katrina," *The Black Scholar*
   36, no. 4 (Winter 2006).

NOTES

1. "Katrina's Strongest Survivors," www.portside.org (accessed September 1, 2006).
2. Adam Rothman, *Slave Country: American Expansion and the Origins of the Deep
South* (Cambridge, MA: Harvard University Press, 2005), 83.
3. Rothman, *Slave Country.*
4. Walter Johnson, *Soul by Soul: Life inside the Antebellum Slave Market* (Cambridge, MA: Harvard University Press, 1999), 6–7.
5. John W. Blessingame, *Black New Orleans, 1860-1880* (Chicago: University of
Chicago Press, 1973), 9–10.
6. Blessingame, *Black New Orleans,* 113.
7. Pierce F. Lewis, *New Orleans: The Making of an Urban Landscape,* 2nd ed.
(Santa Fe, NM: Center for American Places, 2003), 125.
8. Lewis, *New Orleans,* 52.
9. Jonathan Alter, "The Other America," *Newsweek,* September 19, 2005, 42.
10. Alter, "The Other America."

11. Kristin Lavelle and Joe Feagin, "Hurricane Katrina: The Race and Class Debate," *Monthly Review*, July/August 2006.

12. Lewis, *New Orleans*, 123.

13. Lavell and Feagin, "Hurricane Katrina," 59.

14. John Barnshaw, "The Continuing Significance of Race and Class among Houston Hurricane Katrina Evacuees," *Natural Hazards Observer* 30, no. 2 (2005): 12.

II

STRATEGIES
FOR SOCIAL CHANGE

7

Strategies for Combating Racism

Individual and Group Approaches

This chapter focuses on approaches the reader can take to combat racism individually and through group action at the local level. It is not sufficient to be able to describe racism, or to understand its invisible interweaving through the political, economic, and social fabric of American life. Nor is it enough to document its vestiges in social institutions. The question in the end of this philosophical and intellectual exercise must be, therefore, *"What must be done?"*

FACING UP TO RACISM

Minorities expend much psychic energy coping with individual and institutional racism, energy that could be used creatively to improve one's quality of life. American society has conducted a covert action of misinformation to avoid owning up to the reality of racism and the incredible damage it has done to the American psyche. Medical and social scientists now document that one of the reasons for the preponderance of high blood pressure among African Americans has do with the stress of coping with racism on a regular basis. Not only can stress bring about hypertension but also it can produce an overall emotional malaise or depression, putting a cloud over much of the activities of daily life. How much of the debilitating social problems in poor minority communities can be assigned to this overall malaise caused by racism? How large a part does racism play in the high alcoholism rate on Indian reservations? What is the role of racism in the depression exhibited by low-income minorities? Is the use of drugs a method of medicating oneself against feelings of hopelessness? Many social scientists suggest that racism indeed plays a major role in the overall emotions of American minorities.[1]

Our society also fails to understand and acknowledge the detrimental effect racism has on whites. The Michael Richards hostile harangue and the Mel Gibson drunken accusations are simply the tip of the iceberg. Much of the denial of racial hostility in America is the desperate desire to repress the feelings of guilt felt by the dominant group regarding past wrongs. However, the wrongs that have been done to minorities cannot be rationalized and forgotten. Indeed, whites, not from want of trying to forget, are aware of both past and ongoing injustices. The distortion of American life is attested to by the convoluted shaping of social institutions discussed in earlier chapters. The myths that abound in our society regarding race relations are attempts to distort the reality of past and present widespread exploitation of minority groups. Just as the underlying criminality within the Los Angeles Police Department finally exploded into public awareness, so does the periodic scandals of ongoing practices of racism in our social institutions continue to unsettle the public peace, such as we learned in the case study of Hurricane Katrina.

CONFRONTING RACISM AT THE INDIVIDUAL AND GROUP LEVELS

If we are to attack racism at the individual and the group level, we must address the three pillars of its operation: policies, practices, and procedures. For sixty years, our society has not needed to use overt violence or individual acts of racism to perpetuate widespread inequality. The existing policies and procedures have done this exceedingly well. We can only stop racism by taking into account past and present activities within our social institutions and at all levels of social intercourse. We will be able to gauge our success through the social justice that we produce. As we have discussed extensively in this text, due to the vast disparities in wealth, education, and political control, racism has become a self-sustaining social phenomenon. Due to a long history of injustices, racism is entrenched. And we cannot rely on race-neutral social policies alone or on prohibitions against overt acts of racism, or the prospect of individual whites unlearning racist behavior. All of the above actions are necessary ingredients for social change, but not sufficient. Individual, group, and societal concrete means, constructed on a clear vision of the "positive uses" of institutional racism, are required. The remainder of the chapter will focus on some concrete measures that committed individuals and groups can use to battle racism. Many of the action items come

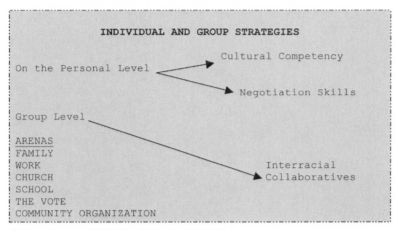

Figure 7.1. Individual and Group Strategies

from my own experience of twenty years of involvement in the civil rights movement and additional years as an educator and activist.

Individual and Group Strategies

First, we must realize there is no single strategy will rid our society of institutional racism. The problem is very complex and must be addressed in multiple ways. We must attack it on all fronts: family, school, work, church, and community. Figure 7.1 charts the various strategies that can be undertaken by individuals and groups.

DEFINING CULTURAL COMPETENCY

Inculcating individuals with cultural competency and incorporating this skill in group activities and organizations is an effective and productive approach to reducing individual racism. In order to ensure that everyone is respected and valued for their uniqueness, we need to become "culturally competent."[2] **Cultural Competency** is a set of congruent attitudes, practices, policies, and structures that come together in personal interactions, organizations, and systems to allow for positive relationships and outcomes in cross-cultural situations. Competence begins as an inside-out process. We first need to know our own culture; all of us are raised with a race/ethnic culture. Within the nurturing of our unique culture, we each develop values, beliefs, and a way of looking at the world around us that is specific to that culture. Within our nurturing culture, we learn a language, we learn of the acceptable roles for males and females, we are taught what our own place in the culture will be or can be. We wear our culture daily as a comfortable garment.

The ability to understand another culture well enough to be able to communicate and work with people from that culture that is the hallmark of a culturally sensitive person. Rather than wail, "Why can't we all be alike?" persons who are striving for cultural competency embrace the opportunity to associate with persons from different cultures. This book has focused on diversity as it relates to race and ethnicity; however other cultures that shape an individual's values and beliefs are organizational, occupational and social in nature.

Understanding Culture

Culture is both objective and subjective. The subjective aspect of culture is our beliefs, values, and patterns of behavior that we learned through social interaction in the family and in the social environment in which we live. The objective aspect of culture relates to the outside social environment that makes our culture unique: theater, literature, art, and the political system. Culture is multileveled, dynamic, and ever-changing. The conservatives in our society aver that our culture is a melting pot, that all differences have been dissolved in the cauldron of Americana. The liberals lament, "Can't we all just get along, can't we all just be alike?" Each of these statements ignores the reality of culture. Each person is raised within their own unique surroundings, their culture. Each person's culture profoundly influences his or her values, beliefs, and how she or he sees the world. Figure 7.2, developed by Milton Bennett, diagrams the distinct parts of culture and how individuals respond.[3]

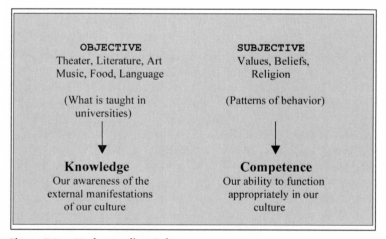

Figure 7.2.   Understanding Culture

Dominant View of American Culture

Figure 7.3 suggests that Euro-Americans, the dominant group, prefer to see American culture as a "melting pot." The term **melting pot** relates to the societal pressure that all residents of the United States adopt and conform to Anglo-Saxon values, language, and lifestyle. However, the assimilation is only one way. All persons are to merge into the dominant culture, originally based on the core culture of England. This mainstream culture is referred to as dominant because it is institutionalized in all major organizations and systems. On the other hand, diversity or the acceptance of different cultures as being just as viable in American society is resisted. It is often suggested that acceptance of multiculturalism or diversity will ruin the country and that it will lead to fragmentation or "balkanization" of American society. This American tendency to obfuscate the reality that the United States has always been a multicultural society is to be overcome as the first step toward cultural competency and ultimately racial pluralism, which will be discussed later.

Essential Elements of Cultural Competency

The essential elements of cultural competency are: valuing, assessing, managing, institutionalizing, and adapting.[4]

Valuing. Valuing relates to an awareness of the importance of difference as a major component to creativity and problem solving. Valuing comes from increased knowledge and understanding of cultural diversity. First, we must be able to define our own culture and exhibit awareness of self as a cultural being. We must be aware of how our culture influences our interactions with people from other cultures. Cultural competence begins with an awareness

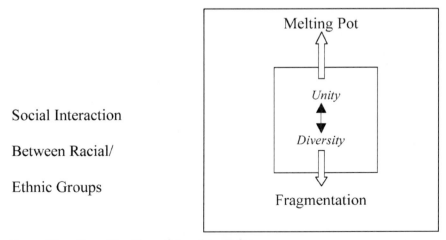

Figure 7.3.   Normative View of American Culture

of the ways culture influences one's behaviors. As we increase our own level of cultural awareness, we are more conscious of personal responses to issues of multiculturalism, diversity, and oppression. With cultural competency comes an appreciation that within-group differences may be as great or greater than across-group differences.

There is much to value in diversity. If everyone thinks alike and sees problems alike there is little creative problem solving or progress. Historically, persons who were the inventors and paradigm shifters of their time were persons who were able to see the world differently and were able to create new solutions to problems based on that ability. The first step in gaining cultural competence is to see the importance of differences to our own well-being. Individuals who seek persons different from themselves and value these contacts are on the way to cultural competency.

Assessing. Second, we must evaluate differences in positive ways. When we are aware of differences, we must examine how the differences can be used to enhance our own experience—how it can be an asset for an individual. For example, speaking English with a non-Anglo accent should not be viewed as a flaw, but as an asset, for it means that the person can share with us a culture with which we are unfamiliar. In that sharing, our own knowledge of the world increases.

Managing. When we encounter persons from other culture, we need to find ways to incorporate their differences so that they enrich our lives. In the workplace, the ability to communicate (verbal and nonverbal) genuinely, nondefensively, and effectively with culturally diverse groups enhances the work environment. Managing skills should include the ability to tolerate conflict in interracial relationships and appropriately resolve it so that creative energy blossoms.

Institutionalizing. In the workplace, accepting and valuing cultural differences should be grounded in the policies and practices of the organization. Management and line staff should be discouraged from establishing informal practices that frown on differences.

Adapting. Individuals, groups, and organizations must be willing to change so that those from different cultures and racial backgrounds are not alienated. Policies, practices, and procedures should be monitored to ensure that cultural differences are not only accepted but also embraced. Individuals desiring cultural competence will increase their intercultural experiences with the goal of increasing familiarity with and gaining comfort from interactions with diverse groups.

Skills of Cultural Competency

Hogan-Garcia suggests that there are four skills of cultural competency: understanding culture as it operates on different social levels, understanding barriers to effective communication and relationships, practicing personal and interpersonal cultural competence, and practicing the design and implementation of organizational strategies.[5]

Skill 1

Understanding Culture was discussed earlier in this chapter, and is the most important skill to develop on the road to cultural competency. Sue et al. suggest that there are three characteristics a culturally competent person who is a counselor must possess,[6] and I have added a fourth; these same traits I believe are essential for all persons committed to social change in America. The suggested four traits are:

1. Beliefs and attitudes about racial and ethnic minorities that facilitate effective cross-cultural relationships, plus a positive orientation toward multiculturalism.
2. Knowledge and understanding of one's own worldview, cultural group, and the sociopolitical influences that shape one's view of the world and one's culture. One needs to be able to define one's own culture and exhibit awareness of self as a cultural being. From this knowledge comes the awareness that one's culture influences one's interactions with people from other cultures. We can use our own experiences of feeling "different" as a foundation for empathy with other racial and ethnic groups.
3. Knowledge of past and current sociopolitical issues relevant to racial and ethnic groups in America. Those of us educated in American schools have generally had to wait until college history classes to learn of the positive contributions of non-European groups to the progress of America. Often world history was a recitation of how Europeans conquered Africa and Asia; we learned little of the contributions of non-Europeans to world progress. Thus the knowledge of the past and current sociopolitical issues relevant to any specific cultural group is important.
4. Intervention techniques and strategy skills that support the ability to work successfully within task groups composed of individuals from different ethnic and racial groups to produce social change. To be an agent of change in this arena, one must be able to adapt intervention strategies to accommodate the diverse cultural beliefs, values, and practices of others. Intervention techniques must be grounded in awareness of the ways that our actions and life choices conspire with the maintenance of various forms of oppression: sexism, homophobia, classism, ageism.

Some trainers in this area suggest that to reach cultural competency in America, it will be necessary to bring ethnicity to the dominant group.[7] They suggest and I agree that Euro-Americans must see their own culture before they can deal with institutional racism, because they will need to see that they control the culture (subjectively). Presently, Euro-Americans do not see themselves as a part of the "Good Ole Boys Club." They do not see themselves as involved in the persistence of a culture of racial inequality in America.

Skill 2

Understanding common barriers to effective communication and relationships increases the chances of success. Personal and interpersonal barriers to cultural competence include language; nonverbal communication; preconceptions, stereotypes, and discrimination; judgments; and stress.

Language is a formidable barrier for most Americans who are monolingual. Certainly, if one is working with or some other reason will be in regular contact with a person or groups that do not speak English well, learning a few phrases in the group's language can go a long way in building rapport. Immigrants know the value of speaking English and are probably hard at work learning the language. Our nonverbal communication tells much about our inner feelings. Though we think we have our feelings concealed, often we are revealing ourselves like a blinking neon sign. If our body language, eyes, and facial expression broadcast our level of intolerance, all the words in the world will not overcome that reality. We examined earlier the potency of negative feelings in the form of prejudice, bias, and hatred. We have also explored how these feelings support both individual and institutional racism. Persons who are committed to cultural competency will begin the task of examining their own prejudices; they will begin to root these negative attitudes out of their consciousness.

Hogan-Garcia states, "Related to *preconceptions, stereotypes, and discrimination* is the *judgment* barrier (italics in the original). This barrier is an unconscious and automatic tendency to pass negative judgment on people who look and behave in unfamiliar ways."[8] As one advances in competency, the tendency to be judgmental will lessen and the ability to relate warmly to persons of different cultures will increase. Finally, much can be said about stress and its contribution to barriers. When people are confronted with unfamiliar language, dress, values, and lifestyles it produces discomfort or stress. Most individuals feel a level of anxiety when confronted with new experiences. For some persons, any unfamiliar occurrence produces fear and anger; it is as if the person who comes from another culture is an immediate threat to one's well-being. Awareness of such tendencies is a crucial step in erasing these feelings of trepidation.

Members of ethnic and racial minority groups in America are cautioned not to assume cultural competence because of minority status. Most minorities are competent in their own culture milieu, and those minorities successful in mainstream America have had to learn to be culturally competent in the Euro-American social context as well. They are adequately bicultural. That does not mean that minorities have not been infected with the prejudices and biases of our society. It is likely that most minority groups have accepted at least a few of the stereotypes about other minority groups. Minority members often are surprised that even they experience stress in the company of a minority member from another culture. Consequently, the lessons of cultural competency need to be learned by all.

Skill 3

Practicing personal and interpersonal cultural competence should be a constant task. To move toward cultural competency, one must practice specific behavior while one examines personal values and attitudes. Behavior changes needed include:

- *Being nonjudgmental.* One of the most important ingredients of modifying behavior is to begin by pushing aside all preconceived notions and accepting persons on their own terms.
- *Being flexible.* You need to readjust to this new contact as often as is necessary to develop a positive relationship. Since each person is unfamiliar with the other, there will be some missteps in the contact.
- *Personalizing the interaction.* Expressing your personal feelings appropriately in a warm and open fashion encourages frank personal discussions.
- *Getting in touch with your feelings.* Examine your inner reaction as you interact with a person from different culture. Accept that you may have some uneasy feelings that may spring from negative messages you received in the past about the culture. Don't allow those feelings to prevent you from making contact. Accept the stress of the unaccustomed.
- *Listening carefully.* Be sure you understand the other person, and when in doubt, ask for clarification. Words have different values in different cultures.
- *Observing attentively.* It is important not to take for granted a common worldview. Each of our cultures teaches us how to see the world; thus, if we are to be open to new contacts, we must be careful of assumptions.
- *Keeping a sense of humor.*
- *Being respectful.* A mutually fulfilling relationship must be built on respect. While noting the unfamiliar, one must remember that each

person holds his or her own culture in high esteem and we must do
no less.

- *Showing empathy.* Whenever possible, put yourself in the other person's shoes; that is, try to see the situation from their point of view. It is important to be able to "feel" with another even though the cultures are different. We are, after all, human beings with basically the same biological, social, and psychological needs.

Cultural Competency Continuum

Terry Cross suggests that cultural competency, or as he labeled it, cultural proficiency, can be viewed as a progression of change.[9] **Cultural proficiency** is a point on a continuum that represents the *policies and practices* of an organization, or the *values and behaviors* of an individual, which enable the agency or person to interact effectively in a culturally diverse environment (see figure 7.4).

Cultural destructiveness: see the difference, stomp it out. Attitudes, policies, and practices that are ruinous to cultures represent the most negative end of the continuum. The most extreme practice in this category is genocide, such as the annihilation of American Indian tribes. Other examples include the exclusion laws focused on Chinese immigrants and restrictive immigration quotas, such as those directed at non-Europeans during various eras of American history.

Cultural incapacity: see the difference, make it wrong. In this category, members of the dominant group see themselves as superior to other ethnic groups. Ethnic minority groups are seen as deficient, deviant, and sometimes dangerous because of their "differentness." One example of this category is the theory of social Darwinism, which suggests that whites are destined to be superior for they have evolved into superior status, and are the fittest of racial groups. Another example would be the devaluing of the historical contributions of minority groups.

Cultural blindness: see the difference, pretend that you don't. This category avers the belief that race, ethnicity, and culture make no difference and that all people are the same. Values and behaviors of the dominant cul-

Continuum of Cultural Proficiency

Figure 7.4.   Continuum of Cultural Proficiency

ture are presumed to universally applicable and beneficial. It is assumed that members of minority groups do not meet the cultural expectations of the dominant group because of some cultural deficiency or lack of desire to achieve, rather than the barriers of structural discrimination.

Cultural pre-competence: see the difference, respond to it inappropriately. This category acknowledges an awareness of limitations in cross-cultural communication and contact. There is the desire to provide fair and equitable treatment with appropriate cultural sensitivity. However, this is coupled with the frustration of not knowing exactly what is possible or how to make the appropriate contact. An example of this section would be the belief that the completion of a single goal fulfills any perceived responsibility to minority groups, such as pointing with pride to the hiring of one fully assimilated Asian as proof of an organization's cultural competency.

Cultural competency: see the difference, understand the difference that difference makes. In this advanced category, there is acceptance and respect for difference. Individuals in this area are continually self-assessing regarding culture and their response to differences. Competent persons are regularly engaged in expanding their cultural knowledge and make regular adaptations to their belief systems, policies, practices, and procedures.

Cultural proficiency: see the difference, respond positively in a variety of environments. Terry Cross suggests that at this level persons hold culture in high esteem. Here individuals seek to add to the knowledge base of culturally proficient practice and advocate for culturally proficient practices in all arenas.

Skill 4

Practicing the design and implementation of organizational strategies and actions corresponds with the discussion later on interracial collaboratives. It is not sufficient to focus on only interpersonal interactions; it is vital that the skills of cultural competency be the cornerstone for group and organizational endeavors. For this skill to be viable, the organization must work to be culturally competent internally. The following attributes are to be acquired:

- Performance standards for culturally appropriate behavior
- Modeling of appropriate behaviors
- Risk taking, speaking on issues that may cause tension and conflict
- Formally and informally increasing the knowledge of others about culture and the dynamics of difference
- Fostering change in the people and the organizations' processes

Skill 4 suggests that all that has been learned is taken forward to engage organizational and institutional tasks. It is important to develop action plans with an organizational context that will assist members to practice cultural competency. The goal would be to develop culturally sensitive personal interaction while developing action agendas that will overcome individual and institutional racism.

Guiding Principles of Cultural Competency

Some individuals view cultural competency as an unrealistic ideal put forward by left-wing liberals and progressives. In the highly competitive atmosphere of American capitalism, some feel it is unrealistic to suggest that cultural sensitivity can reduce racist actions in any way. There are others, myself included, who feel that cultural competency is one of several effective tools to reduce individual racism, and can be reached over time with determination and goodwill. Remembering the five essential elements of cultural competency and its four skills, I suggest the following principles to individual and group behavior that will bring our society closer to a society that is meritorious.[10]

Culture Is a Paramount Influence

Be aware that culture is a predominant influence on behaviors, values, organizations, and social institutions. Although one might be inclined to take offense at certain behaviors that are different from our own, remember that the action may not be a personal attack but may rather be a cultural difference. Remember that people of color have to be bicultural at least to some extent to be successful in this society. This bicultural requirement comes with its own set of problems and conflicts. Style of speech, body language, and dress do not convey stupidity or incompetence. Americans must remember that persons from other cultures have mastered one culture and are striving to master a second one.

Euro-Americans rarely experience the process of acquiring another language or a new set of values, norms, or behaviors, while seeking appropriate places for using their first language and culture. The absence of this experience leads to misunderstanding and devaluation of persons from different cultures. It also protects members of the dominant culture from the negative judgments ascribed to people because of their language and cultural differences.

Minority Groups Are Stratified Differently by the Dominant Culture

Minority groups are stratified in American society. All minorities are not treated the same by the dominant group. For example, Asians may be more easily integrated into a white community than African Americans. Therefore, strategies that work well for one minority community may not work well for another ethnic group. Insensitivity to this axiom leads to the development of a model minority group or model minority individual. The dominant group uses success stories of those who have made it though the current system, rather than examine the system for racial stratification. These success stories reaffirm for the dominant group that the system works well and that there is no need to alter the current distribution of goods and services. These success stories put the burden on minority groups to change rather than forcing the society to review inequality. It supports the status quo and promulgates the false notion that it is the minority group that is deficient in some way.

Acknowledge the Group Identity of Individuals

Although it is important to treat all people as individuals, it is also important to acknowledge the group identity of individuals. Singling out assimilated members of ethnic groups and telling them they are *different*, thus implying that their differentness somehow makes them better, or more suitable, to the dominant group is insulting and demeaning to that person's group. For example, praising a highly trained Latino attorney as being different from all other working-class Latinos is to suggest that the attorney is an exception to the rule that Latinos are intellectually inferior. Cultural sensitivity requires awareness that the dignity of a person is not guaranteed unless the dignity of his or her people is also preserved.

Awareness That There Is Diversity within Cultures

Ethnic groups are not monoliths. Within each ethnic group there are subgroups that are distinctly different. Due to the class differences in the United States, there will be more in common across ethnic lines than within them. Those who are upper class may have more in common regardless of their race or ethnicity, than those who are in the same ethnic group but different social classes. For example, middle-class Latinos and African Americans may be more alike in regards to lifestyle, beliefs, and values than first-generation immigrant Latinos and upper-class third-generation Latinos. Thus, it is important to value both the individual differences and group differences.

Barriers to Cultural Competency

Ultimately, cultural competency creates an appreciation of the values of another culture. Cultural competence is reflected in development of personal skills in interacting and responding to individuals from other cultures. One of the problems in addressing culture openly is the unwillingness of our society to value personal conflict. It is to be expected that persons from different countries, and different racial and ethnic groups, will have tensions and some disagreements, primarily because their culture has taught them to see the world from their unique perspective. However, in our society, overt personal conflict and tension, especially in the workplace, is frowned upon; we are encouraged to shun it and pretend that everything is fine, even though some lively disagreement might clear the air and lead to a better understanding. We are admonished not to discuss race relations in mixed company, just as we are warned to not discuss politics and religion, for any discussion will lead to unalterable harm. However, religion and politics are entirely different from race relations. With a discussion of and action on race issues in America, we can change the course of our country. This would ultimately benefit everyone who lives here. Another barrier to cultural competency is our society's pressure on persons of mixed heritage to see themselves as either black or white. That is, there must always be two opposite halves. Only in recent years has our society begun to tolerate the diversity in many Americans.

A PERSONAL RESPONSE TO INDIVIDUAL RACISM

In many ways, it's easier to confront individual racism because it is often overt. One is aware of being denied goods and services because of minority status. There is generally an identifiable person who has initiated or executed the negative action. What must be done about it? Some would say that the minority person must battle racism each and every time his or her rights are denied. Of course, there is much merit in this. My hesitation in endorsing this wholeheartedly has to do with the psychological price most minorities pay for confrontation, even when they are dead right. For some persons, the ego cannot withstand the daily battle. Consequently, some individuals need to choose their battles, so as to conserve energy for the most important wars. What can be done when confronted by individual racism?

Let me take a personal tone in this discussion: one should determine a response to individual racism by first calculating the level of importance the incident holds. Take a deep breath, control your temper. You cannot win the battle when completely out of control. Remember this is their problem, not yours. You are not less of a person because of another's unscrupulous action. Verbally point out to the perpetrator how their behavior is perceived. Do this, take that deep breath, say nothing until you are in control. Then, look the person in the eye and point out to him/her how the actions have the outcome of disadvantaging you. Question the person as to whether this is what he or she was planning to do. Explain how their action should be different and tell the person exactly what should be done differently to ensure that you are treated fairly. This will take practice, because the first response is to seek vengeance either verbally or physically.

We can accomplish a lot more by forcing the individual to look at and possibly acknowledge how they are perpetuating inequality. At the least, this will take away the normative feature from individual racism; that is, the individual confronted by you will not be able to blithely continue racist behavior with no consequences. At the most, your showdown will force the individual to deal with the exposure of his or her behavior. Don't underestimate the power of exposure. Much racist behavior has been practiced by the dominant group as a partial payment of their privileged position in American society. It is important to force awareness of this assumed privilege. Racism was legally sanctioned and supported by vicious, brutal behavior by individuals to force minorities to accept the behavior as a norm. By nonviolent confrontation, we are saying "business as usual" will not be allowed. The personal code of conduct below, I believe, will help you to deal with the frequent encounters with racism.

Putting on a Personal Armor

Members of minority groups need to re-examine how they can empower themselves, and not be overcome by racism. Here are some strategies to do battle with racism at the internal, personal level:

Re-evaluate everything. Reappraise all that you have been taught that leads to the premise that people of color are not as capable as whites. Review mentally those ideas that have led you in the past to consciously and unconsciously denigrate persons of color. Minority groups who are engaged in intra-racial conflicts should practice this as well.

Develop a profound ability to know what not to believe. Some African Americans have called it "Thinking Black." There are several levels to cognitive thinking:

- Literal level: one accepts what is told, or one believes unquestionably what is read.
- Inferential level: one is able to move from one judgment considered true to another decision whose truth is derived from facts or particulars.
- Evaluative level: at this stage, one weighs carefully and determines after consideration what is significant, and discards erroneous data.

Success is assured when the evaluative level of cognition is the dominant thought pattern.

Know yourself. You are accountable for everything you think, say, and do. Consequently, you are responsible for controlling your thinking, that is, bringing your thoughts in line with who you want to be. Thoughts are things. Your thoughts influence your attitude, your attitude; influences your behavior. To help you to grow in self-discipline, keep a personal journal. That is, begin a ledger/diary in which you write down your thoughts about your daily life and how you feel about what your life is and what you want it to be. Do this for three months, to get in touch with you. You are guaranteed to know yourself a lot better. The better you know yourself, the more your self-control will grow.

Take personal responsibility to know the history of your people. Knowing your people's history must become an overriding task—if you are to know yourself. You are the essence of all of your people who came before you. This means taking courses in what we euphemistically call "ethnic studies." All Americans should take courses focusing on other racial and ethnic groups to increase awareness and sensitivity. Being a member of a racial minority group does not insure a heightened sensitivity to other ethnic groups; this attitude must be cultivated. American educational institutions stress the importance of knowing American history. American history is taught from a Euro-centric framework; it focuses on the European viewpoint or slant on historical events. American history is a required course in every American school. Certainly, it is just as important for minorities to know their history. Euro-Americans and American minorities have also suffered from miseducation. Routinely, European immigrants were pressured to give up any connection with their former country quickly if they were to thrive in America. Euro-Americans are encouraged to follow the same guidelines offered to minorities to rid themselves of the indoctrination of white supremacy. This brainwashing has contributed to an American history riddled with brutality and exploitation of racial and ethnic minorities.

Honor your ancestors. You honor them and yourself by remembering your past and promoting your culture. Support and participate in the celebrations of your ethnicity. Accord these celebrations the same respect Americans accord Thanksgiving. Support and attend celebrations of other ethnic and racial groups as well. By according these groups your support and attendance, you reinforce multiculturalism for all. You move from the point of tolerance of differences to embracement of cultural diversity.

Know that we are living in a constant state of struggle for equality and equity in American society. Thus, everything you do has political and social implications. In a society in which economic inequality is a social value, each person is in competition for society's goods and services. One needs to be aware at all times that the distributions of these goods and services have been distorted. They are diverted from distribution based upon merit to a system whereby racism, sexism, ageism, classism, and homophobia has been allowed to determine to a large degree how the final distribution will be made. How you deal with racism on the job orat the grocery store is all a part of the ongoing struggle for equality. Voting is also a part of this unending struggle.

Nurture your spirit. Given the ongoing negative messages that we receive regarding the desecration of the environment and worldwide warfare and our own national problems, we need to devote time not only to material gains, but also spiritual enhancement. We are spiritual beings and we need to surround ourselves with persons who nurture us. Learn to detect persons who will attempt to do harm to your spirit and avoid them. For American minorities, nurturing our spirit is especially crucial due to the unrelenting negative messages from the media, in the form of negative stereotypes and demonization of minority males. In the past, minorities have inoculated themselves against these realities through strong family and community ties. This continues to be the case; however, to a lesser degree. Thus, we must also use close relationships with friendship groups to supplement our contact with family members.

Treat yourself with respect. Exercise greater control of your thinking process and your actions. Refuse to play the victim. Require of yourself a level of excellence for your performance at work and at home, and know when you are living up to that standard. When you don't meet your own standard, you should have a good reason for not doing so.

Manage your time. Everyone has the same amount of time—twenty-four hours a day. Structure your time to allow for at least a half-hour of creative thinking time—time that is used to get in touch with feelings, time to review goals for the future, time to do some problem solving. For example, when you first wake up in the morning, take some time to think about the life goals you have decided on. What will you do today to further those goals? (Have you taken time to establish goals for your life?) Where do you plan to be one year from now? Five years from now? Ten years from now? You can only reach your life goals if you chart a path to follow.

SUMMARY

This chapter has explored a key method of combatting racism on the interpersonal and group level: cultural competency. Cultural competency begins the process of change with the individual modifying from the inside out by examining their personal shortcomings. The section on cultural competency first explains the importance of understanding culture and its conscious and unconscious influence on our values, beliefs, and behavior. Skills are offered for improving competency in interactions with persons from other racial and ethnic groups. The chapter avers that cultural competency also has its limitations and is one tool among others that should be used to create positive change. The chapter ends with an admonition to clothe oneself in a personal armor so that the poison of racism does as little damage as possible.

KEY TERMS

cultural competency. A set of congruent attitudes, practices, policies, and structures that come together in personal interactions, systems, and organizations to allow for positive relationships and outcomes in cross-cultural situations. It is a developmental process based upon the belief that all individuals can learn to embrace differences.

cultural proficiency. A point on a continuum that represents the *policies and practices* of an organization, or the *values and behaviors* of an individual, which enable the agency or person to interact effectively in a culturally diverse environment.

melting pot. The societal pressure that all residents of the United States adopt and conform to Anglo-Saxon values, language, and lifestyle.

GROUP ACTIVITIES

1. Complete the Exercise 1: Cultural Identity. Discuss your choices within the group. What does the exercise tell you about yourself?
2. Complete Exercise 2: My Culture. How does this exercise help you to understand the influence of culture on your life?
3. Review the section entitled "Essential Elements of Cultural Competency." Each person will receive an index card. Each person will write down an example of the element written at the top of the index card. When completed, pass the card to the next person in your group to do the same. After everyone has written an example, read all the cards aloud to the group to stimulate further discussion.

STUDY QUESTIONS

1. What are the three strategies suggested for individual and group action against racism?

2. Define cultural competency. In what ways does cultural competency reduce the external vestiges of individual racism?
3. Discuss the normative view of American culture.
4. Why is multiculturalism seen as a threat to some American citizens?
5. Why is it important for Euro-Americans to recognize their culture before institutional racism can be overcome?
6. Explain the difference between cultural destructiveness and cultural competence.
7. Why is understanding the nature of culture crucial to becoming culturally competent?
8. Identify and discuss two examples of barriers to cultural competency.

NOTES

1. James Blackwell and Philip Hart, *Cities, Suburbs, and Blacks* (Bayside, NY: General Hall, 1982); Robert Staples, *The Urban Plantation* (Oakland, CA: Black Scholar Press, 1987); Derrick Bell, *Faces at the Bottom of the Well: The Permanence of Racism* (New York: Basic Books, 1992).

2. A much more detailed examination of cultural competency can be found in Mikel Hogan-Garcia, *The Four Skills of Cultural Diversity Competence* (Belmont, CA: Brooks/Cole, 1999); Milton J. Bennett, *Basic Concepts of Intercultural Communication* (Yarmouth, ME: Intracultural Press, 1998); Doman Lum, *Culturally Competent Practice: A Framework for Growth and Action* (Pacific Grove, CA: Brookes/Cole Publishing Co., 1999).

3. Diagram was created by Milton Bennett in a seminar on Intercultural Competency.

4. R. Lindsey, K. Nuri Robins, and Raymond Terrell, *Cultural Proficiency: A Manual for School Leaders* (Thousand Oaks, CA: Corwin Press, 1999).

5. Hogan-Garcia's book also provides a number of worksheets in each chapter, which can used as group exercises in the classroom or in individual study.

6. D. W. Sue, P. Arredondo, and R. J. McDavis, "Multicultural Counseling Competencies and Standards: A Call to the Profession," in J. G. Ponterotto, J. M. Casas, L. A. Suzuki, and C. M. Alexander, eds., *Handbook of Multicultural Counseling* (Thousand Oaks, CA: Sage Publications, 1992), 624–640.

7. Bennett discusses this in his training seminars at the Intercultural Communication Institute held in Portland, Oregon, yearly. See also his book, *Basic Concepts of Intercultural Communication.*

8. Hogan-Garcia, *Four Skills.*

9. Terry Cross developed the Cultural Proficiency model in 1989.

10. Lindsey, Robins, and Terrell, *Cultural Proficiency.*

Exercise 7.1.   Cultural Identity
In the right column, list the microcultures or cultural groups to which you belong.
Leave the column to the left empty at this time.

_____ Nationality   _____

_____ Ethnicity   _____

_____ Race   _____

_____ Religion   _____

_____ Gender   _____

_____ Socioeconomic Status _____

_____ Age Group   _____

_____ Geographic Region _____

_____ Urban-Suburban-Rural _____

_____ Sexual Orientation _____

_____ Profession   _____

_____ Other   _____

_____ Other   _____

After you have completed the right column, use the left column to rank order the three cultural groups you feel have influenced you the most or to which you identify more strongly.
Do these three microcultures alone adequately define who you are?

Source: These subcultures are taken from the discussion microcultures in _Multicultural Education in a Pluralistic Society,_ 2nd ed., by Donna Gollnick and Philip Chinn (Charles E. Merrill Publishing Company, 1986). Adapted for this activity by Teresa M. Hudock and used with her permission.

Exercise 7.2.   My Culture

	How I see or experience this aspect of my culture	How I believe others see this aspect of my culture
My cultural identity (includes the top three micro-cultures from Exercise 1)		
Three values I learned from my culture as I grew up		
How these values impact the expectations I have for myself and others in my family, at work, and in my community		
How these values shape my view of the world		

8

Strategies for Combating Racism

Macro Approaches

NEGOTIATION

The Need for Negotiation

Race relations must not be a zero-sum game. It is necessary to move away from the belief that if one race or ethnic group is making gains, another group is being sacrificed for those gains. Our capitalist society fosters a zero-sum theory. The MIT economist, Lester Thurow, first put forth the theory. The **zero-sum concept** suggests that there is a finite or limited amount of resources; thus, the concept supports the belief in scarcity. It suggests that to succeed one must be assured of receiving more of the resources through competition; only the strongest competitor will receive an adequate portion of the resources. Built into our capitalist society is a high level of competitiveness supported by our value of "rugged individualism."

This leads to high levels of competitiveness among individuals. If we do not win, we lose. If I do not defeat you, I lose. To a large extent this competitiveness is locked into our culture and cannot be erased. However, Americans also desire to see the society as a meritocracy. The unfair competition, which is supported by racism, must be erased if we are to work together for social justice. Our intergroup conflict, which in large part springs from our competition over a piece of the American pie, can be curbed. Conflict resolution must be a focus of intra-ethnic group relations. Competition should be built on the principle of fairness to all cultural groups. Conflict that grows out of competition should be open to negotiation. We need to move to the goal of win-win.

Conflict is a very basic and natural aspect of life. Without tension and the friction that accompanies it, we would lose the rewards of creative problem solving, brainstorming, and consolidated decision making. The potential positive aspects of conflict include:

1. Allowing important issues to be aired
2. Producing new and creative ideas
3. Releasing built-up tension
4. Encouraging groups and organizations to reevaluate and clarify goals and missions
5. Stimulating social change to eliminate inequities and injustice

It should be expected that racial and ethnic diversity would produce conflict, as each group accommodates to the cultural difference in others. Further, as we know, our society has encouraged stratification of minority groups that produces envy and anger. It is how we adjust to the conflict that makes it negative. The win-lose formula needs to be eliminated for a more useful model for handling conflict.

Acts of racism come from the desire for economic advantage, social privilege, and or psychic reward. Challenging persons physically or humiliating them verbally when confronted with racist acts should not be a choice. Even though persons from minority groups may feel justified to inflict any pain possible to persons who deny them their rights, one cannot nor should one go through life with clenched fists. As stated earlier, psychologically the price is too high. To accept the choice of violent confrontation means that one's creative energies are spent in constant battle, not moving toward one's self-actualization. Negotiation is another skill that can accelerate the movement to racial pluralism.

Negotiation Defined

Negotiation is the process of conferring with another so as to arrive at the settlement of some matter. It should be at the heart of individual activity to create a new social environment. I am not suggesting that equality and equity are negotiable, only that our communications focus on win-win outcomes. We have used the sociology of dichotomy, the division of two mutually exclusive or contradictory groups, for too long as a means of communication. This dichotomy of whites versus people of color has been in every sphere of American life. In the political arena racism has been used successfully as a wedge issue to separate Southern whites from their traditional alliance to the Democratic Party. Racism has been used to reinforce segregation in the school system and to maintain spatial separation throughout the United States.

Through negotiation, we can begin on a one-to-one and group level to improve our social relationships. There is much to be said for form and socially sanctioned behavior. Even though these outward gestures of civility will not change institutional racism, they will help to calm the atmosphere. Remember the civil rights rulings in the 1960s probably did not change the hearts of racists in the South. Nor did it eradicate racism in the institutions. However, it did reduce lynching of black males, it mandated voting rights for African Americans, it provided access to all public facilities and governmental areas, and it reduced the amount of public harassment visited on minorities, thus reducing the societal humiliation heaped upon African Americans daily. Improved superficial social discourse is to be valued. The win-win approach of ameliorating social conflict begins with the goal for each of the parties to come out whole and intact. Neither party should come away feeling cheated, or humiliated. The old adage "a person convinced against his or her will is still to be convinced" still holds.

The Goal of Negotiation

The goal of the negotiation is to improve social relationships. Further, skillful negotiations will create an atmosphere that will support positive communication in the future. This will assist in building an alliance that will continue to attack societal injustices, not individuals. Only when one is assured that his or her own vested self-interest will be accommodated will a person be open to join in an alliance for social justice.

In regard to race relations, conflict occurs around values, perceptions, facts, and personalities. If values are the source of the conflict, it is important to clarify them and understand that it is almost impossible to change another person's values. One should seek to understand, but not waste time trying to change them. Values are the filters through which we observe facts. Perceptions are our interpretations of the facts. Our view of social phenomenon is colored by our cultural upbringing. If differences in perception are the cause of the conflict, check perceptions and share them. Use empathy to improve communication; put yourself in the other person's shoes and try to understand the situation from their viewpoint. Encourage the other person to do the same. Clarify perceptions so that you can understand why each of you has taken your respective positions. Facts are indisputable truths. If the conflict is over facts, do the research and share the facts. Differentiate between facts and perceptions and values.

Through win-win negotiations, it is possible to create positive personal relationships. Both sides through this process learn more about the other on a personal level and gain more knowledge about the vagaries of race politics.

I acknowledge that negotiation will not ease tensions in situations where goodwill is nonexistent. Individuals, groups, and social systems that support racism for social and economic gain will be intractable. However, those persons who commit racist acts because of psychic rewards may be persuaded to change, as many Southern whites did during the civil rights movement in the 1960s.

INTERRACIAL COLLABORATIVES

Societal change, which moves away from the investment in whiteness, will entail concerted effort by negotiation groups and organizations through interracial collaboratives. Past collaboratives were instrumental in fostering human rights for women, people with disabilities, and gays and lesbians. The most monumental example of the power of an interracial collaborative is the civil rights movement.

One of the most valuable strategies to overcoming racism and creating racial pluralism is the development of joint projects and action plans across racial and ethnic groups. **Racial pluralism** is a state of society in which members of diverse ethnic and racial groups maintain an autonomous participation in and development of their traditional culture within the boundaries of a common society. As concerned individuals, we can further the goals of racial pluralism by our commitment to group action as well as individual actions. Figure 8.1 shows the United States as a multicultural society with all racial and ethnic groups actively involved and equally rewarded based upon merit. Racial pluralism as a goal will be discussed in depth in the next chapter.

The Need for Macro Strategies

The normative view of racism in America is that it is an individualized problem. The idea that racism can be solved by person-to-person interaction fits into our ethos of rugged individualism. It is comforting, though patently false, to suggest that the problem of racial justice hinges simply on individual behavior. It also spares us the acknowledgment that institutional racism is deliberately and deeply embedded into our social systems. Fortunately, in America there is a growing awareness of social problems as community problems; this is witnessed in the developing consensus on the part of some policy makers, in public and private sector organizations. There are a number of such groups/collaboratives in this area. (See the appendix for a partial listing of such organizations.)

There is a broad range of strategies to use when initiating macro change. One way of looking at this broad range is by placing these strate-

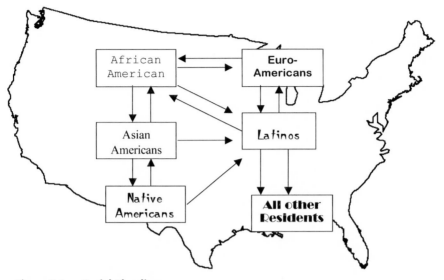

Figure 8.1.   Racial Pluralism

gies on a continuum. Cultural competency and negotiation is at one end of the continuum and interracial collaboratives at the other. If we want to create a world that embraces the creativity and unique problem-solving successes that come from diversity in brainstorming, then we must build on multicultural problem-solving groups, beginning at the local level. It has been suggested that current dispute resolution strategies focus on one-on-one conflicts, rather than inter-group and community conflicts.[1] As a part of the effort at the local level, we will discuss how collaboratives in our communities can be vehicles for dispute resolution. Later, we will examine how these collaboratives can be used as mass movements for societal change.

After the 1992 Los Angeles riot, inter-group collaboratives were limited in scope and focused on dialogue. This has been the character of most racial interactions held in cities after racial outbursts. While interracial dialogues are useful, they have generally been sporadic and not geared toward long-term goals. The Multicultural Collaborative avers, "Such efforts have not engaged grassroots leadership in concrete, mutually beneficial community-building activities."[2] Current collaborative efforts are often halfhearted because of fear, guilt, or shame of what will be discovered if the truth is revealed in interracial conversations. Some persons who have joined such dialogues have not been ready to accept the inevitable call for systemic institutional change in America; they continue to harbor the delusion that racial conflict can be fixed if we all get to know each other and we talk pleasantly to each other.

Defining Interracial Collaboratives

A collaborative is simply groups or organizations that work jointly in an intellectual endeavor. The definition of collaborative I find most informative is one offered by Bonnie Benard:

> Collaborative, defined as a group of individuals who work together on common goals, is a process that exemplifies the principles of prevention philosophy: empowerment, mutual problem solving and decision making, and mutual respect. In fact, the very process of collaboration, of coming together out of mutual concern and agreeing to work together, is doing prevention, for we're actually creating a more supportive environment by this action.[3]

The interracial collaboratives I am suggesting begin with the acceptance of the reality of institutional racism and the desire to eradicate it in our society. The collaboratives would include persons from all racial and ethnic groups, and it would ensure that persons from all socioeconomic levels would be involved in all planning and execution. And it goes without saying that Euro-Americans who support social justice and social equity are a necessity. However as Bong Hwan Kim states, "The toughest part will be convincing those with the most that even if a redistribution of power means no gains for them in the short term, the society as a whole will be better for everyone in the long term."[4] The long-term purpose of interracial collaboratives in local communities is to be a preemptive force to deter signs of racism and to use group problem solving and group pressure to reduce the economic advantage gained by maintaining racism within community and municipal social institutions.

The collaborative I envision will have spent considerable time studying and understanding what institutional racism is and how it moves through our social institutions. Members would begin to confront their own prejudices. They would have explored the pain they experienced from being exploited or of having been part of a group that exploited. Members would be prepared to embrace differences, having already moved from the stage of toleration of differences. Members would be in training to be culturally competent. Members would also be prepared to be activists, not simply well-wishers.

An issue that will frequently need to be negotiated with collaboratives is the rank order of actions. For some issues, all members cannot share the same emotional attachment. For example, Asians and Latinos will find immigration issues of vital concern, while African Americans, Latinos, Euro-Americans, and Native Americans will be unable to feel much positive concern. On the other hand, African Americans would probably be more concerned about the three-strikes law than would be Euro-Americans or Asians.

Benefits of Collaboratives

Collaboratives have many benefits, including a reduction in duplication and overlapping of efforts. Collaborating for problem solving breaks down the isolation people often feel working alone, and creates empowering experiences while building rapport among the members. The following qualities have been mentioned consistently as necessary for successful collaboratives:

1. Shared interests and needs before joining if the group is to be successful
2. Sufficient time for the group to do joint planning and consensual decision making
3. Frequent group meetings
4. Mutual goals and objectives
5. Mutual respect at the heart of all endeavors
6. Shared power, control, and responsibilities; even leadership should be rotated to ensure that all segments of the organization buy into the group's effort
7. Equal participation by collaborating partners in order to develop commitment
8. Built-in incentives and rewards to the membership for their efforts[5]

What Interracial Collaboratives Can Do

The Multicultural Collaborative remarked,

Compared to the costs of intervening and arbitrating racial conflict through law enforcement and the legal system, very little private or public sector funding is dedicated to building neighborhood, community or individual capacity to peacefully resolve interethnic conflicts or cooperatively address the conditions at the root of such conflicts.[6]

The key responsibilities of an interracial collaborative would be to:

1. Develop a network that would be involved in crisis intervention and long-term mediation of intergroup community conflicts
2. Provide ongoing training that exposes to individuals, groups, and communities the underlying causes of racial conflicts
3. Engage in community-based activities that have the goal of exposing and eradicating institutional racism

Collaboratives would provide training and support for grassroots leaders in effective interracial community organizing. Si Kahn suggests a number of skills for grassroots organizers.[7] They include working well with people, being able to define issues in a community, skillfully conducting meetings, understanding how organizations work, knowing how to do investigative research, maintaining a system of communication within the organization, and knowing how to maintain contact with the media. The collaboratives would provide models that promote solutions and identify skill-building tools. It would confront fundamental economic and social issues that undergird racism and racial conflict. The strength of a collaborative is the uniting of organizations across the spectrum of race, ethnicity, and class. This network of organizations has the benefit of developing long-term projects, rather than being limited to crisis intervention that is the present focus of many such entities.

Racial conflict in communities is likely to erupt within the context of increasing competition over scarce resources. Interracial collaboratives that spring from the desire to eradicate racism are appropriate mechanisms for reducing such strife, and using the incident as a teaching and building opportunity. While the public media focuses on racial strife, there are many neighbors and communities fighting against youth violence, housing discrimination, and poor working conditions. These informal endeavors can be the building blocks to more focused group action zeroing in on racism. The goal should not be to simply bring about more harmony in social relationships, but to mobilize intergroup cooperation into strategies for economic and political advancement of all groups with the ultimate goal of creating racial pluralism.

Limitations of Collaboratives

In many instances, there will be varied degrees of resistance to macro change, for too many Americans only perceive a loss to their social and economic status when asked to give up white skin privilege. Many will need to understand how their advantage is a disadvantage to others and ultimately a disadvantage to the community. Another barrier may be demographics itself. Has too much time passed for Latinos, African Americans, and Asians to believe that they gain by joining such groups? In California, Latinos are the largest ethnic group in the state. While their numbers also include undocumented immigrants who cannot vote, Americans who count themselves as Latinos are growing ever powerful in the political arena. Will Latinos come to the conclusion that they no longer need to form alliances with Asians and African Americans to increase their social, political, and economic power? There is no way to answer this question at this point in time.

There is also the issue of whether Latinos will eventually be declared "white," thus eliminating their need for useful connections with racial minorities. Some Latinos will fervently deny their willingness to give up their rich culture to fully assimilate into Anglo culture. Other Latinos may feel that they have truly been accepted as Americans if they are fully assimilated. Only time will tell how this will play out. It is my belief that such acceptance is unlikely, for it would seriously reduce the numbers of persons on the bottom rung of the economic ladder. This is the group required by the society to do the jobs that no one else will do for such low wages. Further, those on the bottom continue to be the spur that keeps the rest of the society fully involved in the capitalist system of rewards and punishments.

Interracial collaboratives, by the nature of their membership and their thorough understanding of the persistence of institutional racism, are in a good position to help bring about racial equality at the local level. They can show through their actions how everyone can gain from racial pluralism. It should be realized, however, that systematic change will only occur incrementally, over time. There is no quick fix to racial equality and no swift route to racial equity.

SUMMARY

This chapter continues the examination of individual and group strategies to combat racism by focusing on negotiation skills and interracial collaboratives. Negotiation skills are suggested as a tactic to employ to overcome our zero-sum approach to human relations. The importance and usefulness of negotiation is discussed as a method to combat social tension that accompanies increased cultural diversity. A strategy offered at the group level is interracial collaboratives. Interracial collaboratives have proven their potency within the civil rights movement. They combine the skills of cultural competency, negotiation, and social action.

KEY TERMS

collaboratives. Groups or organizations that work jointly in an intellectual endeavor.

negotiation. The process of conferring with another so as to arrive at the settlement of some matter.

racial pluralism. A state of society in which members of diverse ethnic and racial groups maintain an autonomous participation in and development of their traditional culture within the boundaries of a common society.

zero-sum concept. Suggests that there is a finite or limited amount of resources, thus the concept supports the belief in scarcity.

GROUP ACTIVITIES

1. Review "Putting on a Personal Armor" and discuss how you can personally use the concepts in your personal life. Do you envision any handicaps to using theses edicts in your life?

STUDY QUESTIONS

1. Explain how the zero-sum theory leads to tensions between minority groups and the society at large?
2. Why is negotiation a skill useful in racial relations in America?
3. How do negotiation skills assist in building interracial collaboratives?
4. Why is a macro intervention required to combat institutional racism?
5. Discuss how interracial collaboratives have proved successful in the past.
6. List and discuss three benefits accrued through collaboratives.
7. What are the limitations of interracial collaboratives?

NOTES

1. Carol Dowell, ed., *Race, Power and Promise in Los Angeles* (Los Angeles: Multicultural Collaborative, 1996).
2. Dowell, *Race, Power and Promise,* 5.
3. Bonnie Benard, "Collaboration Fosters Creative Problem Solving," *Western Center News* 4, no. 2 (March 1991).
4. Elaine Kim, "Between Black and White: An Interview with Bong Hwan Kim," in, *The State of Asian America,* K. Aguilar-San Juan, ed. (Cambridge, MA: South End Press, 1994), 70–74.
5. Kim, "Between Black and White."
6. Dowell, *Race, Power, and Promise.*
7. Si Kahn, *Organizing: A Guide for Grassroots Leaders* (New York: National Association of Social Workers Press, 1991).

9

Arenas for Individual and Group Strategies

We have discussed in chapters 7 and 8 the activities that should take place if institutional racism is to be subdued in American society. This chapter will explore the arenas where combating racism should take place. The arenas explored are home and family, the workplace, religious communities, schools, the vote, and the community.

HOME AND FAMILY

Euro-American Home and Family

The social dilemma of racism is often thought of as a problem out there—in the inner city, on the job, in politics. However, the issue of racism both individual and institutional must also be addressed in the home. Is cultural blindness and cultural deafness prevalent in your home, your community, and your job? When was the last time you discussed the issue of racism in America with anyone in your family? Have you ever listened intently to the point of view of a person of color on the issue of institutional racism in America? Possibly all your family members are white and you live in a community that is considered white and most of your friends are white. Consequently, you may feel insulated from the issue of racism and its ramifications. However, our homes are not as insulated as you might think. The world comes into our homes via the television, music, the Internet, toys, CDs, books, magazines, and the daily newspaper; an example of the phenomenon is rap music. More white suburban teenagers buy rap music than any other segment of American society. Each of these purveyors of American culture provides the vehicle for racism to enter your home and opportunities to respond to it.

As mentioned earlier, talking about racism is not easy for us to do. Few whites have grown up in homes that have openly discussed the prevalence of racism in America. Many Euro-Americans have been raised to believe that racism is only prevalent among ignorant, mentally ill persons or ill-advised white supremacists. The prevailing norm within the dominant culture is to see any vestige of racism as an aberration. Some persons come from families who believe that to acknowledge and discuss racism is to further it. However, Euro-Americans can admit and overcome these past experiences and create an atmosphere in the home where issues of race, gender, class, can be honestly discussed. Those who are concerned about ending the disparity between the races should seek opportunities to discuss issues of race with family members and coworkers.

We have an impact on our family and friends by the atmosphere that we create in our home. Do we have positive images of people of color? Not only minority children need African American/Asian American/Latino dolls; white children need them too. Euro-Americans who often enjoy ethnic music should also ensure that there are books, art works, magazines, and books that portray positive images of minority groups. Bookmark equity and diversity websites on your home computer. This does not mean that you need to turn the home into an ethnic museum or discard favorite toys or games. However, establishing a multicultural environment can be accomplished with little fanfare. Children do not need to be protected from racism; they see it often on television, in the movies, and possibly in the classroom. They just may not have the appropriate words for what they see and feel. What they do need is a balance that shows positive aspects of minorities. They need tools to critical think about their social environment. Discuss with them the racism they find in books and instill in them the desire to ensure social justice for all.

Paul Kivel suggests that children be encouraged to participate in how the home should be made different. He avers that it is much more meaningful when the children and all adults in the family become involved in creating "an anti-racism multicultural environment."[1] As Kivel states, "the goal is not to create an ethnic museum but to acknowledge and celebrate the diversity of people and cultures represented in our society." Such an endeavor in the home should also provide an excellent opportunity for family members to explore the issues of sexism, homophobia, ageism, and issues around physical and mental disabilities. When young people within the family examine these areas of oppression, there is a strong likelihood that they will develop not only values that support social justice, but a willingness to strongly advocate social change.

Minority Home and Family

While people of color are aware of the disparities in our society, there are still skills that must be practiced in the home that will improve the nurturing atmosphere for adults and children. Adults must take a very strong stand to ensure that the home is nurturing. Minorities receive a constant stream of racism from "out there"; thus, minority parents must provide a positive environment that sustenance to the spirit so that the children thrive, even in a racist atmosphere. Minority parents should place special emphasis on teaching children to honor and respect their cultural heritage. Moreover, minority children need to be exposed early to the positive contributions of their culture to world civilization. Minority adults must provide an armor but not blinders for their children. Minority children will experience racism at some point no matter what parents do in an attempt to shield them, for there is no way to completely insulate them from painful experiences. In addition, point out the stereotypes and cultural misinformation depicted in movies, TV shows, computer games, and other media. Minority parents should use "teaching moments" earlier discussed to teach their children to be aware of and to respond to racism in appropriate ways. The home should include books, magazines, and artwork that celebrate their culture. Along with evidence of these contributions should be artifacts of other minority cultures. This provides an inclusive way for the young to appreciate our country's multiculturalism. Enroll your children in schools, daycare centers, after-school programs, and camps that reflect and celebrate differences. Minority families produce healthy children when they reinforce their feelings of empowerment. Emphasizing personal attributes and encouraging children to build on these strengths while overcoming areas of weaknesses increases self-empowerment.

THE WORKPLACE

The Historical Connection between Work and Racism

As was discussed in chapter 2 and chapter 4, institutional racism strives because of the desire of the dominant group for economic, social, and psychological advantage. Employment in America is intricately tied to the economy of this country and the world. It has been explained earlier that racism gives the advantage to white males through the two-tier labor market. The two-tier labor market in America is the most visible structure of a highly segregated economy, one that is stratified by race/ethnicity, gender, and class. From the inception of the Industrial Revolution, racism has been used in America to tie workers to the company and exploit them when possible. Capitalists lured white male workers from the agricultural domain into industrial jobs during the nineteenth century with the rationalization that at least they would be better off than the slaves. They could preserve their maleness while giving up their economic independence because being a worker in a factory was not the same as being a slave for a master.[2] We discussed in chapter 4 the history of minorities being exploited in the economy to provide advantage for both native and immigrant white males. Employment in America continues to carry the taint of exploitation of minorities, women, the disabled, and older workers.

Signs of Racism in the Workplace

Since institutional racism is perpetuated by the need for gain (economic, social, and psychological), confronting it at the institutional level of employment requires a macro approach. In other words, it will be necessary to formulate a strategy at the policy level or administrative level of the institution. How do we detect institutional racism in social institutions? First, we remember the definition of institutional racism offered in this book—policies, practices, and procedures that operate in such a way as to consistently disadvantage members of racial and ethnic minorities. With that in mind, we examine those processes within the social institution. Are the guidelines for hiring and promotion structured in such a way that is difficult for minorities to thrive in the setting? Are few members of minority groups ever elevated to decision-making positions? Is the work environment hostile to minorities? David Wellman, a white sociologist who has done extensive research on racism, suggests several key clues to workplace racism: "Is the employer's decision supported by fact? Does the employer apply its standards consistently among people of different races? Did the employer's explanation of its decision change when the employee challenged it?"[3]

Watch for signs such as how people are grouped or group themselves in the organization: Are all top decision-making positions nonrepresentative of the population served by the organization? In an agency that serves Latinas, are there Latinas on the governing board and in leadership positions at the agency? In those situations where there has been a demographic change in the community that has altered the client base, is the agency aggressively seeking to hire persons representative of the new reality of the community population as positions become available? Is there continuous turnover or attrition of minority workers? Are informal gatherings in the agency, such as coffee breaks, after-work activities, and lunches noticeably separated by race and gender? In any plenary meeting, is there noticeable separation and tribalism? All of the above situations may be indications that racism exists. Unfortunately, the training of executives and others in corporations in race relations has focused only on appreciation of diversity and not on eliminating the root causes of inequality. The curriculum must be changed.

Combating Racism in the Workplace

The following guidelines are offered for fighting racism on the job:

1. Understand that institutional racism is a norm in American society. Therefore, it exists everywhere.
2. Examine how the workplace benefits from the persistence of institutional racism. For example, does the practice insure more jobs available for certain groups to the disadvantage of other groups? Has it operated in such a way to ensure that whites maintain the most lucrative positions? The reasons for the racism have to be the core of what must be done to combat it. For example, if the purpose appears to be the latter, that is, to keep the most lucrative positions for white males, then the approach might include strategies that point up the absence of women and minorities at the higher levels. When possible recruit trustworthy white females as true allies. They also stand to gain by confronting discrimination.
3. Understand the culture of the powerful in the organization, and determine how racism serves to maintain that culture. Point up the long-range harmful effects of racism on the agency/ corporation. A strong argument has to be the demographic changes in our society, which preclude a corporation from being homogeneous.
4. Make it your business to learn the policies and procedures of the corporation. Be so well versed that you will know when a racist practice is being instituted and how it is in violation of the existing policy. Use organizational tools (the status quo) against racists whenever possible. The status quo is often the weapon of the powerful to maintain their control. *Be aware that the powerful may change the rules whenever the status quo is threatened.*
5. Understand the interrelationship between racism, economic issues, sexism, and other oppression inside the organization. Take some time to analyze its nuances in your organization. The theme of this book is that *all major social institutions operate together in an invisible way to reinforce racism.*
6. Minority males and females can be their own worst enemies. Sometimes, minority males insist upon subservience from minority women as their due, having experienced many barriers on their way up. Thus, they often perpetuate inequality, distancing minority women from them and arousing their wrath. This impedes the opportunity for minority groups to work cooperatively.
7. Revel in moving up in the organization, because you are now in position to make policy and determine its implementation. Often, minorities and females shun higher positions fearing that they will be

more visible for racist attacks. Since you will probably experience racism at whatever level you are, you might as well move up and use your higher status in the company as an opportunity to improve the climate for those women and minorities who will follow you.

8. Teaching moments: While it may not be possible to change the hearts of powerful whites, often we can curtail their actions, which, after all, is much more important to our livelihood. For example, when a racist exhibits behavior thoughtlessly, use that opportunity to point out in a nonconfrontational way that the behavior ultimately disadvantages you. Ask the person if that was his or her intention. Since racism does not function well in the light, the person will most likely say, "no." What you have done is made the person more sensitive to their behavior. Further, you have put him or her on notice that you will not tolerate inappropriate actions. Remember the guidelines offered for fighting individual racism.

9. Use your skills to point up how racist practices disadvantage the agency. Always focus on the vested self-interest of the agency or corporation. Shame has limited effect. Spend as much time as necessary to point up the losses of not having a diverse workforce. The crux of your argument is always the bottom line. The bottom line is always financial gain or loss for the corporation.

10. Don't do it alone. You must form alliances with like-minded individuals. Get to know colleagues. Gauge where they are in their understanding and militancy toward combating racism. Form partnerships with them to address crucial issues of inequality.

11. Don't become abusive verbally; try to remain calm when confronting institutional racism. Remember one of your advantages is that racism, both individual and institutional, does not stand up well when dragged into the light of awareness. Again, use the status quo, that is, use the stated policies that generally are written and executed as neutral to racism. America wants to perceive itself as a just society; use this to your advantage.

12. Encourage opportunities to keep the dialogue going.

13. Whenever possible, spearhead interracial collaboration on organizational planning and tasks.

FAITH COMMUNITIES AND SCHOOLS

The Role of Faith Communities

The end of separatism and racism in our faith communities and schools must be a top item on America's agenda. Sunday is the most segregated day in America. Only a few of our churches, synagogues, and mosques boast an integrated congregation. This reality tells us a lot about our culture. Often because of spatial segregation, neighborhoods are dominated by a particular racial or ethnic group. Persons tend to go to churches in their neighborhood, so we find that places of worship, like public schools, are racially segregated. What can we do as members of faith communities to improve race relations and reduce racial exploitation? We have committees in places of worship to help the poor; why not have church committees to focus on social injustice? It should be said that there are places of worship that are doing just that, but the magnitude of the racism calls for more members to be involved.

Examine your faith's congregation; how diverse is it? When there are meetings, are there members of minority groups in leadership positions? Faith communities must take up the challenge of moving beyond superficial involvement, such as Thanksgiving and Christmas baskets to the inner city, into a solid and consistent force of protest against the status quo. Faith communities can be a very powerful political force. One need only refer to the power of the *Religious Right*, which has influenced the election of Republican presidents and has kept abortion and right to life as a front-page issue for some years. The church and other faith communities can use this same power to promote racial pluralism. One committed church person can begin the process of religious involvement in social justice.

Evidence of Racism in the Public Schools

Chapter 3 explored the hidden face of racism in America's educational system and offered some remedies to the social problems. Structural racism in our schools can be seen in school funding, curriculum development, resource allocation, teacher training, and control and administration of educational programs. At the individual and group level, additional strategies need to be mounted. Most children continue to attend segregated schools. This separation has supported the disparity in funds available for suburban and inner city schools. White schools, within middle-class communities, receive greater funding for schools than do the inner-city poor schools. The disparities in funds available are reflected in the quality of teachers, availability of textbooks, maintenance of the physical plants, and existence of enrichment programs. When we look at the disparities in income, we have to acknowledge that most white students have tremendous educational advantages over students of color.

This is not to suggest that enough money is spent on the middle class; what is necessary is more money available to better educate all of our children. Parents know that money does make a difference in the education available. Why else would parents move to certain neighborhoods that boast better schools or sent their children to private schools? All of our schools need improvement, and one of the areas of immediate need is to reduce the differential in funding minority schools.

Another area of glaring need is the curricula. Generally, the textbooks have been written from a Eurocentric perspective. This has lead to a distortion or absence of the contribution of non-Europeans to the advancement of world civilization in the curricula. Our textbooks neglect to explain white colonialism in America as colonialism. The contributions of people of color are trivialized and reduced to the marvelous feats of one person who is seen as an exception. Parents who are committed to cultural competency and social justice must be more involved in insisting that textbooks have a multicultural emphasize. Schools need to spend more time celebrating the contributions of people of color beyond the festival of food and music. Parents must urge teachers to research and provide evidence of the major contributions to science, math, and literature of people of color and use ethnic holidays to celebrate how these contributions have enriched all of civilization.

Finally, teachers must strive to be culturally competent if they are to reduce the amount of racism operating in the schools. Consequently, teacher education must emphasize cultural competency in the curriculum. Fortunately, there is more awareness in universities of the need to overhaul teacher education. Teachers need to be taught that contact with persons of different backgrounds does not necessarily reduce the amount of individual racism, and that close contact has little effect on institutional racism. More in-depth study of the roots of institutional racism will better prepare teachers to educate their charges to be critical of the American norm of racism.

Current Strategies to Combat Inequality in Schools

There are two strategies presently being used in public education to combat racism at the individual and group levels. One approach is to provide individual assistance to minority children in the form of after-school tutoring, scholarships, Saturday schools, and other special training programs. These interventions are helpful, but they do not address systemic racism in the schools. Kivel suggest that these interventions also have had negative consequences as a few fortunate people of color are praised by the white community while the rest of the community is put down and blamed for their lack of success.[4] The second intervention is the attack on the causes of racism in the schools. Fortunately, this is increasingly being done in minority communities. People are organizing around correction of sexism and racism in the textbooks, supporting legislation that provides more funds for building new schools and renovating existing schools in the inner city, and pressuring for more funds at the local and state level. These battles by local communities are paying off; local communities have gotten the attention of the mayors and governors, and presidential contenders.

THE VOTE

The Importance of the Vote

My reason for including the vote is a personal strategy related to the accepted importance and power of the individual to influence government. Through the vote, each person is able to influence policies, practices, and procedures, and thereby reduce structural oppression, including racism. I had not planned to write anything on this topic. That was before the presidential post-election contest in December 2000, which focused primarily on the state of Florida. Most Americans have been considerably naive about the politics of voting in current American society. My students, who are generally in their mid-twenties, have accepted those events of the presidential elections as a much-needed civics lessons, and so should all Americans. They now tell me they will register to vote because they realize how important every vote can be. That election was a wake-up call. The 2006 elections, which put the Democrats in the leadership in both the House and the Senate, should cement the notion for all Americans the power of the vote.

The Right to Vote

According to the Supreme Court, it interceded in the 2000 election vote count dispute in Florida in part because a recount, which did not have uniform guidelines for every county, would violate the "equal protection" clause in the Constitution. Ironically, the clause was primarily designed to remedy the inequalities piled upon African Americans. The Fifteenth Amendment erased this by prohibiting race discrimination with respect to the vote. However, the South refused to honor the amendment for most of the twentieth century. African Americans were simply disenfranchised by racist policies such as the poll tax and individual racist acts such as intimidation or violence. It was only through the pressure of interracial collaboratives such as the civil rights movement and National Council of Churches that African Americans secured the right to vote with the Voting Rights Act of 1968, often with the backup of federal troops.

The civil rights movement pointed up how the politics of voting can be crucial to the well-being and upward mobility of minorities, and how even voting procedures in a highly democratic society can be entangled in the web of racism. A newspaper article in December 2000 stated that African Americans leaders from Jacksonville, Florida, filed a lawsuit contesting the presidential election because minorities were systemically denied the right to vote.[5] The article alleged that blacks felt there was a miscount in Duval County. In that county, Texas governor Bush received 58 percent of the vote; Vice President Gore received 41 percent. However, an unusually large number of votes were thrown out, because they were either "undervotes," and did not contain a presidential vote that a machine could read, or were "overvotes" invalid because they contained more than one vote for president. Interestingly, those votes came from the county's four black city council districts, created to ensure a minority voice when Jacksonville combined with Duval County more than two decades ago.

Many African Americans equate the 2000 presidential election with the voting injustices they experienced prior to the 1960s. Unfortunately, there continues to be concern about the efficacy of our present voting system. A nationwide survey in 2001 found that the types of foul-ups that threw Florida's presidential election results into doubt were most common nationally in congressional districts whose populations were relatively poor and heavily minority, and whose voting equipment was old.[6] A poll by Harvard University's Shorenstein Center found that 90 percent of African Americans thought the results were unfair, compared with 60 percent of whites. Some feel that there is a concerted effort to reduce the right to vote of minorities.

New regulations are being considered in Alabama, Missouri, and Georgia ostensibly to prevent fraud, such as requiring photo identification, proof of citizenship, and restrictions on driver registration. However, these restrictions could have the effect of disenfranchising minorities, the elderly, and the poor. Some states are pushing these new restrictions to prevent fraud; however, there is no research which supports the idea that there is widespread voting fraud. Florida now rules that there will be no registration before the primary and that huge fines will be assessed to voluntary organizations that do not turn in voter registration forms within ten days of signing up a new voter. The cost of citizenship is going up as states institute increases in fees for citizenship application. This is of particular concern to Latino immigrants, for fee hikes and the plan to have all filing online may seriously reduce the ability of legal immigrants to become U.S. citizens—furthering reducing the Latino vote.

African Americans chronicle the following incidents on Election Day 2000. In Miami, Atlanta, St. Louis, and Jacksonville the "get-out-the-vote drive" headed by the NAACP found that polling places were totally unprepared for the large numbers of persons who arrived to vote. Many people were turned away. In South Carolina, Democratic officials filed a complaint with federal authorities regarding Republicans who were said to be wearing shields that looked like police badges and challenging black voters in Charleston and Sumter counties.[7] Of course, some may say that African

Americans are being too sensitive about the matter and overreacting to commonplace foul-ups. However, remember that for decades African Americans protested brutal treatment by municipal police, and many outside the inner cities waved off such protest until the Rodney King beating was aired on television across the country.

There is one last area of concern—there are seven states that impose a lifetime ban on voting for ex-felons. Nearly 2 million adults in the 17 states are ineligible to vote because of felony disenfranchisement laws in those states. Nationally, about 4.7 million Americans cannot vote because they have a felony conviction.[8] It is impossible to discuss this issue separate from race; black men make up 30 percent of disenfranchised voters, but only 6.1 percent of the U.S. population.[9] In Florida and other states, Latinos are disproportionately in prison, on probation, or parole. The hurdles to regain the right to vote for ex-felons are formidable. Considering that the majority of former inmates come from poor, often uneducated families, only a small fraction will probably ever see a voting booth again.[10]

The Weaknesses in Our Voting Process

A provocative article by Alex Keyssar, professor of history and public policy at Duke University, suggests that the 2000 presidential election pointed up a glaring issue of possible disenfranchisement for many Americans in the following ways:

- If you registered to vote, your name may or may not be on registration lists when you arrive at the polls. Registration lists are periodically expunged and mistakes happen. Forms filed at the Department of Motor Vehicles may not have made it to the voter registration office, thus you will be unable to vote.
- If you vote, your vote will probably be counted, but maybe not. Hundreds of thousands of ballots are tossed out at each election because of improper marks or machine malfunctions. You may or may not be told that your ballot has been rejected.[11]

These voting problems continued with the 2004 and 2006 elections in varying degrees across the country.

The Use of the Vote by Minorities

Despite the problems of the 2000 and 2004 presidential election, the vote continues to be a powerful tool of individual action and social change in America. Both Jews and African Americans have used the block vote as means of being heard even though their numbers in the population continue to be small. Jews represent approximately 2 percent and African Americans less than 13 percent of the total population.[12] In the 2000 presidential election contest, political scientists and pundits examined openly the necessity of a large African American vote for Vice President Gore to win the White House. In California where the Anglo and Latino vote is volatile, with a percentage split between the Republicans and the Democrats, African American voters emerged as the state's most crucial swing constituency. David Friedman, a Markle senior fellow at the New America Foundation, suggests that "If African Americans continue to strongly favor Democrats, as they have historically, statewide Democratic and urban candidates would almost certainly win most elections, and by a comfortable margin, even if Latinos should turn markedly Republican."[13]

Many Americans see the right to vote as sacred. In the twentieth century, women and African Americans through women's suffrage and the civil rights movement paid a heavy price to secure this hallowed right. The recent presidential elections suggest that we should look at the vote in two ways: as a means of influence and as a sacred right that can be contaminated with racist activities. And while I initially saw the vote as a tool to increase social justice, these elections remind me that we must always be vigilant to ensure that the vote is protected from not only racism but also partisan politics. Through individual efforts of citizens who are concerned about advancing social justice, the battle must be joined to ensure the right to vote and that the vote is counted.

Across the country we learned that the presidential election was plagued by faulty election machines, and tainted by protests of exclusion by minorities and the elderly. We have learned that some poor communities across the country are saddled with the most dilapidated voting machines. In the 2006 election, California witnessed a Republican Vietnamese candidate sending letters to Spanish-surnamed citizens advising them that illegal immigrants could be prosecuted if they voted in the election. There was temporary concern that Latino citizens might be afraid to vote. Overall, there is considerable concern about mismanagement of the election process that is controlled by the states and the counties.

The fact that faulty and antiquated voting machines are prominent in low-income and minority communities is a glaring example of a policy or procedure within a social institution that has a negative outcome on minorities. Because of undermaintenance and chad buildup, these machines may skew an election. The judges, fixating on the glitches in the recount in 2000 rather than looking at the larger picture of faulty machines that contributed to long waiting lines as well votes being thrown out, missed an opportunity to repair a large breach in the cloth of equality. Instead they ignored the real inequality and asked the legislative bodies to remedy the problem. We are now moving to electronic voting machines for future elections. There is concern that reported malfunction of these machines may effect elections.

Making Every Vote Count

Interracial collaboratives could take on the task of monitoring counties in their area to ensure that voting machines are adequate to the task. More minorities will need to insist on a presence on the election commissions around the country. The beginning of reform should be a national commission to complete an exhaustive investigation into election procedures across the country. It would make recommendations for change to Congress to help guarantee fair national elections. Each state should do the same, as there are many more local and statewide elections that are supervised by the counties. While modernizing voting machines, states must ensure that they work properly. Counties are responsible for buying and maintaining this equipment; however, many are financially unable to do so, thus state and federal governments must step in and ensure that the necessary funds are made available.

THE COMMUNITY

The Goal of Community Organization

Community organization is one of the macro practice skills of the social work profession and is practiced by persons from all walks of life. **Community organization** relates to the practice of mobilizing persons of a community to increase their problem-solving skills, to increase their ability to make group decisions, and to take concrete action to resolve issues of importance to the community. There are two major types of communities: geographical and functional. A geographical community is one that is designed by political entities. Examples of a geographical community include Chicago, Los Angeles, and municipal councilmatic districts. A functional community is one that consists of individuals who share in common certain attributes, such as language, place of origin, religion, race, ethnicity, gender, and sexual orientation. Examples of a functional community would be women, Catholics, gays and lesbians, and Latinos.

Persons join community organizations when they realize that their individual actions cannot be as effective as action by a group. Persons who see themselves as sharing similar concerns see the power of group action. Further, they see their own vested interest will be served by joining with a group. We discussed earlier the advantages of collaboratives; those assets are the same when we speak of community organization. Community organization as a process or action is also the work of collaboratives.

Strategies and Tactics

Three basic models of community organization designed by Jack Roth-man delineate the most appropriate action to take in a given situation.[14] This book focuses on "model c: Social Action" for it suggests a process that is appropriate to functional communities that are marginalized, poor, and exploited. Model c suggests that this community needed to be "organized, perhaps in alliance with others, in order to make adequate demands on the larger community for increased resources or treatment more in accordance with social justice or democracy."[15] Its strategies are overt and activist, or-ganizing people to take action against a foe. Its goal is to aid the exploited, promote social justice, and spearhead specific changes in power relation-ships and resources within the society.[16] The tactics employed are con-frontational, and involve conflict or contest if necessary, to get the attention of those in power and insist they make the needed changes.

In Rothman's model, Social Action, the design for action encompasses the following:

1. The community organizer views himself or herself as an advocate, ac-tivist, agitator, broker, and negotiator as his or her role within the or-ganization.
2. The organizer assists in developing formal organizations and guiding the organization toward the goal of social change.
3. Mass organization is seen as necessary because the members generally have limited resources: money, political influence, or influential con-nections. Their greatest resource is their numbers and their power to disrupt.
4. The power structure is viewed as the external target; that is, the persons in control are not within the community of activists. The power struc-ture is viewed as the enemy, as the ones perpetrating the injustice.

Who Should Do It?

When one views mass protest in a society, such as the student protest at Tiananmen Square in Beijing, China, or the Million Man March in Wash-ington, D.C., one naturally assumes that organizers of social action must be of a certain ilk. Uninitiated people may assume that these leaders must be extroverted, completely confident in themselves, gifted speakers, and charis-matic. All of these qualities would be of great assistance to a community or-ganizer, but they are not required in order to begin to mobilize people to take action. The most essential qualities are commitment and willingness to work with others in a democratic way to produce change. There have been successful organizers from all walks of life and with a variety of personal strengths and weaknesses. It is important to learn the skills and the tools of community organization, and I suggest two texts, *Community Organizing in a Diverse Society* and *Organizing: A Guide for Grassroots Leaders,* which will increase the success of an organizer.[17]

Culture and Community Organization

We discussed in chapter 7 the meaning of culture and how it relates to the strategy, cultural competency; it is also an important ingredient in community organization.[18] In organizing individuals to take action, we will find that they will only organize around actions that fit within their value systems. Each minority group will create its resistance in ways that fit into its view of the world, values, and sense of right and wrong. Sometimes individuals are unsure of the real values of their culture because they have received so many conflicting interpretations of their culture.

Most Americans have accepted the many myths spun about our country in general and their own ethnic or racial group in particular. We have noted the need of the dominant group to weave negative stereotypes of minority groups in America: the Indians scalped white settlers and raped their women for no reason other than that they were savages; Africans were lazy and violent; Latinos come to this country to live off the hard work of Americans and not contribute to the society; and on and on. As we have learned, the dominant group has needed these stereotypes to justify exploitation of minority groups.

Further, the dominant group has striven to have these stereotypes accepted by the minority group. Why? The more the group accepted the denigrated portrayal of their community, the more likely they would behave within the stereotype. A person tends to behave in ways that are based on how he or she perceives others see him or her—the looking glass image. As these groups at least acquiesced to the caricature of themselves, their behavior became shaped by that image. The American myth that blacks acquiesced to their subordinate position was reinforced by the elevation of Booker T. Washington. Washington urged that blacks could move ahead without challenging the racist policies within all the social institutions. He averred that success for the individual black came from individual effort within the racist system. This myth of personal success was promulgated as a means of keeping African Americans from acting as a community. Much of the history of widespread and frequent resistance to slavery was hidden to reinforce in the black community that cooperation was the only and best way to succeed.

One sees from this discussion the crucial link between culture and community action. Functional communities will be better able to organize themselves as a force for social justice, if community activists take into account the importance of culture to the growth and development of social action.

SUMMARY

This chapter examines the various ventures or arenas for social action against racism. The key arenas for social action are the home and family, the workplace, faith communities, and the schools, whether public or private. After the presidential campaign of 2000 and 2004 it is clear that citizens must closely monitor elections to ensure their power to influence public policy is not abrogated. Finally, a group strategy historically successful in confronting the power elite is community organization. Persons are encouraged to first examine their immediate surroundings for signs of cultural insensitivity and then look at the wider communities of job, school, and religious organization to effect social change. Each of these arenas poses unique opportunities at both the individual and group level. It is important to use individual and group strategies in tandem for more lasting impact.

KEY TERM

community organization. The practice of mobilizing persons of a community to increase their problem-solving skills, to improve their problem-solving skills, improve their ability to make group decisions, and to take concrete action to resolve an issue of importance to the community.

GROUP ACTIVITIES

1. Take turns discussing your last experience of an in-depth conversation about race relations with a person from a different racial or ethnic group. If you have not had such an experience, commit to doing so during the week and report the experience to the group.
2. Describe to the group how you would augment your living quarters to reflect your commitment to multiculturalism.
3. Describe the changes you would make at your former high school to reflect multiculturalism.
4. Discuss what you think the role of the faith community should be in combating racism.
5. What are your feelings about the last three national elections? Did you vote? If not, why not?

STUDY QUESTIONS

1. What were the suggestions for modifying the home to reflect multi-culturalism?
2. List the suggestions for creating a positive atmosphere in a minority home.
3. What is the historical connection between work and racism?
4. What are the signs of racism in the workplace?
5. List three actions you can take to combat racism in the workplace.
6. Why is the vote important in combating racism?
7. How have African Americans and Jews successfully used the vote even though their numbers are small?
8. How does community organization relate to interracial collaboratives?
9. What are the strategies and tactics of model C: Social Action?

NOTES

1. Paul Kivel, *Uprooting Racism* (Philadelphia: New Society, 1996).
2. David R. Roediger, *The Wages of Whiteness* (London: Verso, 1991).
3. From an article by Erin Texeira, "The Subtle Clues to Racism," *Los Angeles Times*, January 11, 2001, A1. David Wellman is the author of *Portraits of White Racism* (New York: Cambridge University Press, 1977).
4. Kivel, *Uprooting Racism.*
5. Scott Gold, "Black Leaders Sue to Overturn Election," *Los Angeles Times*, December 8, 2000.
6. Esther Scrader, "Congressional District in L.A. Had Voting Glitches," *Los Angeles Times*, July 9, 2001.
7. Scrader, "Congressional District in L.A."
8. Bonnie Winston, "More Blacks Going to Prison in 17 Key Election States," www.blackamericanweb.com (accessed September 24, 2004).
9. Winston, "More Blacks Going to Prison."
10. Ann Louise Bardach, "How Florida Republicans Keep Blacks from Voting," *Los Angeles Times*, June 9, 2003.
11. Alex Keyssar, "One Man, One Vote?" *Los Angeles Times*, December 10, 2000.
12. U.S. Census Bureau, *Statistical Abstract of the U.S. 2000*, 120th ed. (Washington, DC: 2000), 62.
13. David Friedman, "Don't Write Off State's Black Voters," *Los Angeles Times*, November 19, 2000.
14. This model was first presented in Jack Rothman's "Three Models of Community Organization Practice," in *Social Work Practice* (New York: Columbia University Press, 1968; 1978). Rothman is the author of several articles and books on community organization.

15. Rothman, "Three Models," 26.

16. See Rothman's discussion of this model in *Reflections on Community Organization* (Itasca, IL: F. E. Peacock 1999).

17. There are two excellent books on community organization: Felix Rivera and John Erlich, *Community Organizing in a Diverse Society* (Boston: Allyn and Bacon, 1998); and Si Kahn, *Organizing: A Guide for Grassroots Leaders* (New York: National Association of Social Workers, 1991).

18. See chapter 18, "Culture," in Kahn, *Organizing*.

10

Racial Pluralism

From the late 1960s to the middle of the 1970s, large numbers of African Americans were convinced that there was the possibility that they would be rounded up by federal troops and ensconced in concentration camps, forever isolated in American society. At the same time, many were convinced that "when the revolution comes," African Americans would rise up and fight back and vanquish racist America. Racist America would be no more. Suddenly, we woke up and looked around us, saying "We live here too. If America goes under where will we be? We are Americans, not motivated to live in Africa." The reality hit us—we are all in this together. *The antidote to institutional racism is racial pluralism.*

RACIAL PLURALISM DEFINED

Racial pluralism is a state of society in which all persons are valued and rewarded according to their efforts. In such a society, need and merit dictate distribution of goods and services. Because in American economy individual effort and private ownership dominate, persons would continue to be responsible in large part for their own advancement. Those unable to care for themselves would be provided for through various public and private social welfare programs. In this reformed society, persons would continue to compete and merit whatever they receive. However, there would no longer be the unfair barriers of racism to artificially limit the chances to succeed. *Racial pluralism equates to equity, not equality.*

Racial pluralism is the exact opposite of the institutionalized oppression (sexism, racism, homophobia, classism, and ageism) under which American society now metes out goods and services, and social status. Racial pluralism, like cultural pluralism, would embrace diversity at all levels. The ultimate solution to social ills enunciated in this book is a remolding of our current society to reject the cultural and economic acceptance of racism. Of course, detractors will state that racial pluralism is an unrealistic utopia that will never exist, and reluctantly I agree. There will never be a perfect world because humankind is imperfect. There is, however, the need to examine what the ideal society would be and then work to achieve as much of it as we can. Certainly, there is palatable distress over the constant stream of racial eruptions and animosity as detailed in this book. Our society is forced to examine the ramifications of diversity as more and more persons who are non-European enter the United States legally and illegally. America is becoming more diverse, ready or not. *There will be diversity, but will there be pluralism?*

DIVERSITY IN CURRENT SOCIETY

There has been a long-running debate regarding how diversity should be addressed in this country. Historically, in these political and economic debates, "nonwhites" routinely lost. They were exploited and forced into subordinate roles to Euro-Americans, even as religious and philanthropic groups decried the harsh treatment accorded them. As European immigration increased to this country, each group had to fight for the privilege of being considered "white."[1] The Irish, Italians, and Jews were not considered "white" during the early 1800s. Those not considered "white" were relegated to second-class status.

One of the early solutions to diversity caused by the influx of persons from non-English backgrounds was the "melting pot" mentioned in chapter 7. It usually took at least one generation for European immigrants to learn to speak Standard English and to incorporate the lifestyle and values of the Anglo-Saxons. Although some Americans continue to state with pride that America is a melting pot for all groups, this has never been so. The forced assimilation to whiteness was only accessible to the certain groups. It was not available to Native Americans or to Africans in the beginning or to Asians later on. Policies, practices, and procedures were used for more than two hundred years to ensure that these groups were isolated and separated from Anglo life. These formal and informal means corrupted all the social institutions and subsequently created a thoroughly racist society that has had periodic eruptions, sometimes violent ones, ever since.

The Civil Rights Movement as a Vehicle for Social Change

The civil rights movement of the 1950s ushered in the beginnings of a protracted struggle to bring about an integrated America—racial pluralism. This movement increased the legal sanctions against discrimination in many areas: education, voting, public accommodations, housing, and employment. The early 1960s was a time of integrationist idealism fostered by Dr. Martin L. King, Jr., and Baynard Rustin. The goal of the movement was Dr. King's dream that race and ethnicity would no longer be a barrier to full access to the nation's fruits.[2] The first battlefront was education, when the Supreme Court ruled that "separate but equal" was unconstitutional. The second battlefield was public accommodations: the integration of seating on municipal buses and interstate travel. This battlefront also included the removal of separate public facilities for white and blacks, and the requirement to provide equal services to blacks in public and private accommodations. Before the civil rights battle, African Americans would not be served in restaurants and hotels; and they were not allowed to try on clothes in department stores.

The civil rights interracial collaborative fought a hard-won battle, with resistance on the part of whites in both the North and the South. Southern whites rioted to prevent black children from integrating public schools. The deployment of the National Guard was required initially to protect blacks that integrated interstate transportation and public schools. The third front of the civil rights movement was in the area of politics. Harsh social and legal sanctions were employed to exclude Southern blacks from the political process. Social sanctions included intimidation in the form of firings, eviction from tenant farming, beatings, and sometimes lynchings. Legal sanctions to prevent African Americans from attempting to vote included the poll tax—a levy of a fixed amount on every voter. However, blacks were the only persons required to pay the tax. In the Southwest, the poll tax, along with gerrymandering, was used to prevent Mexican Americans from gaining political power.

Much of America's attention was on the battle in the South, not acknowledging that the North was also guilty of egregious social practices. It came as an unwelcome reality that the cities of the North had serious racial problems. When the interracial collaboratives turned their attention to the North and organized against racist practices, there was a thunderous white backlash. In the North, African Americans moving into white neighborhoods were attacked and their homes marred or crosses burned on their front yards. African Americans in the North protested job discrimination, spatial isolation, and de facto segregated schools. Whites in the North resisted the fight for racial pluralism. From 1950 to 1975, there was tremendous resistance in the South and the North to providing the same opportunities in housing, employment, and education to Native Americans, African Americans, Latinos, and Asians.

The only area fairly free from racist procedures in the North was in the area of voting; there were no poll taxes or other visible barriers to voting. In fact in the 1940s and 1950s, the Democrats courted the vote of African Americans in the Northern ghettos. African Americans tended to vote almost exclusively for Democratic candidates because of the Roosevelt era when federally subsidized social programs were created, giving blacks hope that the federal government would be their ally against racism. Because of the spatial separation, African American votes could overwhelm any Republican candidate who ran in their area.

Minority Separatist Response to White Resistance

African Americans were deeply disillusioned by the intense white resistance to full integration across all the social institutions, which would have been a crucial step toward racial pluralism. This disillusionment led to the sometimes violent black backlash of the separatist movement, the Black Power movement. In the 1960s, the Black Panthers, founded in Oakland, California, formed the backdrop for the separatist movement. Black militants viewed racial oppression in America as "internal colonialism." For them, "equality meant self-determination for blacks as a colonized people in America."[3] African Americans who identified with separatist thought turned their backs on the opportunity to continue the struggle to amalgamate into an Anglo-Saxon culture. Other militant groups argued for a separate homeland inside the United States. During this period, other ethnic groups turned their backs on assimilation, "the melting pot," as well. In the 1970s, Native Americans, through the American Indian movement (AIM) and Mexican Americans in the Southwest (the Chicano movement) argued for acceptance of their culture as essentially American and not in need of alteration. The Brown Berets, a militant offshoot from the Chicano movement, was created in the Southwest. They vigorously protested the broken treaties between the United States and Mexico. Moreover, they protested their second-class citizenship in an area that had formerly been a part of Mexico.

White Separatist Response to Pluralism

The transracial ideal of the civil rights movement, and the separatists movements of Native Americans, African Americans, and Mexican Americans, are not the only ideologies introduced to address the diversity of America. In chapter 1, there was some discussion of the white supremacists who also have a different vision of how diversity should be handled. They have suggested that there be no mixing of the races. Some members of this persuasion endorse the murder of Jews, Catholics, and all nonwhite ethnic groups. The less extreme of this group endorse separate living areas for whites and nonwhites, but no pressure to eliminate them. Among white supremacist groups, there are many variations on how diversity should be addressed in American society.

Much of the rancor felt by white supremacist groups can be traced back to economic issues. Since the 1980s, immigrants have begun to replace natives as the cheap and exploited labor force at the lower tier. Some poor whites and blacks perceive both immigrants and the ruling class as squeezing them out of the marketplace and threatening their social standing. Economic uncertainty is the crux of the anger of some poor and working-class whites who have turned to militias and white supremacist groups. This book avers that institutional racism is one of the time-honored formulas to ensure economic, social, and psychological advantages for whites over people of color in American society; this advantage has been disturbed by calls for racial parity and the torrent of Asian and Latino immigration. Economic exploitation of Africans and Native Americans began the process of white skin privilege, and is the foundation of much of the wealth of the country today. Thus, a societal transformation to embracing racial diversity would most certainly engender fear, hostility, and violence in some groups. Note the extreme actions of some white supremacist groups. A deplorable example is the bombing of the federal building in Oklahoma City. When racial pluralism is suggested as a remedy, there is no illusion that this is an easy task, or that it could be accomplished in the near future. I am not at all sure that a sufficient number of whites will have the political will to make such a radical social change, even if it is incremental.

BARRIERS TO RACIAL PLURALISM

There are many built-in barriers to full-scale racial pluralism, and some are the same ones that led to institutionalizing racism in the first place. Institutional racism is so difficult to overcome because of the zero-sum theory, and the economic process that spurs the capitalist system of this society. The capitalist economic system draws its vitality from the principle of vested self-interest and scarcity. Americans prosper on their ability to be competitive and productive vis-à-vis others who are also competing. As stated throughout this book, the desire for economic advantage created institutional racism, and our society has built its wealth and current economy on the maintenance of an unequal and unfair stratified society. These factors support the broad-based nullification process that keeps racism locked in place.

Loss of Economic and Societal Privilege

Another major obstacle to change is the feeling of loss of economic and societal privilege that Euro-Americans experience each time more equity and equality is promoted. In most cases, I would say that whites have not identified or named this feeling; nevertheless, it is a prominent drive that ultimately sabotages sincere efforts to equalize the society. White males have been quite vocal regarding affirmative action. In an article, four white males discussed their fear of loss of power that would come with the actualizing of affirmative action.[4] They suggested that affirmative action was denying white males jobs and giving goods and services to persons who did not deserve it. Numerous articles have been written on the reaction of whites to affirmative action. Overall, these studies reaffirm that whites acquiesce to affirmative action only when they perceive that it will not disadvantage other whites regardless to the issue of fairness.[5] Few white males have taken a stand for affirmative action. Beyond lip service, liberal white males have not taken the role of allies for equity and equality inside the corporation.

White Skin Privilege

A third barrier is the sense of loss by Euro-Americans of their present sense of self as embodied in white skin privilege. Whites have historically measured their own status and self-worth through comparison with the ultimate other—the African or the African American. The measurement could be achieved by external differences that allowed them to think well of themselves as Euro-Americans. Whites could look at their housing, schools, jobs, and their prominence in policy making and determine their value. Consciously and unconsciously, Euro-Americans have believed themselves to be superior to all people of color. There will be tremendous resistance to surrendering that feeling of superiority. With the advent of legally sanctioned racial pluralism, white male prerogative and white skin privilege would be greatly reduced and eventually eliminated.

Fear of Change

A fourth barrier to racial pluralism is fear and resistance to social change itself. Everyone tends to look at change with trepidation. Humans are comforted when society is predictable. Moving to a society that advocates and promotes pluralism at all levels would be a sea change for America. The preferred answer to multiple races and cultures has been the drive to "Americanize" all ethnic and racial groups. Many will refute the value of cultural pluralism by pointing to the recent crises in Kosovo, Serbia, and Rwanda. They will suggest that to keep our country from falling into the same quagmire, we must insist on only one cultural identity—Anglo-Saxon. However, the paradigm shift for racial pluralism will be from a goal of "creating harmony" to that of managing the permanent tensions that diversity creates. Americans will need to acknowledge and accept that our differences will always create some level of disharmony and discomfort. Moreover, I counter the argument that pluralism will cause unacceptable dissonance by insisting that racial and cultural pluralism does not erase our common identity as Americans. What pluralism will do is level the playing field so that race and ethnicity can no longer be used as a mechanism for distribution of goods, services, and social status in the society. Pluralism will reduce much of the social discord created by structural oppression.

THE CURRENT STATUS OF RACE

Challenges to White Hegemony

This century will see momentous changes in the status of race in America and around the world. The shift probably began in the last century with the end of World War II, according to Howard Winant, the coauthor of *Racial Formation in the United States.*[6] At that time the ordering of the racial power began to change, as colonies in Africa and Asia challenged the control of Europeans. India and most of the countries of Africa fought bloody battles of liberation against European rule. The civil rights movement of the United States in the 1950s and 1960s challenged white supremacy in the United States, and the rebellion of Africans against apartheid in South Africa in the 1970s and 1980s continued the struggle against white supremacy. These events were the biggest challenges to white rule in modern times. Global immigration from the South to the North has opened formerly homogeneous European countries as well as the United States to a more multiracial population than had ever been envisioned; this has been an additional challenge to white rule. England and Europe are wrestling with the social and economic consequences of residents from their former colonies entering their countries in large numbers. The riots in 2005 in the Paris ghettos by African and Arab youth against their second-class status and spatial isolation confirm European concerns. Immigration has forced all countries of the Northern Hemisphere to focus on the ramification of race. Finally, the American invasion into Iraq has increased the tensions between religious groups, Christians and Muslims, adding a new dimension to the challenge of white rule.

The New Racism: "Color-Blindness"

Because overt racism failed to control the external and internal challenge to white hegemony, a new form of racism has emerged in many parts of the world. The "color-blindness" ploy of the American neoconservatives is an example of the "new racism" being employed to stunt the growth of affirmative action and pluralism. Earlier in this book, I labeled this social phenomenon as cultural blindness and cultural deafness. Kent, for example, states that on American college campuses, whites and blacks are talking at cross purposes, unable to reach common ground. He states that whites see the past as of marginal importance, while blacks see U.S. history as the central core of present-day realities. Whites suggest that color consciousness reinforces racism and its absence reduces it.[7]

However, most American minority group members have gone beyond individual issues or physical characteristics and have long included social institutions as the dominant example of racism. They stress that this condition must be brought into the open to effect positive social change. Kent suggests another form of the "new racism" which combines negative minority stereotypes with the glorification of individualism and meritocracy. In this new ideology, minorities are made the scapegoat for the social ills of society—poverty, crime, and violence—while at the same time suggesting that individual effort is the only requirement for success in America. This belief is put forth even with the widespread awareness of the erosive corrosive effects of poverty, and how the lack of access impacts the upward mobility of young people of color.

The New Racism in Europe and United States

Winant suggests that other examples of the new racism can be found in Europe where "respect for difference" is used to reinforce ideas about the "integrity of national cultures" and is a method of stemming the flow of immigration and reducing the possibilities of citizenship.[8] There is insufficient mobilization against this new racial nationalism of the right in either Europe or the United States. Possibly this is because the neoconservatives have redesigned their rhetoric to disguise their goal of maintaining economic and social privilege. Further, it is evident here in the United States and in some European countries that the centrists in power do not want to redistribute goods and services, which would create more equity, nor want to offend capitalists. Unfortunately, as has been noted throughout this book, white liberals or "the left" are still invested in white supremacy. The capitalists have been able to continue to divide the workers in the unions of the North. The unions have always been leery of racial and ethnic change in the workforce because of its effect on lowering wages or reducing jobs. Furthermore, the liberals, now threatened by the leaner and meaner form of capitalism that has taken hold, and are experiencing a great deal of economic uncertainty. Perhaps they do not have the will for sustained battle against economic exploitation of the poor when their own economic stability is in doubt. Thus, we find a global social and economic unease that narrows the base of liberals and progressives to launch the mobilization of positive pluralism.

INCREMENTAL RACIAL PLURALISM

Incremental Change as Viable Solution to Racism

Racial pluralism, accomplished incrementally, is probably the only macro process that can transpose the country to the full meritocracy envisioned by the Constitution. While people of color have fought valiantly, at times with violence, throughout their sojourn in America for equity and equality, violence as a tool for change is rejected here as untenable. In reality, minorities have no military might to match the power of the state or federal government. Such a militant solution would only results in protracted armed struggles similar to those in Northern Ireland or the Gaza Strip.

Nor will concentrating on the uplifting of the most vocal of the ethnic or racial groups foster positive social change throughout the society. This "divide and conquer" ploy, often used by the British in their colonies to separate and cause dissension between ethnic groups, led to ethnic genocide long after the British surrendered their claims on the country. Witness the genocide between ethnic groups in Southern Africa or the genocide among ethnic groups in Sub-Saharan Africa. In America, skin color was used as the ploy to divide the African Americans internally. African Americans of lighter hue were given a higher social status than darker-skinned ones. With this status came certain privileges that were not accorded to darker African Americans, such as having lighter working duties or working in the residences rather than the backbreaking fieldwork. It has taken many decades to overcome these artificial barriers among African Americans. Because abrupt change is impossible, violent uprisings are untenable, and elevation of one ethnic/racial group has long-term consequences, incremental change is the only suitable method.

Strategies for Incremental Change at the Macro Level

To influence change at the governmental or macro level, there must be a focus on the existing public policy enactment and the monitoring of new policies. Interracial collaboratives must work not only at the neighborhood or community level, but oversee actions at the municipal, state, and federal level. Strategies that should be adopted are:

- Timely response to proposed legislation, state initiatives, nominations of public officials, public planning documents, and public hearings on proposed urban planning.
- Constant petition of public officials to pass legislation that promote massive reinvestment in the inner cities to compensate for the massive neglect and ill use of the communities of color. Figure 3.2 aptly depicts this ill use. Such reinvestment would be an example of retributive justice long overdue. It is important to remember that indiscriminate pumping of money into the community will not be helpful. Public reinvestment needs to be focused and accountable. The residents of the communities must be involved in the planning and the decision making. The involvement of community not only ensures community "buy-in," but increases the resident's feelings of self-worth, empowerment, and improves their decision-making skills. Hopefully, the government's partnership with the community will ensure that funds are focused on the infrastructure of the community.
- An examination of policies to determine their effect on communities of color. Kivel avers that public policy issues change but almost all have racial implications.[9] We have noted in several chapters how policies, whether intentionally or not, have been paired with racist underpinnings to gain support for the policy from a public trained to accept exploitation of minority groups. Consider the policy decisions regarding crack cocaine, juvenile crime, and the death penalty. Conservatives with the overt purpose of reducing crime have created these policies. However, the result has been the incarceration of disproportionate numbers of minority males. There has been little discussion of how these policies have benefited the criminal justice system with a flood of new jobs, and a stream of contracts for prison construction. We can look also at the highly punitive drug laws themselves and note that many segments of society, both legal and illegal, are making millions from the drug trade while the policies have not eliminated drug use.

To counteract the tendency to use racism as a way to enact policies that are lucrative to the power elite, but detrimental to ordinary citizens, the following tactics are suggested:

1. Assume that there is a substantial racial connotation for every policy and determine what effects these policies will have on people of color and the poor.

2. Understand the ways the issues are framed in racial terms—in code or openly—to build support for an upper-class agenda.
3. Constantly review current policies that we thought had been settled, because there will always be attempts to underplay the gains of minority groups until we reach a society based on racial pluralism.
4. Be patient, and accept small changes as we pressure for larger ones.
5. Become involved in public action, not just talking about injustices. We can only influence public policy by discourse and collective action. Collective action, possibly through interracial collaboratives, is what influences and molds policy debates in the first place. In the nineteenth century, it was the sustained discourse and public protest, which finally brought about the emancipation of African Americans from slavery. The sustained Japanese American struggle during many years produced reparations for their treatment during World War II. We must be prepared for sustained discourse and collective action to bring about social justice for all people of color in America.

FROM INSTITUTIONAL RACISM TO RACIAL PLURALISM

While a litany of obstacles to racial pluralism has been listed throughout this chapter, we must believe that concerted efforts can make a difference. The expertise and the power to change reside in every American citizen. Behind every successful transformation is a sense of vision. We must demand that the society change to a more just one, and we must start the process with those around us. *Racial pluralism is diversity with justice.* This book has charted some of the strategies at the individual, group, and societal level. The strategies are doable, though the journey to racial pluralism will be a very difficult one.

We have a moral imperative. We must change to a meritocracy because it is the right thing to do. How long can our country continue to hold its breath waiting for the next riot? It's as if we are a household that has a much-abused dog chained up somewhere in the house. We tiptoe around the dog that, over time, has turned violent. We fear what will happen if it ever breaks the chain that it is straining against. There is an unspoken tension always in the house. Why not feed the dog, treat it humanely, take off the chains, and live in the house without rancor and fear? *We will have diversity but will we have pluralism?* In striving toward a meritocracy, we must maintain our commitment and our patience. It will be an incremental change in America, not a violent revolution.

Sports: A Metaphor for Pluralism

The move from institutional racism to racial pluralism will require a personal and institutional conversion. Sports can be a metaphor for how meritocracy (racial pluralism) can work and equalize the playing field. We are witnessing the incremental move to that point in men's sports: basketball, football, and track. The NFL, for example, is about 68 percent African American. American owners and coaches opened up the game because of the pressure to win. There was not a sudden conversion on the part of team owners, but recognition that their chances were enhanced if they eliminated the racial bias that denied them the best-qualified players. They learned over time that diversity and meritocracy was the superior method to be successful. An excellent example of such a transformation is American professional football and basketball. Here, men are selected for the teams based on skill, talent, and work ethic. African American males who have changed the nature of basketball now dominate the sport at 68 percent. I have heard some young African American males quip that they do not want football to be dominated by black males because it would be a less interesting sport. Again, diversity rules. Most sports lovers will agree that diversity has created an exciting dimension to football, basketball, and track. The two social institutions that have visibly moved toward racial pluralism are sports and the armed forces. Though neither have complete pluralism, they exemplify the merits of pluralism. A sign of the merit of diversity is the reality that for the first time two black coaches faced each other in the 2007 Super Bowl.

The Current Movement toward Pluralism

Change is unsettling to people generally and is threatening to some; racial diversity has been unsettling to the United States. Although whites have benefited for centuries by maintaining the present system, there are some indications that Americans believe in the value of diversity. A study conducted by DYG, Inc., a New York polling firm, for the Ford Foundation found that 91 percent agreed that "our society is multicultural and the more we know about each other, the better we get along."[10] However, we can take only small comfort in this survey of American attitudes because the hard questions were not asked. The pollsters deliberately shied away from using the term, "affirmative action." The poll did not deal with the hard issues of white skin privilege or overhauling American social institutions to increase racial parity.

However, American society is changing regardless of our readiness. Witness the fact that Census 2000 offered the first opportunity for persons to identify themselves as members of more than one race. The increase in interracial marriage is a positive sign toward pluralism. It is estimated that 21 percent of the U.S. population will claim mixed ancestry by 2050. However, pluralism will not rely on biological intermixture, although the voluntary personal commitment and embracement of "the other" is a hopeful sign of individual change. Some liberals have suggested since the 1970s that pluralism would come as there were more interracial unions. However, I counter that unless we change the trappings of unmerited privilege in our society, inequity will continue. We will become a majority nonwhite nation sometime around mid-century. The huge immigration of the 1980s and 1990s has forced the country to discuss diversity and its ramifications in every sphere of American life. Immigration has challenged the status quo, for Americans can no longer claim that the United States is a white country. It has forced the country to examine the values and lifestyle of non-Europeans and begin to view their differentness as an American reality. Importantly, immigration challenges the idea of assimilation. More and more immigrants are maintaining many of their native countries' values and ideologies while incorporating useful American lifestyles and beliefs. Assimilation has lost much of its currency with many of the new arrivals. All of this has set the society on its ear and forced new thinking about how we shall live together.

Another factor to consider in the inevitable march to diversity in the United States and worldwide is the fertility rates. It has long been known that those with the highest income and educational attainment tend to have fewer children, while the poorest segment has higher birth rates. The poorest segments in our society tend to be disproportionately people of color. As Pinkerton opines, "Nationwide, about 44% of women aged 15–44 are childless, but those childlessness numbers skew above average in high-income, high-tech states such Massachusetts, Vermont and Colorado. By contrast, the lowest percentages of childless women are in downscale states such as Alaska, Mississippi, and Wyoming."[11] Thus, as we move through the twenty-first century, if trends continue there will be an increase of persons of color in both the North and the South hemispheres of the globe.

EMBRACING RACIAL PLURALISM

How can we help persons to embrace the change? If something is taken away, something else must be put in its place. The replacement has to be economically viable, must not lower the individual self-esteem, and must foster meritocracy. The reality of the high cost of maintaining a society with a great racial divide has not been a deterrent for a sizable segment of American society. The dominant society has been willing to pay for imprisonment of large and disproportionate numbers of minorities. It has been willing to live with the certainty of future racial eruptions. It has been willing to compartmentalize basic American values to hold on to racism. But there is a limit to how much the country will pay. The criminal justice system, for example, is showing change. Even neoconservatives are questioning the huge numbers of inmates being housed in prisons for drug addiction. In

November 2000, California passed Proposition 36, which will funnel drug users who are guilty of no other crime into rehabilitation programs rather than prison. Under Proposition 36, the maximum penalty for a small-time user convicted of possessing heroin, crack, or other drugs will be a drug rehabilitation program. The rehabilitation program is operating in fits and starts seven years later. In February 2001, a California Court of Appeal struck down a key portion of a tough new juvenile law, ruling that prosecutors should not be able to decide unilaterally whether teenagers are tried as adults.[12] Since this law disproportionately affects minority youths, its repeal will have a significant consequence for minority families and communities. Hopefully, this is a first step to rethinking the existing draconian policies within the criminal justice system. This alteration can spread to other social institutions just as meritocracy has spread through the sports. What is taken away is unjust advantage, and the replacement is a more vibrant society, one that can be less violent and more creative. The urgency of the reality of diversity can be the spur to produce change.

Inner City Interracial Collaboratives

At this moment, America's inner cities are practicing pluralism; inner cities are home to newly arrived immigrants, the elderly, large numbers of minorities, the poor, and the working class. While the media concentrates on sensationalizing violence and crime in the inner cities, the majority of the residents, Latinos, Asians, and African Americans, share the same space and work on community issues together.

Some urban communities are learning to negotiate their differences and accept a certain level of tension that accompanies differentness. Communities are discovering that while there are differences in their beliefs and values, there are community issues upon which they can coalesce. Unfortunately, too many politicians use identity politics as a wedge because they believe this enhances their standing in ethnic communities. At the same time, many human service agencies and community-based organizations are suspicious of each other. Politicians and professional human service workers have not been as helpful as one would expect as inner city communities have become more diverse. Neighbors have often had to initiate community gatherings to discuss community issues. Many community groups with diverse membership are beginning to take up the challenge of improving their environment with the help of their neighbors. Locally based interracial collaboratives can be useful in assisting communities to discover their mutual interest. One such group in Los Angeles, Community Coalition, has mobilized the bicultural community of South Central Los Angeles to ban the proliferation of liquor stores. A interracial collaborative, The Bus Riders Union, mobilized poor whites, Latinos, and African Americans to confront the powerful Los Angeles Metropolitan Transit Authority. Through their efforts they ensured that funds were moved from subway construction to the purchase of more buses to service bus riders who were predominately poor and minority members.

The Evolution of American Social Policy Regarding Racial Pluralism

Figure 10.1 shows the evolution of social policy over the decades and points to the type of society to be sought. In this figure, racial pluralism is translated to mean equality of opportunity. Van Dyke explores this concept, stating that liberals want liberty to have worth. Freedom, as an ideal, is the opportunity to reach your highest potential that is equality of opportunity. Van Dyke explains his thesis as it relates to racism:

> Liberals are not willing to define it simply as the absence of discrimination. A person with a broken leg scarcely has equality of opportunity in a race even if, like all the others, he has an open lane ahead of him on the track. . . . To promote equality of opportunity, you need to not only eliminate discrimination but insofar as possible, to make up for special disadvantages, both those

Social Policy	Relative Time Period	American National Motivation	Label for Historically Oppressed People	Societal Response by Historically Oppressed People
Segregation	before 1950s	Legal separation Normative view of white supremacy	Genetically inferior Culturally inferior	Alienation
Desegregation	1950s	Separation illegal	Culturally deficient	Dissonance
Integration Equal access Equal rights	1960s	Civil Rights Movement Women's Movement Gay Rights Movement	Culturally deprived	Marginality
Equal benefits Multicultural education	1970s	Education	Disadvantaged	Dualism
Diversity	1980s	Economic	Different	Negotiation
Cultural competency	1990s	Moral acceptance	Diverse	Bicultural transformation
Racial pluralism	2000s	Ideal	Citizens	Multicultural transformation

This chart is a modification from the original conception by Randall Lindsey and Alberto Ochoa. Source: Lindsey, R., Robins, K. Nuri, and Terrell, Raymond. *Cultural Proficiency: A Manual for School Leaders* (Thousand Oaks, Calif.: Corwin Press, 1999).

Figure 10.1.   Evolution of Social Policies and Equity

for which society is responsible and those for which the individual is not responsible.[13]

We can continue to move toward a society that is a meritocracy. The November 2000 election seemed to indicate the uncertainty of what would be the best course for the country. However, in the November 2006 election, the country seemed to be clear that it wanted a change, not only as it relates to the war in Iraq, but regarding domestic issues. This time of transition should be used to revisit the issues of equity. Now is the time for those who are committed to a racially pluralistic society to mobilize. We must become involved in social change, not just talk about it. We want to shape policies, practices, and procedures by discourse and collective action. We must judge policies based on whether they help or hurt communities of color, regardless of the intentions. It is important to advance proactive, race-conscious policies that define the role of government in promoting racial equity and protecting against discrimination.[14] Collective action—through collaboratives—is the force that has been used successfully by marginalized groups in America to shape policies in the first place, and it continues to have the power to produce social change. Finally, our concern should be to deal with personal and community responsibility, not victimization. We must understand social structure barriers, but focus on what can be done. Figure 10.2 provides graphically the silhouette of such a society.

SUMMARY

This chapter examines an antidote for institutional racism: racial pluralism. It provides a historical review of how American society has responded to racial diversity, and how white and black separatists have attempted to wall themselves off from integration. The current barriers to racial pluralism are formidable, and a new form of racism has risen in both the United States and Europe: color-blindness. However, there is a growing resistance to white hegemony by developing countries through the world. The chapter ends on a hopeful note, pointing out the areas in America where racial pluralism is being practiced.

GROUP ACTIVITIES

1. Identify one corporation or nonprofit organization that the members are familiar with and discuss practices that could be enacted to produce more racial pluralism within.

Pluralism	Institutional Racism	Racial
Beliefs	~The presumption of white supremacy ~Acceptance of social, economic inequality ~Championship of "colorblindness"	~Assumption of racial equality ~Acceptance of the need for equality of opportunity ~Realization that diversity produces creativity ~Assumption that there is only the human race
Attitudes	~Commitment to inequality between the races/ethnic groups ~Supports individual effort as the result of economic status ~Accepts negative stereotypes as truly representative of minority groups ~Hostility, fear, intolerance	~Welcoming of differentness ~Shuns forced assimilation ~Positive management of differentness ~Support of ethnic celebrations ~Empathy, concern, support ~ Uses negotiation appropriately
Practices	~De facto segregation ~Spatial isolation ~Informal methods to maintain white skin advantage ~Hostile acts to maintain white supremacy	~Embracement of multicultural society ~Informal methods to actively increase racial pluralism ~ Cultural competency ~ Acceptance of level of tension that accompanies differentness
Structures	~Formal policies, practices, and procedures to maintain racism ~Organizations and social institutions that maintain white male advantage ~*The Web of Institutional Racism*	~Formal policies, practices, and procedures to enforce racial equity and equality ~Interracial collaboratives ~Multiracial community organizations

Figure 10.2. Toward Racial Pluralism

2. Using your own employment discuss the current barriers to racial pluralism you have noted. What, if any thing, is being done by the administration to correct inequality?

STUDY QUESTIONS

1. Explain the different approaches to pluralism effected by both white separatists and black separatists.
2. List and describe the major barriers to racial pluralism.
3. List examples of how the civil rights movement served as a medium of social change.

4. List five factors that contribute to the current thinking on race.
5. Explain why it would be impossible to eliminate social tension in a pluralistic society.
6. How have Europe and England responded to increased diversity inside their borders?
7. Why is incremental racial pluralism the only feasible solution for institutional racism?
8. What can communities do to foster interracial collaboratives?
9. What tasks are necessary for sustained response to public policy initiatives that have negative outcomes for people of color?

NOTES

1. Read chapter 1 in Andrew Hacker, *Two Nations* (New York: Ballantine Books, 1992) for an expanded discussion of race identification in the United States from colonial times to the 1850s.

2. See the newspaper article by Michael Lind and Sean Wilentz, "And the Beat Goes On: The Continuing Power of the Liberal '60's," *Los Angeles Times* Sept. 12, 1999, for their discussion of liberalism.

3. See "Through a Glass Darkly" in Ronald Takaki's *A Different Mirror* (New York: Little, Brown, 1993). The quotation is taken from page 408.

4. Eric Rofes, David Keiser, Tony Smith, and Matt Wray, "White Men and Affirmative Action: A Conversation," *Social Justice* (Summer 1997): 133–46.

5. Thomas C. Wilson, "Whites' Opposition to Affirmative Action: Rejection of Group-Based Preferences as Well as Rejection of Blacks," *Social Forces* 85, no. 1 (September 2006): 111–20; David Harrison et al., "Attitudes on Affirmative Action," *Journal of Applied Psychology* 91, no. 5 (September 2006): 1013–36.

6. Howard Winant, "Race in the New Millennium," *Colorlines* (Spring 2000): 5–7.

7. Noel Jacob Kent, "The New Campus Racism: What's Going On?" *NEA Higher Educational Journal*, 10, no. 5, 1996.

8. Winant, "Race in the New Millennium."

9. Paul Kivel, *Uprooting Racism* (Philadelphia: New Society, 1996).

10. Sam Fulwood III and Kenneth Weiss, "Public Values Ethnic Diversity, Survey Finds," *Los Angeles Times*, Oct. 7, 1998, A4.

11. James P. Pinkerton, "The Stork Now Delivers a Stark Reality," *Los Angeles Times*, January 2, 2001, B7.

12. Maura Dolan, "Justices Curb Law on Prosecution of Youth as Adults," *Los Angeles Times*, February 8, 2001.

13. Vernon Van Dyke, *Ideology and Political Choice* (Chatham, NJ: Chatham House, 1995), 265.

14. Applied Research Center, "Working Principles for Racial Equity," Race and Public Policy Conference: Proactive Agenda for 2005 and Beyond, April, 2005.

Appendix:
Interracial Collaboratives

Applied Research Center
25 Embarcadero Cove
Oakland, CA 94606
510.534-1769
www.arc.org

Center for New Community
6429 W. North Avenue, Suite 101
Oak Park, IL 60302
708.848-0319

Center for Third World Organizing
1218 E. 21 Street
Oakland, CA 94606
510.533-7583

Coalition for Economic Survival
1296 N. Fairfax
Los Angeles, CA 90046
323.656-4410

Coalition for Human Dignity
P.O. Box 21266
Seattle, WA 98111
306.756-0914

Facing History and Ourselves
16 Hurd Road
Brookline, MA 02445
617.232-1595

Floridians Representing Equity
  and Equality
1333 West Cass Street
Tampa, FL 33606
727.464-4880

National Association for the
  Advancement of Colored People
4805 Mt. Hope Drive
Baltimore, MD 21215
410.358-8900
www.naacp.org

The National Coalition Building
Institute
1835 K Street NW, Suite 715
Washington, DC 20006
202.785-9400

National Council of Churches
475 Riverside Drive, Room 670
New York, NY 10115
212.870-2376
www.nccusa.org

National Institute Against Prejudice
and Violence
31 S. Greene Street
Baltimore, MD 21201-5170
301.328-5170

Pennsylvania Network of Unity
Coalitions
P.O. Box 8168
Pittsburgh, PA 15217
412.521-1548

Southern Catalyst Network
MR Box 1692, 31 McAlister Drive
New Orleans, LA 70118-5555
504.865-6100

The Southern Poverty Law Center
400 Washington Avenue
Montgomery, AL 36104
205.265-0286

Bibliography

Administration for Children and Families, U.S. Department of Health and Human Services. *Change in Numbers of TANF Families and Recipients, 12/2002–12/2003.*

Allen, Theodore. *The Invention of the White Race.* New York: Verso, 1994, 1997.

Anderson, Troy. "Perverse Incentive Factor Rewards County for Swelling System, Critics Say." *Daily News.* December 6, 2003.

Applied Research Center. *The False Foundations of Welfare Reform.* Oakland, CA: Applied Research Center. 2001.

———. "Working Principles for Racial Equity." Race and Public Policy Conference: Proactive Agenda for 2005 and Beyond. April 2005.

Bacon, David. "Black/Migrant Rivalry for Jobs Can Be Eased." *Los Angeles Times.* August 22, 2004.

———. "Immigration Reform: Uniting Black and Immigrants." *ColorLines.* Winter 2004–2005.

Bagaza, Angelo. "I Don't Count as 'Diversity.'" *Newsweek.* February 8, 1999.

Banton, Michael and Jonathan Harwood. *The Race Concept.* New York: Praeger Publishers, 1975.

Bardach, Ann Louise. "How Florida Republicans Keep Blacks from Voting." *Los Angeles Times.* June 9, 2003.

Barrera, Mario. *Race and Class in the Southwest.* Notre Dame: University of Notre Dame Press, 1979.

Benard, Bonnie. "Collaboration Fosters Creates Problem Solving." *Western Center News* 4, no. 2. March 1991.

Bennett, Milton J. *Basic Concepts of Intercultural Communication.* 1998.

Blackwell, James. "Looking for the Working Class," *New Society* 61. September 1982.

Blash, Gary. "Far Along Yet Far From Equal." *Los Angeles Times.* January 11, 2004.

Blauner, Bob. *Racial Oppression in America.* New York: Harper & Row, 1972.

Brownstein, Ronald. "Minorities' Home Ownership Booms Under Clinton but Still Lags Behind Whites." *Los Angeles Times.* May 31, 1999.

California Budget Project. *Will Proposition 21, The Gang Violence and Juvenile Crime Prevention Act, Decrease Juvenile Crime in California?* 2000.

Center on Budget and Policy Priorities. "Mothers Fell Substantially During Recent Period of Labor Market Weakness." June 22, 2004.

Center on Urban Poverty and Social Change. "Metropolitan Inequities and the Ecology of Work: Implications for Welfare Reform." *Social Service Review* 77:7. June 2003.

Chambers, Bradford. *Chronicles of Black Protest.* New York: New American Library, 1968.

Children's Defense Fund. "New Census Data Show 1.3 Million Children Have Fallen into Poverty Since 2000." http://www.childrensdefense.org (accessed September 22, 2006).

———. *Quality Child Care Helps Parents Work and Children Learn.* 2002.

Cowen, Tyler and Daniel Rothschild. "Unskilled Doesn't Mean Unnecessary." *Los Angeles Times.* May 15, 2006.

Cuban, Larry. "Housing, Not School, Vouchers are Best Remedy for Failing Schools." *Los Angeles Times.* January 31, 1999.

———. "Needed: Watchdog for Standardized Test Makers." *Los Angeles Times.* December 12, 1999.

Cyrus, Virginia. *Experiencing Race, Class, and Gender in the United States.* Mountain View, CA: Mayfield Publishing, 1993.

Davis, C., C., Estes, and V. Schiraldi. *Three Strikes: The New Apartheid.* San Francisco: Van Loben Sels Foundation. 1996.

Deitch, Elizabeth, et al. "Subtle Yet Significant: The Existence and Impact of Everyday Racial Discrimination," *Human Relations* 56, no. 11. November 2003.

Dolan, Maura. "Justices Curb Law on Prosecution of Youth as Adults." *Los Angeles Times.* February 8, 2001.

Dowell, Carol, ed., *Race, Power and Promise in Los Angeles.* Los Angeles: Multicultural Collaborative. 1996.

Downs, Anthony. "How America's Cities are Growing." *Brookings Review* 16, no. 4. Fall 1998.

Editorial. "Getting to the Bottom and the Top." *Los Angeles Times.* February 11, 2000.

Fagan, Patrick F. and Robert Rector. "The Effects of Divorce on America." Heritage Foundation paper. June 5, 2000.

Ferber, Abby L. *White Man Falling.* New York: Rowman & Littlefield, 1998.

Fox, Sue. "Overhaul of Poster System Wins OK." *Los Angeles Times.* February 18, 2004.

Friedman, David. "Don't Write Off State's Black Voters." *Los Angeles Times.* November 19, 2000.

Fulwood, Sam and Kenneth Weiss. "Public Values Ethnic Diversity, Survey Finds." *Los Angeles Times.*

Gans, Herbert J. "The Positive Functions of Poverty." *American Journal of Sociology* 78, no. 2: 75–289.

Gobodo-Madikizela, Pumla. "White People Just Don't Get It About Racism Culture." *Los Angeles Times* (July 12, 1999).

Gold, Scott. "Black Leaders Sue to Overturn Election." *Los Angeles Times.* December 8, 2000.

Goldberg, Mark. "Losing Students to High-Stakes Testing." *Educational Digest* 70, no. 7. March 2005.

Hacker, Andrew. *Two Nations: Black and White, Separate, Hostile, Unequal.* New York: Ballantine Books, 1995.

Hannaford, Ivan. *Race: The History of an Idea in the West.* Baltimore, MD: John Hopkins University Press, 1996.

Harrison, David, et al. "Attitudes on Affirmative Action." *Journal of Applied Psychology* 91, no. 5. September 2006.

Haskins, Ronald. "Statement before the Committee on House Ways and Means." *Congressional Quarterly.* July 19, 2006.

Hayes-Bautista, D. and G. Rodriguez. "Killing Minorities Softly with Words Intended To Be Helpful." *Los Angeles Times.* April 15, 1997.

Hill, Herbert and James Jones, Jr., eds. *Race In America.* Madison: University of Wisconsin Press. 1993.

Hogan-Garcia, Mikel. *The Four Skills of Cultural Diversity Competence.* Boston: Brooks/Cole. 1999.

Houppert, Karen. "You're Not Entitled." *Nation.* October 25, 1999.

Howard, Lamar. *Texas Crossings: The Lone Star State and the American Far West, 1836–1986.* Austin: University of Texas Press, 1991.

Human Relations Commission. *The State of Race Relations in Los Angeles.* Fall 1985.

Independent Commission on the Los Angeles Police Department. *Report of the Independent Commission on the Los Angeles Police Department.* Los Angeles City Council. 1991.

———. *Summary.* Los Angeles. 1991.

Jencks, Christopher and Meridith Phillips, eds., *The Black-White Test Score Gap.* Washington, D.C.: Brookings Institution Press, 1998.

Kahn, Si. *Organizing: A Guide for Grassroots Leaders.* New York: National Association of Social Workers Press. 1991.

Katz, Bruce. "Enough of the Small Stuff: Toward a New Urban Agenda." *Brookings Review* 18, no. 2. Summer 2000.

Keyssar, Alex. "One Man, One Vote?" *Los Angeles Times.* December 10, 2000.

Kim, Elaine. "Between Black and White," *The State of Asian America.*

Kim, James S. and Gail Sunderman. "Measuring Academic Proficiency Under the No Child Left Behind Act: Implications for Educational Equity." *Educational Researcher* 34, no. 8. November 2005.

Kivel, Paul. *Uprooting Racism: How White People Can Work for Racial Justice.* Philadelphia: New Society Publishers, 1996.

Knowles, Louis and Kenneth Prewitt, eds. *Institutional Racism in America.* Englewood Cliffs, NJ: Prentice-Hall, 1969.

Kozol, Jonathan. "Confections of Apartheid Continue in our Schools." *Educational Digest* 71, no. 6. February 2006.

Kromkowski, John. *Race and Ethnic Relations 95/96.* Guilford, CT: Dushkin Publishing, 1996.

Ladner, Joyce. "A New Civil Rights Agenda." *Brookings Review* 17, no.1. Spring 2000.

Lamb, David. "Workshop on Whiteness Explores Unearned Rights." *Los Angeles Times.* November 19, 1996.

Lehr, Robert. "A Brief Critical Look at Affirmative Action." *Social Work Perspectives* 4, no. 1. 1993.

Levenson, Michael. "Drug Tally Shoots Down a Racial Myth; Whites Top City's Rising Toll From Abuse." *Boston Globe*. March 25, 2006.

Lind, Michael and Sean Wilentz, "And the Beat Goes On: The Continuing Power of the Liberal '60's."

Lindner, Charles L. "The System Has Become Dysfunctional." *Los Angeles Times*. March 19, 2000.

Lindsey, R., K. Nuri Robins, and Raymond Terrell. *Cultural Proficiency: A Manual for School Leaders*. Thousand Oaks, CA: Corwin Press. 1999.

Lipsitz, George. *The Possessive Investment in Whiteness*. Philadelphia: Temple University Press, 1998.

Loprest, Pamela. *Families Who Left Welfare*. Washington, DC: The Urban Institute. 1999.

Los Angeles Times Staff. *Understanding the Riots*. Los Angeles Times. 1992.

Lum, Doman. *Culturally Competent Practice*. 1999.

Machan, Dyan. "Habitation, No Rehabilitation." *Forbes* 90. 1998.

Maldonado, Marilyn. "Harvesting the Fruits of Color Blindness: Racial Ideology in Employers' Discourse and Everyday Production of Racial Inequality in Agricultural Work." *Dissertation Abstracts International A* 66, no. 2. 773A–774A. Aug. 2005.

Males, Mike A. "The Scapegoat Generation: America's War on Adolescents." *Journal of Psychohistory* 25, no. 2. Fall 1997.

Manglitz, Elaine. "Challenging White Privilege in Adult Education: A Critical Review of the Literature." *Adult Education Quarterly* 53, no. 2 (February 2003).

Mauer, Marc.

McRoy, Ruth G. *The Color of Child Welfare Policy: Racial Disparities in Child Welfare*. Austin: Center for Social Work Research, University of Texas. 2000.

Mohammed, Mima. "U.S. Prison Numbers Up 35% in 10 Years.," *Los Angeles Times*. December 1, 2006.

"Myths That Explode Like Firecrackers." *Los Angeles Times*. May 2, 2000.

Neubeck, Kenneth and Noel Cazenave. *Welfare Racism*. H.W. Wilson, 2002.

——. "Welfare Racism: A Force in the Rise, Demise, and Aftermath of AFDC," 2000.

Orfield, Gary and Chungmei Lee. "*Brown* at 50: King's Dream or *Plessy's* Nightmare?" Civil Rights Projects, Harvard University. 2004.

Pettigrew, Thomas. "Justice Deferred A half Century After the Brown Board of Education." *American Psychologist* 59, no. 6. September 2004.

Pinkerton, James P. "The Stork Now Delivers a Stark Reality." *Los Angeles Times*. January 2, 2001.

Platt, Anthony, ed. *The Politics of Riot Commissions*. New York: Collier, 1971.

Pope, C. and W. Feyerherm. "Minorities and the Juvenile System." *Final Report*. Washington, DC: Justice and Delinquency Prevention, 1991.

Popple, Philip and Leslie Leighninger. *Social Work, Social Welfare, and American Society*, 2nd ed. Boston: Allyn and Bacon, 1993.

Powell, John. "Race and Space." *Brookings Review* 16, no. 4. Fall, 1998.

Report from the Federal Reserve Board. Associated Press. September 8, 2006.

"Report of the National Advisory Commission on Civil Disorders." New Times Co., 1968.

Report from the National Institute of Drug Abuse, 1990.

Rivera, Felix and John Erlich. *Community Organizing in a Diverse Society*. Boston: Allyn and Bacon, 1998.

Rivers, Eugene. "The 3 M's Help Keep Youth Violence at Bay." *Los Angeles Times*. October 2, 2000.

Roberts, Dorothy. *Shattered Bonds: The Color of Child Welfare*. New York: Basic Civitas Books. 2002.

Roediger, David R. *The Wages of Whiteness*. London: Verso. 1991.

Rofes, Eric, David Keiser, Tony Smith, and Matt Wray. "White Men and Affirmative Action: A Conversation." *Social Justice*. Summer 1997.

Rothman, Jack. *Reflections on Community Organization*. Itasca, IL: F. E. Peacock.

———. "Three Models of Community Organization Practice." In *Social Work Practice*. New York: Columbia University Press. 1968; 1978.

Savage, David. "Cases Retread *Brown v. Board of Education* Steps." *Los Angeles Times*. December 4, 2006.

Scrader, Esther. "Congressional District in L.A. Had Voting Glitches." *Los Angeles Times*. July 9, 2001.

Siegel, Larry J. *Criminology*. New York: West/Wadsworth, 1998.

Simms, Margaret. "The Changing Black Family: Implications for Children." in *Focus*. Washington, DC: Joint Center for Political Studies. 1988.

Skerry, Peter. "The Limits of Black, Brown Solidarity." *Los Angeles Times*. February 1, 1998.

Slater, Eric. "Town Is On Edge After Rioting." *Los Angeles Times*. June 19, 2003.

Smedley, Audrey. *Race in North America*. Boulder, CO: Westview Press, 1999.

Soss, Joe. *Unwanted Claims: the Politics of Participation in the U.S. Welfare System*. Ann Arbor: University of Michigan Press. 2000.

Steinberg, Stephen. *Turning Back: The Retreat from Racial Justice in American Thought and Policy*. Boston: Beacon Press, 1995.

Suchetka, Diane. "From Welfare to Work but Still Not Making It." *Cleveland Plain Dealer*. June 6, 2006.

Sue, D. W., P. Arredondo, and R. J. McDavis, "Multicultural Counseling Competencies and Standards: A Call to the Profession." In J. G. Ponterotto, J. M. Casas, L. A. Suzuki, and C. M. Alexander, eds., *Handbook of Multicultural Counseling*. Thousand Oaks, CA: Sage Publications. 1992.

Takaki, Ronald. *A Different Mirror: A History of Multicultural America*. New York: Little, Brown, 1993.

———. *From Different Shores*. New York: Oxford University Press, 1987.

Terzian, Richard. "Committed Management Is Needed to Reduce Abuse of Costly Foster Care Programs." *Cal-Tax Digest*. October 2002.

Texeira, Erin. "The Subtle Clues to Racism." *Los Angeles Times*. January 11, 2001.

Thomas, Hugh. *The Slave Trade*. New York: Simon & Schuster, 1997.

Thomas-Lester, Avis. "An Apology for 'America's Holocaust.'" *Washington Post*. June 20, 2005.

Thompson, Tommy. "Capitol Hill Hearing Testimony on Welfare Reform, House Ways and Means." *Congressional Quarterly*. July 19, 2006.

Tonry, Michael. *Malign Neglect*. New York: Oxford University Press, 1995.

U.S. Census Bureau. *Statistical Abstract of the U.S. 2000*. 120th ed. Washington, DC, 2000.

U.S. Commission on Civil Rights, *Civil Rights Issues Facing Asian-Americans in 1990s*. 1992.

U.S. Department of Health and Human Services. "Mental Health: Culture, Race, and Ethnicity." supplement to *Mental Health: A Report of the Surgeon General*. 2001.

Van Dyke, Vernon. *Ideology and Political Choice*. Chatham House. 1995.

Weinstein, Henry. "Illinois Poised to Set Taped Interrogation Rule." *Los Angeles Times*. July 17, 2003.

———. "Justice System is 'Broken,' Lawyers Say." *Los Angeles Times*. June 24, 2004.

Wellman, David. *Portraits of White Racism*. New York: Cambridge University Press, 1977.

Wider Opportunities for Women. "Coming up Short." 2004. http://wowonline.org/docs/dynamic-CITA-43.pdf.

Wilson, Thomas C. "Whites' Opposition to Affirmative Action: Rejection of Group-Based Preferences as Well as Rejection of Blacks." *Social Forces* 85, no. 1. September 2006.

Wilson, William J. *The Truly Disadvantaged*. Chicago: Chicago University Press. 1987.

Winant, Howard. "Race in the New Millennium." *Colorlines*. Spring 2000.

Winston, Bonnie. "More Blacks Going to Prison in 17 Key Election States." www.blackamericanweb.com (accessed September 24, 2004).

Index

Index

About the Author

Shirley Better received her Ph.D. in social welfare from the University of California at Los Angeles. She is a professor in the School of Social Work at California State University at Los Angeles, where she designed and implemented an upper division theme of six courses focusing on Institutional Racism. She is one of the founders of the National Association of Black Social Workers (NABSW), and a founder of ABSW-Los Angeles. Dr. Better serves on the boards of several community-based organizations. For more information you can visit her on the web at shirleybetter.com.